THE ERA OF
FRANKLIN D. ROOSEVELT

VOLUME 52
THE CHRONICLES
OF AMERICA SERIES
ALLAN NEVINS
EDITOR

THE NEW DEAL IN ACTION

THE ERA OF
FRANKLIN D. ROOSEVELT

A CHRONICLE OF
THE NEW DEAL AND GLOBAL WAR
BY DENIS W. BROGAN

NEW HAVEN: YALE UNIVERSITY PRESS
TORONTO: GLASGOW, BROOK & CO.
LONDON: GEOFFREY CUMBERLEGE
OXFORD UNIVERSITY PRESS

1950

Copyright, 1950, by Yale University Press

CONTENTS

ILLUSTRATION

THE NEW DEAL IN ACTION
From a mural by Thomas H. Benton at the
New School for Social Research, New York.   *Frontispiece*

THE ERA OF
FRANKLIN D. ROOSEVELT

..

CHAPTER I

PANIC AND DEPRESSION

1930–1933

IT is seldom possible to identify a single day as the beginning of a new era or cycle, but a date on which the period of the New Deal was born may plausibly be fixed. On October 24, 1929, as panic gripped the New York Stock Exchange, nearly thirteen million shares were sold in the greatest debacle known in the financial history of the United States and the world.

Bitter hindsight was later to make it difficult for many to remember with what blind confidence they had supported the great bull market. Yet ever since the Federal Reserve Board had acted in the summer of 1927 to loosen credit, some critics had expressed apprehension and some men had prophesied distress if not disaster. In the spring of 1928 a sharp recession had shaken out many weak speculators, and suggested to prudent men that the time had come to pocket their profits; but these prudent folk were to be confounded by the experience of 1929, when prices soared higher than ever. They went up and up until they reached their peak on September 19. As they did so, the great majority listened to the "experts" who talked of a new day in American if not world economics.

The attempt of the Federal Reserve Board in 1929 to slow down the bull market had deserved a better response. Just before Hoover became President, it had warned member banks and the public that the Federal Reserve Act did not "contemplate the use of the resources of the Federal Reserve Banks for the creation or extension of speculative credit." But the weakness of mere exhortation was soon manifest. The National City Bank boldly defied the heads of the banking system. So did some great corporations like Bethlehem Steel. The boom market was not to be starved into sobriety; particularly when the profits of feeding it were so attractive, with new call money being lent on the eve of the crash at nearly 10 per cent. Yet the Federal Reserve Board was right in showing uneasiness. Factory production began to decline in

July; the peak of employment came in July and it began to fall early in October; building had been increasingly stagnant since 1925. Prudent European speculators were beginning to take alarm, and before the fatal day there had been several sharp breaks in stock prices. Indeed, though few suspected it, the great boom had reached its peak six weeks before the avalanche swept down on the market.

When the catastrophic nature of the collapse became apparent on October 24, the leaders of the New York financial world took hasty council. Panic had to be halted before it became uncontrollable; so the rulers of the market argued, and on that premise they acted. Morgan, National City, Chase, Guaranty Trust and Bankers Trust put up $240,000,000 and the chief Morgan broker was sent in to buy. The very sight of Richard Whitney, the knowledge of what forces were behind him, stopped the rout. If it was not quite Sheridan on the battlefield of Winchester, at least the bold stroke of the great banks made possible a withdrawal in good order to more defensible positions.

By the weekend the worst seemed to be over. But it was not, for on Monday the retreat was again a rout, and it was obvious that a crisis was developing which would test the American economy.

One of the distinguishing features of the stock-market crash of 1929 was the degree to which it involved millions of Americans who, a generation before, would have had no more direct concern with the latest speculative prices of stocks than with the latest prices of old masters. But the great bond sales of the First World War and the subsequent rumors of easy profits made by investment bred a new attitude toward the fascinating game of playing the market.

Money was sucked into the New York market by all the devices of high-powered salesmanship. It was money, at first, to float great industrial corporations like the Nash automobile company, to develop Cuba, and to fund the debts of Peru; it was money to reequip Germany. Then it was simply money for any promising speculation. By the spring of 1929, gambling had become respectable. Banks and brokers catering to it flourished like faro men in a gold rush. In the single year 1929, no less than $11,000,000,000 of new securities were marketed. Every great city had its jammed, overworked stock exchange, and many secondary cities boasted them too. At least one minor city of Pennsylvania was planning its own exchange as the crash came; it seemed as much a necessity for a rising community as a country club or a chamber of commerce.

There was a rational basis for some of the optimistic boosting of great industrial combinations.

The magical history of businesses like the Ford Motor Company was an example of the possibilities open to investors who got in on the ground floor. Salesmen from brokers' offices, investment departments of great banks, and the new investment trusts were always ready to persuade the doubtful that the day of golden opportunities was just dawning. It was absurd, in such an era, to wonder whether it was wise to pay ten times the issuing price for stock in a corporation that had not yet declared a dividend. It was absurd to inquire closely into the bookkeeping of such towering pyramids as the Van Sweringen railroad systems or the Insull utilities empire; as vain to question their solidity as that of the great terminal in Cleveland or the opera house in Chicago, that were visible monuments to the pride and prosperity of the great promoters.

To be sure, there had been warning voices telling Main Street of the doubtful character of the benefits offered by Wall Street. But men knew that there were great speculators in the market and that prices were made and unmade by their decisions. It was important to know what these manipulators planned, and the revelation of their secrets became an important secondary industry. Apart from the "market letters," and the advice of local bankers and brokers, there was the lure of the private tip. Here a fortune had been made by a prudent butler

who listened to his master's guests. There it was
a caddy who had eavesdropped on a fashionable
golf course. Behind the speculators were the real
rulers of the American economic machine, the
Gods behind and above the Titans, who would not
let anything serious happen.

The public was admonished in October, 1929,
by the New York *World,* not to think that 1920
had come again. There was no post-war inflation
to liquidate; there was comparative stability in the
world markets; there was peace. Above all, there
was the incomparable American productive machine. The great plants still stood, their slight
slowing up in production disregarded. The fertile
lands that had been so lavishly mortgaged were
as fertile as ever. The great office buildings and
apartment houses of so many cities from New York
to Beaumont, Texas, still stood. Still greater towers
were being thrust into the sky. The American
people with its ingenuity, industry, and resources
was unchanged. True, vast paper losses had been
incurred. When a new bottom was reached in late
November, the investors were thirty billion dollars
poorer. But optimists held that it was only a paper
loss. Prudent men like the elder and younger Rocke-
feller were buying good common stocks. Surely
President Hoover was right when he said that the
worst would be over in sixty days; surely Secretary
Mellon was correct when he seemed to welcome

the liquidation of merely speculative elements in the American economy. When Christmas came, the stores were as busy as ever, the worst seemed over, and it was reasonable to expect that in 1930 the short pull upwards would begin again.

Yet for hundreds of thousands the prospect remained grim enough. The fairy gold of easy profits had been counted on, and hostages had been given to fortune. Houses had been bought (on credit); cars had been bought (on credit); jewels had been bought (on credit); sons and daughters had been sent to college (on credit). The very speculations that had turned out so badly had been largely conducted on credit. At the height of the speculative craze it was estimated that 300,000,000 shares were being held on margin, and sometimes the investor's contribution was only 10 per cent. Unable to put up adequate collateral, such men lost their investment. It was the pressure on these borrowing gamblers that had produced the Johnstown floods of liquidation. They did not know they were lucky to have been forced out so soon, and to have been saved the temptation to throw good money after bad. As 1929 ended, they seemed to be the only real victims of a severe but healthy purge.

For those whose index of national health was the stock market, there seemed evidence in the early spring of 1930 that confidence in the power of the American economic machine was justified. Market

prices did recover; there was even a little boom.
The rulers of the nation and the market acted on the
theory that all that was now seriously needed was a
full restoration of confidence. The old Puritan com-
forts were argued: adversity was bracing; the nation
and individuals alike would gain by the sharp lesson administered. For the greater part of the
American population, such admonitions made
sense. It was at worst a case of Paradise Mislaid,
not Paradise Lost.

This optimistic view overlooked the hard fact
that even at the height of the boom there had been
black patches on the golden quilt of national prosperity. In worked-out cotton lands of the South
like Greene County in Georgia, poverty and economic despair were not new. In debt-encumbered
rural areas in the Dakotas, there had been no great
margin since the collapse of the war boom in 1920.
In the declining textile towns of New England
men and women had been despondent for years
before 1929. The peak of the boom had been
reached as far as manual workers were concerned
some time before the stock market boiled over.
There were probably at least two million unemployed even in the best months of 1929. And it
was suspected that millions more were beginning
to put unusual pressure on public and private
charity.

When summer came on, it was evident that

either confidence had not returned or that confidence was not enough. And even though the President's appeal to industry not to cut wages was heeded by many great corporations, it was ignored by others, and in any case was poor comfort for the mounting army of the unemployed. By autumn, faith in the industrial and political rulers of America was ebbing fast. Candid Republican leaders were less surprised at their losses in the Congressional elections of 1930 than gratified that they barely lost control of the House and kept a nominal majority of the Senate.

Affairs did not take a turn for the better, and early in the new year, 1931, the man who had personified the endless golden day, ex-President Coolidge, announced flatly in his daily column: "This country is not in good condition." The statement was now a bitter truism. With the acceptance of that truism, there came into the American mind a growing sense of anger and disillusionment. In vain did President Hoover talk of Valley Forge and preach the self-reliance and self-confidence of the Continental Army. The Continental Army had been a small elite; the dwellers in the new Valley Forge were tens of millions of ordinary American folk, frightened and harassed by two winters of growing want and worry. The tactics of preaching confidence now recoiled upon the heads of the preachers. The Republican promises of 1928 were recalled with irony, and an optimistic statement upon the speedy abolition of poverty once made by Mr. Hoover became a bitter byword.

To the small zealous group of the American Communists, the depression seemed a vindication of their preaching. In vain they had talked about the inherent contradictions of capitalism in the golden day. Now they could point with ironical scorn at the men who had talked of an "economic revolution" which was to abolish class distinctions in a free competitive system. Among the educated classes, and especially the young professional writers, teachers, and technicians, they won some recruits. So did other radical groups. For a moment, the panacea of technocracy seemed the answer to tens of thousands perplexed by the sight of so much technical capacity and material resources unused. The inventor of this doctrine was an enemy of the money system. National accounts should be kept in units of energy, and with the free release of the national resources that would follow from throwing off thraldom to finance, every American family could have the equivalent of an annual income of $20,000. In their despair, thousands clutched at the hopes thus held out, and for months, technocracy was the main conventional theme of conversation. Its popularity was probably significant less of faith in the new doctrine than of doubt in the old order.

The condition of the masses meanwhile went from bad to desperate. Though nobody could do more than guess at the figures of the unemployed, certainly by the end of 1931 they numbered over ten million. Those who had work were often paid miserable wages. Wages in the Pittsburgh steel industry fell from $30 a week in 1929 to $15 in 1932; a worker in a Southern mill who complained that he got only $2 a day was told by an unemployed friend that he would take the job for a dollar a day. Servants were found to be working for their mere keep; shopgirls in New York were hired for $3 a week. In the boom days it could be complacently assumed that, apart from children and the physically handicapped, only the shiftless needed help, save in sudden emergencies of accidents, illness, or the loss of the breadwinner. For dealing with such cases there was an elaborate machinery of organized charity. Akron, for example, had the Family Service Society, which in August, 1929, dealt with 257 cases. What was Akron to do when 5,000 cases a month appeared in 1932? The expenditure of New York City for public relief rose ten times over between 1929 and 1932; but at least New York could spend. What was to be done in Kansas, where counties with less than 140,000 population were limited by law to a tax of one-half mill on the dollar for poor relief, and the more populous areas were allowed only eight-tenths of a mill for this purpose? Prices kept on falling so that the purchasing power of wages rose. But wage rates fell faster than prices; in fact, in three years they fell 55 per cent; and the fall in prices frightened the businessman, making him refuse to manufacture merely in order to sell on a falling market.

By the summer of 1931, nobody could pretend that the unemployed were idle good-for-nothings who preferred not to work. They were everywhere, standing idle in the streets of stricken industrial towns, where one observer saw men "on the sidewalks clapping their hands in a queer way, obviously just to be doing something." The symbolic unemployed man of the depression was the apple seller who bought fruit cheap from worried producers and offered it to the more prosperous, who had, in these outstretched hands, a perpetual reminder of the national sickness.

Clergy and social workers reported with increasing distress on the effects of the depression upon home life. The father of the family, proud to be "a good provider," was now often the dependent of his children and his wife. Some families were strengthened by the ordeal; more were weakened. Tens of thousands of boys and thousands of girls took to the roads. Soon the "hobo jungles" were full of youthful recruits, and the railroad police gave up attempting to keep them from stealing rides. Whole families moved on in a vague search for a better place to live or merely because they had no place to live at all. They begged for handouts; they stole and parched corn. Men lost skill and lost hope.

While it was mainly on the poor that the greatest suffering fell, tens of thousands of once prosperous people were precipitated to the bottom of the economic scale, beyond all hope of recovery. New disasters added to the general misery. The failure of the Bank of United States in New York swept away the savings of multitudes of immigrants who, deceived by the name, felt that the Federal Government or some other official body should make good their losses. The collapse of the Swedish match empire of Kreuger and Toll ruined thousands of a more prosperous and theoretically more prudent class from Boston to Seattle. All over America, banks closed by the hundreds until few of the great cities did not have a record of the sudden suspension or the long and futile struggle of some prominent financial establishment.

Bank failures became so great a threat, indeed, that the Administration was forced to depart from its trust in the curative forces of a free economy. After an ineffective attempt to get the strong banks to support the weak, it set up the Reconstruction Finance Corporation (January, 1932) with Federal funds to support threatened banks, railroads, states, and cities. The social strain of further liquidation might have brought about the collapse of the whole debt structure, for debt was one of the great problems of the crisis. While the national income fell to less than half what it had been in 1929, the burden of debt was little altered. The holders of titles to money were the last sufferers. Indeed, dividends hardly dropped at all in the first two years of the depression. The contrast between the losses of the sellers of money and the sellers of labor was striking. "Whose depression?" asked an indignant economist, contemplating the distorted figures of the national income in 1932, and reflecting that probably one cause of the depression had been the diversion of too much money into profits and dividends after 1925.

Against this background of differential suffering, it was hard to take calmly the refusal of the Federal Government to help alleviate such widespread misery. True, the Reconstruction Finance Corporation was authorized to lend money to states and other governmental units for relief work, but President Hoover stood firmly by the doctrine of local responsibility for relief, regardless of the insolvency of many cities and counties, of the reluctance of bankers to lend, and the frequent constitutional impotence of local governments to borrow. When it was revealed that the head of a great bank had managed to avoid taxes on an immense income by creating fictitious losses, and that much of the income of the richer classes was in tax-free bonds; when a Senate committee began to expose the rigging of the markets, the creation of pools, and the sale of next to worthless bonds, the patience of the people with financial orthodoxy declined. A revolt against Congressional leaders of both parties prevented a general Federal sales tax, and in each year after 1930, the Federal deficit grew to what then seemed astronomically dangerous heights.

Despite the RFC, banks continued to fail and railroads to pass into the hands of receivers. The real estate market was also demoralized. Its ailments had been one of the causes of the depression, and the failure of the investment house of S. W. Strauss and Company was as symbolic a disaster as the closing of the Bank of United States. Socially more important was the long history of evictions. Rents were often unpayable, and all over the country hundreds of thousands of tenants were turned out while hundreds of thousand of owners lost their mortgaged homes. Communists were quick to support resistance and to move tenants and furniture back as fast as they were moved out. But such tactics were no more of an answer than the old spiritual sung by threatened Chicago Negroes: "I shall not, I shall not be moved." They were moved. Others abandoned expensive apartments and unpaid-for furniture and took what shelter they could find. In New York, a reporter found a husband and wife living in a cave in Central Park. Some slept in home-made sheds. Some lived with their families; in many cases they went back to the family farm. But the farmers were often threatened with eviction. Millions of acres were forfeited.

The threatened bankruptcy of local government was one ingredient of the bitter draught. Some cities could not afford an adequate police force. Every luxury of government was ruthlessly pruned. Libraries bought no books; hospitals got along with inadequate staffs and supplies; and even the pride of American democracy, the school system, sometimes seemed threatened with destruction. Teachers' pay was cut and cut again. Schools were opened late, were badly heated and badly cleaned. In some areas they did not open at all. Kansas teachers took salaries of $17 a month as better than nothing. In face of this collapse it was bitter to remember the adoption, after a White House Conference, of a "Children's Charter" on November 21, 1930. Article VIII demanded for every child "a school which is safe from hazards, sanitary, properly equipped, lighted and ventilated. For younger children nursery schools and kindergartens to supplement home care."

By 1932, with all extras pruned away, kindergartens shut down, and children huddled in overcrowded, dirty, understaffed schools to which they had come from cold homes, underclad and underfed, such proclamations of unattainable ideals seemed mere mockery. Actually President Hoover was by no means stupid, idle, or hardhearted. But while he waited for the curative power of nature to work, luck was against him. For a brief moment in the summer of 1931, a bold stroke by the President was seen as a turning point. He induced Congressional leaders to agree to a year's suspension of the European war debts in return for a suspension of the reparations due from Germany. It was becoming an Administration theory that the sickness of Europe was preventing the convalescence of the United States. This belief was in dramatic inconsistency with the policy of prohibitively high tariffs accepted by the President in 1930, a policy that assumed that foreign trade was of little moment to the United States. Now all foreign trade had fallen off disastrously and the American share was down to a third of the figures of 1929. But the debt moratorium of 1931 had no permanent effects. England went off the gold standard, world trade still shrank, and the economic plight of the United States grew steadily worse.

The revolt of the farmers was accompanied by a rising demand of veterans for a war bonus. Congress did something for them. It allowed (over the President's veto) the advancing of 50 per cent of the value of the "adjusted service certificates" of the veterans, a step which led to the underwriting in 1931 of one and a quarter billion dollars' worth of veterans' borrowings. It was unorthodox but it did enable a section of the American people to pay its debts; and that was not unimportant. In 1932 it was estimated that "uncollectible retail debts" amounted to $600,000,000, three times the average of 1929.

Nature seemed to conspire to perplex the leaders of the nation. At a time when oil prices were ruinously low, great oil discoveries in eastern Texas threatened to ruin the already harassed producers in older fields. Cotton dropped from 16 cents a pound in 1929 to 5.4 cents a pound in 1932. Wheat fell from $1.00 a bushel to 31.6 cents. The index of industrial production declined from 119 in 1929 to 64 in 1932. National income went down by more than half, and national wealth by more than a quarter. The growing paralysis was reflected in small things and in big. In Akron, building permits and dog licenses alike declined from 1930 to 1931 by two-thirds. There seemed to be no end to the spiral of decline.

CHAPTER II

THE ELECTION OF ROOSEVELT

In November, 1930, Franklin D. Roosevelt was
elected to his second term as Governor of New
York by a majority of 730,000. His triumph was
so complete that he would have won even without
the immense majorities provided by New York
City. The Democratic State Chairman, James A.
Farley, at once declared that he did not see how
Mr. Roosevelt could escape being the next Presidential candidate of his party, "even if no one
should raise a finger to bring it about." There was
no risk that fingers would not be raised. The prize
was too great and the availability of the candidate
too obvious. The Governor himself had long had
his eye upon the White House, and his unprecedented majority told him that his hour had come.
Even a Governor less promising than Roosevelt
would have been a serious contender, and this would
have been true even if his election prospects had
been entrusted to less zealous and competent men
than his secretary, Louis Howe, his secretary of

state, Edward Flynn of the Bronx, and his friend James A. Farley.

First of all: "The Roosevelt name is magic"—so politicians in the party were told throughout the next two years. Franklin D. Roosevelt was both a kinsman and a nephew by marriage of the former President, and had accepted many of T.R.'s ideas. His name had automatically attracted attention to the young Democratic senator who entered the upper chamber at Albany in 1910, and who within a few days had gained the headlines with an ease and efficiency that seemed a gift of nature. Born to wealth on both sides of his family, educated at Groton, Harvard, and Columbia University Law School, Roosevelt became at once the center if not the leader of the group of young Democrats who defied the Tammany whip and blocked the election to the United States Senate of "Blue-eyed Billy Sheehan." Publicity thus gained was not necessarily helpful. A young Tammany leader in the legislature, Robert Wagner, saw in the campaign against the nominee of Boss Murphy mere publicity-seeking as well as bad discipline—and Tammany Hall had a reputation for a long memory.

The struggle, however, attracted the attention of those respectable if often politically impotent forces known as the "better elements." By January 22, 1911, the young state senator was being written up in the magazine section of the New York

Times. Readers were told how "on the face of this Roosevelt, younger in years and in public service, Nature has lavished all her refining processes until much of the elementary strength has been lost in the sculpturing." Ten years later, nature was to remedy that.

Roosevelt continued to oppose Tammany by giving warm support to the candidacy of Woodrow Wilson for the Democratic nomination in 1912, support rewarded by the post of Assistant Secretary of the Navy. In that office, the aristocratic young politician became familiar with the world of Washington and with the ways of the service to which he had been devoted since childhood. The First World War made the post of great practical importance, and by the time it ended, Franklin Roosevelt was well known in the ranks of the younger Democrats. His personal aide, Louis Howe, not only gave him valuable routine service, but kept his work well publicized. But his one effort to enter national politics from the legislative side had failed; he had been defeated in a contest for the Democratic nomination for United States Senator from New York in 1914. His sole legislative experience was to remain his two terms in the New York Legislature. Henceforward he was to see the political world always from the side of the executive branch.

The year 1920 was not auspicious for the Democrats, and it was a gesture that cost little to make Franklin Roosevelt the candidate for Vice President. Hopes of success for the Cox-Roosevelt ticket cannot have been high, but the catastrophic defeat of November was not anticipated by the younger man. It was more than a personal setback, for the Republican victory marked a complete defeat for American participation in the new world organization to secure the fruits of victory. For twelve years Roosevelt's party was to remain out of power.

In August, 1921, the ambitious, exuberantly healthy young politician was stricken by infantile paralysis in a form so severe that all activity seemed likely to be ended for the rest of his life. It was in the long climb back to health that patience was learned, that the smooth, handsome face was marked with suffering, that there was time to ponder the lessons of affliction. It seemed for years that the lessons would have to be profitable for private life alone: "I spent two years lying in bed trying to move my big toe." But beside the stricken man were three vigilant guardians, his wife Eleanor, his mother Sarah Delano Roosevelt, and his secretary Louis Howe. Mrs. Roosevelt, though not active in Democratic politics, maintained close touch with those social reformers whose spirit she understood and whose ambitions for a better social order she shared. Sarah Delano

Roosevelt kept her son's ambitions alive and his ardors undiminished. Howe had pinned his faith to Franklin Roosevelt when he was a young state senator; he did not lose faith now.

During 1924 had come the first tentative return to politics. In the bitterly contested fight for the Democratic nomination, the heir of a great Knickerbocker family had put before the convention the name of the son of the sidewalks of New York, Alfred E. Smith. In that speech Roosevelt first showed to a national audience his phrase-making power, for he named Smith "the Happy Warrior." Again in 1928 he made the nominating speech, rewarded this time with success. But the nomination was a good deal less than half the battle. It was thought important that the candidate to succeed Al Smith as Governor of New York should bring independent strength to the ticket. Pressure was brought to bear on Roosevelt, then taking treatment at Warm Springs in Georgia; he gave way, and to the general surprise carried New York for himself while his chief was rejected by his own state.

As Governor, Roosevelt had the handicap of succeeding the most popular and successful executive in the recent history of the state. He did not have and did not acquire Smith's deep knowledge of the state administration, and he had to deal with a political and economic situation that grew steadily more difficult. Within a year of his election, the great collapse began; it was soon not a matter of bond issues for hospitals, but of state solvency and the rescue from total destitution of hundreds of thousands of unemployed. Governor Roosevelt showed sympathy and understanding. He began to know the mind and abilities of the social workers with whom his wife had long been associated; two in particular, Frances Perkins and Harry Hopkins, were given important jobs in the administration. But no governor could do much in face of the national character of the economic blizzard; a few windbreaks were the most that any state could erect.

The political situation, too, forced caution on the Governor. The old cleavage between city and "upstate" had been made acutely manifest by the defeat of Governor Smith. The handicap of Tammany associations had been again proved, while Tammany itself was divided within and assailed from without. A Republican legislature launched a general investigation under the direction of an anti-Tammany Democrat, Judge Samuel Seabury. Few great American institutions could afford to have their deeds and misdeeds during the boom years closely investigated. It was soon shown that the famous Democratic organization was highly corrupt, and even the tolerant New York public was much less ready to condone pleasant political vices than in the golden years of the bull market.

As the depression deepened, the political prospects of the Democratic party improved and the nomination in 1932 became a glittering prize. There began to appear in the field not only the usual crop of "favorite sons," but candidates formidable in their own right. Above all, it became clear that the "Happy Warrior" was burning to avenge defeat of 1928. Behind Smith emerged formidable forces. They included his personal devotees, who were passionate, numerous, and powerful, as well as many important politicians of Irish Catholic descent who, like the candidate, thought the manner of his defeat in 1928 a personal affront. Moreover, the Smith forces were in command of the central machinery of the Democratic party.

Normally that control would have mattered little. The National Chairman appointed by a defeated candidate is usually a nonentity once the election returns are in. But John J. Raskob, Smith's nominee as chairman, though new to politics, had the one great qualification of wealth. He was ready to use it in keeping the party machine together and an effective propagandist organization going. The economic collapse created a situation in which even moderately competent campaign material would have been effective, but the chief of the Democratic publicity office, Charles Michelson, was no more a merely competent publicist than his brother had been a merely competent physicist. Every mistake, every misfortune, every instance of bad timing in the well-meant moves of the Hoover Administration was noted with the speed of light, spread on the record, and insinuated into the public mind with a diabolical adroitness.

Chairman Raskob had no desire that his admirable propaganda machine should work for Roosevelt. He, like Smith, was a Catholic; he, like Smith, had wounds to avenge. And he, like many others, distrusted the ideas and doubted the courage of Franklin D. Roosevelt. Such distrusts and doubts were widespread; every apparent hesitation or evasion in Albany was taken to prove the inadequacy of Governor Roosevelt for the Presidency—and the desirability of letting the American voter make amends for the crime of 1928. As Democratic chances grew brighter, the determination of the Smith forces became stronger, although occasionally a politician would beard the ex-Governor to point out that he had had his chance in 1928 and that the party dared not risk providing the Republicans with their only chance of victory, an anti-Catholic scare.

With comparatively little noise, the Roosevelt forces under the leadership of State Chairman Farley were meanwhile at work. Organizations known by their initials were to be a feature of the Roosevelt era, but perhaps the first to matter was the BPOE, the "Benevolent and Protective Order of Elks." Mr. Farley was an eminent Elk and that fact gave him friends in all parts of the land. He began with a visit to a convention of his brethren; then came a series of journeys which made him known favorably to working politicians all over the country, and made his candidate's strength known, too. Most county chairmen and local leaders were frankly attracted by the prospects of victory. Bill Howes, National Committeeman for South Dakota, put the case crisply: "Farley, I'm damned tired of backing losers. In my opinion, Roosevelt can sweep the country, and I'm going to support him." So said hundreds of other local leaders, and by the beginning of 1932 Governor Roosevelt was the obvious favorite in the race.

That position had its advantages. It had its drawbacks, too. All the other candidates entered into a loose alliance to "stop Roosevelt." Enemies of the Governor worked either for delegations instructed to support favorite sons or for uninstructed delegations. The Convention must not open with the necessary two-thirds committed to the favorite. Farley had many triumphs. He had many disappointments, too, notably in Indiana and Illinois. Most of all he had to lament the political condition of his own state.

In vain he had pleaded with the leaders of the

two chief New York boroughs, John F. Curry, boss
of Manhattan, and John H. McCooey, boss of
Brooklyn. They would have nothing to do with
Roosevelt, and revealed a touching if belated devotion to Smith. Only the Bronx, under Secretary
of State Flynn, was safe for the Governor. Roosevelt would enter the Convention the favorite of
more than half the delegates, but not the uncontested selection of his own state. It gave grounds
for the charge that his own neighbors did not think
him Presidential timber. Reports were constantly
being circulated, too, that he was an invalid and
a cripple.

He *was* a cripple. Above the waist he was still a
man of great physical power and energy; below the
waist, his shriveled legs told the tale of the long
illness. But he had learned to live with his handicap; he was still a powerful swimmer, a fine
yachtsman; leaning on the arm of a friend, holding
himself erect by a cane and steel braces, he gave
an impression, wholly justified, of great physical
resilience. He had campaigned in every county in
New York, showing himself to the voters as he
really was, no invalid. But the story was hurtful.

Hurtful, too, was the story of his being a good,
easy man with no power of decision and no political
courage. Otherwise, the indignant critics asked,
why had he not removed the peccant Mayor of
New York? For the Seabury investigation had at

last reached the most conspicuous figure in the Tammany gallery, James J. Walker. On the witness stand, the debonair Mayor had not answered highly damaging questions. Yet the Governor did not remove him out-of-hand, as he had removed lesser sinners. He undertook his own investigation (a time-wasting device, asserted the moralists). He entrusted it to an eminently respectable Catholic lawyer, Mr. Martin Conboy; Mayor Walker must not be made a religious martyr. He examined the Mayor himself, but by the time the Convention met in Chicago, the case was still treated as *sub judice*. This was prudent, it was politics, and it was frequently assailed as proof of timidity and moral indifference.

The Democrats in Chicago met in the hall recently used by their depressed opponents. If there was little in the state of the nation or of the world to gratify them as citizens, there was much to please them as politicians. The Republican Convention, meeting under the shadow of probable defeat, had not improved the party's prospects. It had not thrown overboard Vice President Curtis; it had failed to take any clear stand on the burning question of prohibition. To the general mass of voters, the Republicans were committed to the "noble experiment" of which the country was now profoundly tired. Nothing could save the once dominant party but a series of foreign and domestic miracles, or a new outbreak in the Democratic Convention of the bitter conflict between the industrial East on one side and the South and West on the other that in 1924 and 1928 had wrecked whatever chances then existed of a Democratic victory.

The fear of such a disaster kept the public feuds of the party within bounds. There were present such bitter figures as William Gibbs McAdoo, cheated out of the nomination in 1924 (so he thought) by forces represented by the noisy partisans of Al Smith who now filled the galleries in Chicago. There was Al Smith himself, upsetting the plans of the "Stop Roosevelt" managers by taking his own chances too seriously and too long. The one great absentee was Governor Roosevelt.

His managers, however, were there. Farley was testing the strength of those alliances he had built up by his endless journeys, his innumerable letters and telephone calls, the links he had attempted to create between himself and the 38,000 Democratic party officials all over the Union. Farley was full of hope that his candidate would be nominated on the first ballot. Although the Roosevelt forces secured the choice of Senator Barkley of Kentucky as "keynoter," they were said to have done it only by promising their support to the Smith candidate for chairman, Jouett Shouse. The bargain, if made, was not kept, and the senior Senator from Montana, Thomas Walsh, became Chairman. The tempers of the opposition were not improved; and there was worse to come. Under pressure from a fiery leader of Louisiana Democrats, Senator Huey Long, the Roosevelt forces were stampeded into coming out for abrogation of the century-old two-thirds rule. To use their majority to get round the rules in the middle of the game was a mistake, and Roosevelt had to disavow the maneuver.

The party platform was mercifully brief. And it was definite on one important topic, straight repeal of the Eighteenth Amendment.

Despite Farley's proclaimed hopes, no nomination was made on the first ballot. There was a handsome majority but it was not overwhelming, and the tactics of the opposition were obvious. The impression must grow that Roosevelt could be beaten, then the switches could be made, the delegates released, and the rush made to the new band wagon, almost certainly drawn by a dark horse. One name in particular began to be mentioned, that of Newton D. Baker of Ohio, Secretary of War in Wilson's Cabinet, and a man famous for devotion to the international ideas of his dead chief. That fame was in a sense his undoing, for it alarmed William Randolph Hearst, the chief supporter of Speaker John N. Garner of Texas. It soon became evident that the way to break the deadlock in favor of Roosevelt was to win over the

Garner forces, which included the California as well as Texas delegates. The Speaker could have little real hope of nomination; he was from a Southern state, and one that had bolted the party in 1928. His nomination would add even more bitterness to the open conflict between the South and the Northeast, inflamed by the angry utterances of Al Smith.

Farley had kept in close touch with the Texas leaders, and with McAdoo and other Californians. If no bargain was made, there was a clear, implicit understanding. On the fourth ballot, the Garner votes were released to Roosevelt; the stampede was on. Only the unrelenting Smith partisans refused to make the nomination unanimous. Farley played his part; Garner got the Vice Presidential nomination that he did not particularly want. The favorite had won.

Before the Convention adjourned it had one last sensation. Defying "the absurd traditions that the candidate should remain in professed ignorance of what has happened," Governor Roosevelt flew out to Chicago to confront an audience which for the most part did not know him and was not free from skepticism about its choice. But the man who addressed the Convention was already a different figure from the aspirant for the nomination. He was, in his own mind, already President-elect, and it was with no doubts that he proclaimed to the exhausted delegates his pledge of "a new deal for the American people." The magic phrase-maker who had twice launched the campaign for the Happy Warrior was now battling for himself.

His first and most important decision was to take the battle to the country. Prudent counselors advised a dignified "front porch" campaign; they remembered the disasters that had befallen other politicians "swinging round the circle"—the way they had made enemies and lost friends. But the candidate was firm. He must go and show himself to the electors; he must fight the rumors of his physical condition. He must, at the risk of making them worse, try to mend the rifts in party unity, and, more important still, win over the millions of doubting Republicans and independents who would decide the issue.

The decision was a triumphant success. From the Atlantic to the Pacific, the candidate was seen, liked, and trusted. His skill in soothing local leaders and tying their fortunes to his own was in marked contrast with the record of Al Smith in 1928—and with that of President Hoover. These leaders felt that they were backing a winner whose strength was transferable to them. The greatest local handicap was removed by the timely exit of Mayor Walker; Roosevelt gave him the choice of resigning or being removed, and he resigned. A reconciliation took place with Al Smith; it was more formal than hearty, but they *were* united in one special cause, for together they broke an attempt by Tammany Hall to prevent the nomination of Herbert Lehman for Governor of New York, a triumph that made the vote of the Empire State secure.

While the public activities of the candidate stole the limelight from all other politicians and forced Hoover belatedly to take the field himself, behind the scenes the party machine was being taken over by the new National Chairman. Farley inherited from Raskob the services of Michelson, who showed that the change of commanders had not in the least affected his virtuosity. True, the Republicans were in disorder and gloom; attacking them was like pressing on a swinging door; but the door was never allowed for an instant to swing back.

While Farley encouraged the party workers in Chicago and Kokomo and even in normally neglected areas like the South and Maine, the policy of the candidate was being devised by another group of workers, the experts and professors christened by James Kieran the "Brain Trust." (The variant "Brains Trust" came to be used later.)

Close counselor of the candidate as Governor of New York was Samuel Rosenman, and a new adviser on policies was Raymond B. Moley, expert on criminal law, and soon Chief of Staff on the policy, as apart from the political, side of the campaign.

Leaving Farley to attend to his job, and getting equal immunity from interference in return, Moley began to provide help in the writing of speeches. He brought the candidate into touch with many academic colleagues, most of them, naturally, fellow faculty members at Columbia University. Experts on agriculture, electric power, and finance were consulted, and many had the satisfaction of seeing some of their ideas embodied in speeches. There were ghost writers and idea men in plenty, but the final speeches bodied forth the prophetic soul of the candidate.

Although Hoover had shown great respect for academic research and had employed many teams of experts, the idea of consulting theorists instead of practical men seemed to some Republicans funny and likely to be politically hurtful to the Democratic candidate. But as 1932 went on, as the economic situation grew worse, it was discovered that, for once, the American people were in no mood to laugh, even at professors.

The public was moved by the ingenuity with which the Democratic candidate managed to weave together theories and facts, and color them with genuine emotional fervor. This man, they felt, knew how the crisis hit *them*. He was no mere experimenter, but a leader of heart and courage. When on April 7, 1932, in the first important speech of the campaign year, Roosevelt declared that he would not make the mistake of Napoleon at Waterloo and forget the infantry, the masses took up the phrase; they were "the forgotten men," forgotten by the Hoover Administration that spent its main efforts on the needs of the man at the top, who had not suffered the dire penalties that their blunders had inflicted on millions of the helpless.

They took, also, to the phrase "the New Deal"; to "social justice" (a phrase destined to a strange history); to the campaign against the Republican "Four Horsemen," "destruction, delay, deceit, despair." The public began to appreciate the matchless art of the candidate's voice on the radio. The opening call to fellowship, "my friends," the warmth and vigor of the delivery, the skill with which local allusion was mingled with national policy, soon made the campaign of 1932 the nearest approach to the Bryan campaign of 1896. It appealed largely to the same elements, but the distressed Republican farmer, the harassed Republican small businessman, too, wavered and were won. In vain President Hoover and Secretary Ogden Mills of the Treasury threatened that a change of Administration meant the killing of the tender plant of confidence and recovery that they asserted was just thrusting through the soil. The answer was given in the Maine elections, for the Democrats carried the state.

The Republicans were the victims of their own

policy. From the beginning of the depression, the Hoover Administration, while taking some constructive steps, had relied too heavily on the creation of confidence as the way to recovery and on optimistic prophecy as the way to confidence. Now, too many checks had been drawn on the bank of public faith.

Governor Roosevelt was vigorous in affirmation if not wholly consistent. He defended and adopted as his own the party platform. He promised rigorous economy (a reduction of 25 per cent in expenditure); a rigorous adherence to sound finance and a sound currency; a turn away from the high tariff policy of the Republicans (but not at the expense of the farmers); Federal aid for the relief of the distressed, especially children; rigorous regulation of the stock market; and control of the production and marketing of electric power. For the power industry, the "birch rod" of state or Federal operation was to be kept in the cupboard, for use if the utility magnates did not reform. There was no promise or threat of revolutionary change; America was to be saved and restored, not made over.

So far as the candidate had a political philosophy, it was revealed in a speech whose later fame was greater than its contemporary impact. Speaking to the Commonwealth Club of San Francisco on September 23, Roosevelt went further than in any other campaign speech to declare the convictions that were in him. He recalled the happy age of the open frontier that made the day of individualism "long and splendid." That day was done. "Our industrial plant is built; the problem just now is whether under existing conditions it is not overbuilt. Our last frontier has long been reached, and there is practically no more free land. . . ."

The shades of the prison house were closing round the small businessman, too. "We are steering a steady course towards economic oligarchy, if we are not there already." There was still hope in better discipline, better standards, and a partnership in reform. "As yet there has been no final failure, because there has been no attempt." There would be such an attempt to save the American capitalist system, despite its rulers, if the electors gave the mandate.

They did. Nearly 23,000,000 voters chose the prophet of the New Deal. It was the greatest vote ever cast for a Presidential candidate, and, very significantly, it was the widest-spread in modern times. Roosevelt carried 2,721 counties; Hoover 372 counties and only six states. This was a dramatic change from 1928, when Hoover had polled a higher percentage of the vote than Roosevelt did in 1932. Only eight Republican Governors were elected. It was not a mere revolt; from a political point of view it was a revolution. But not from any other point of view. The Communists, who asked for a real revolution, got only 100,000 supporters; the Socialists, who proffered a complete remedy for the economic catastrophe, polled proportionately far less than in 1912. The American people were ready for a New Deal that would give capitalism another chance.

On December 10, 1932, Hoover made his last speech as President to the Gridiron Club. It was a dignified plea for cooperation in the face of the great common danger. "During the past two years we have been fighting to maintain the very foundation of our own stability. That front can be held if no mistakes are made." As he spoke, the President knew that the front was buckling under unprecedented pressure. There had been signs, in the autumn, of a genuine upturn in business, but it had come too late in America (and in Germany) to save the old political order. The banks, the holders of fixed-interest securities, the men at the top of the economic heap, had so far managed to pass most of the cost of the depression on to others. The steadily contracting circle of the depression was now squeezing them.

The banking structure of the United States was in danger of collapse. Bank failures in 1932 had not been as numerous as in 1931. But the drop in deposits was now affecting all banks, even the most secure. Not till January, 1933, were figures released that showed how far the shrinking had gone. An additional blow fell when, in February, the Reconstruction Finance Corporation made its quarterly report revealing to what extent the banking structure was already a building threatened with collapse and only shored up by Government loans.

The country now faced panic as complete as in 1873. Even before the election, Nevada banks had been shut down for a time by the Governor's proclamation. "Bank holidays" began to spread, credit to freeze up, and substitutes for currency to be sought for in local scrip. Areas tried to insulate themselves from the creeping paralysis, and hatred of the men who were thought to have exploited and then betrayed the country spread like a fever. If there was no revolutionary temper in November, it was not so certain that none existed in January.

In such a crisis it was unfortunate that a gap of four months still lay between the election and the inauguration of the new President. A series of crushing problems faced the executive authority of the United States, and this authority was in fact divided between President and President-elect. Hoover was fully conscious of this and anxious to secure from his successor pledges of a continuation of his policy. The President-elect was equally determined to have a new policy. He consulted such veterans as Justice Brandeis; but no more than

Lincoln in the same situation was he willing to underwrite the efforts of the outgoing Administration to cure the crisis or keep it from ending in collapse. It was true that the mounting crisis was largely an affair of panic, was irrational, was curable by faith. But faith and the Hoover Administration had been severed by three years of increasing disillusion. The faith that the American people might have in the new Administration must not be squandered now.

Hoover and Roosevelt had two conferences, but they broke down. Hoover wanted a guarantee that his medicine would still be administered; Roosevelt felt that there must be a dramatic and obvious change in attitude as well as personnel, if the patient was not to die in the process of cure. The contrast at one White House conference between the two leaders and their aides was significant of much. On the one side the plodding, tenacious Hoover and on the other the resilient, imaginative Roosevelt; on one side the still confident, energetic representative of the discredited old business order, Secretary of the Treasury Ogden Mills, and on the other the professor of law and reformer of the criminal courts as adviser to the President-elect, Raymond Moley.

And while the fruitless negotiations went on, the crisis deepened. Louisiana, then, more ominously, Michigan, declared bank holidays. On February 14 the news from Detroit shook the nation. On February 15 came more startling news from Miami. A madman had attempted to assassinate the President-elect and had mortally wounded Anton Cermak, Mayor of Chicago, who had gone to Miami to make his peace with Roosevelt—and Farley. "It was providential that my car went about thirty feet ahead before the crowd closed in." So the President-elect put it next day. It was providential indeed, for what little hope the shattered nation then had was being concentrated, in default of any other object, on him.

In the three weeks just before the inauguration, the need for hope grew greater and greater. There could be no pretense now; Chicago, Philadelphia, and, at last, New York followed Detroit. On March 4, the banks in all states but one were completely or in great part closed. The central nervous system of the greatest capitalist country in the world had ceased to function.

CHAPTER III

MEETING THE CRISIS

FRANKLIN D. ROOSEVELT was fifty-one when inaugurated President of the United States; a year younger than Lincoln at his inauguration. And he was inaugurated in circumstances that had no parallel in American history except in the inauguration of Lincoln. In a sense the conditions were more critical, for it was as if Sumter had been fired on the day before Lincoln became President. The new President had one great quality, a courage that was spontaneous and infectious, an enjoyment even of the greatest emergencies, a physical and moral resilience. While he was still President-elect, a friend condoled with him on the terrible burden that he would have to bear for the next four years. "I shall enjoy every minute of it," was the answer. That ease and confidence were not always welcomed by the critical; his gaiety, Justice Frankfurter later wrote, was "at times easily taken for jauntiness." But on the whole it was an asset, and his countrymen soon slept better, as someone said, because they knew that President Roosevelt slept well.

There was no jauntiness on March 4, 1933, though there was a great deal of confidence. Roosevelt waved and grinned both before and after the ceremony, but he delivered his speech without a trace of a smile or any relaxation of the note of high seriousness. He began with a new appeal for confidence. "The only thing we have to fear is fear itself." There followed, what was most necessary, a disengagement of the new Administration from the leaders and the system that had gone down in ruin. "The money-changers have fled from their high seats in the temple of our civilization. . . . We may now restore that temple to the ancient truths. . . . This nation asks for action, and action now."

Certainly the nation needed action. Till the very end, the Hoover Administration had clung to the hope that a general bank closing could be averted. But the Acting Attorney-General, Homer S. Cummings of Connecticut, who had been called to fill the gap caused by the sudden death of Thomas Walsh, was ready with legal opinions assuring the new President that he had the powers he wanted. The few doubts about his power to shut Federal Reserve Banks were brushed aside, and all the banks of the United States were closed. Concessions were made to soften the blow: banks could admit clients to their own safe deposit boxes and could cash checks on the Treasurer of the United States; postal savings banks remained open. While the new and old Secretaries of the Treasury and their aides were in continual conference, the President, for five hours, reviewed the inaugural parade. No doubt he did this to restore confidence in the permanent order of things; but, as a close admirer wrote, "Mr. Roosevelt really wanted to see the parade." That enjoyment of all parts of his office was to be of immense advantage to him, just as the sense of its burdens had been of great disadvantage to his predecessor.

In addition to closing the banks, the President's proclamation forbade the withdrawal of gold or silver and imposed very severe penalties for violation. At first it was planned to issue "scrip," but it was decided to permit the issue of Federal reserve notes against the sound assets of the banks; the new notes would look like the old notes while unusual "scrip" would have fed fear. The Bureau of Printing and Engraving ran day and night turning out the new currency. When Congress, summoned in special session, met on March 9, a banking bill was ready for it, though such had been the speed with which the work had had to be done that a rolled-up newspaper had to serve as a symbol of the bill which was not yet printed for distribution to the members. In a few hours the bill was passed.

It gave the President power to reopen closed banks that were wholly solvent; to appoint "conservators" (a word avoiding the ugly sound of "receivers") for the doubtful banks; and to keep the really insolvent banks shut. The rediscount powers of Federal Reserve Banks were greatly extended and the RFC could buy preferred stocks in national banks, thus providing capital for sound but anemic institutions. On Sunday, March 12, the President gave the first of his "fireside chats" reporting to the nation on the progress that had been made. Next day, the twelve Federal Reserve Banks would reopen; on Tuesday the reopening of other banks would begin. State banks would get help from the RFC as well as from members of the Federal Reserve System, although the responsibility for letting them reopen was a matter for the state authorities. The "confidence of the people," for which the President again asked, was being given; the first battle with fear had been fought and won.

The legislation for the immediate banking crisis was followed at once by legislation dealing with what many thought an equally serious crisis, the problem of Federal deficits. Faithful to the party platform and his own campaign promise, the new President demanded that Congress pass a measure with the significant title of "A Bill to Maintain the Credit of the United States Govern-

ment." The bill authorized an immediate cut of
$100,000,000 in the Federal payroll (including the
pay of Congress) and, more startling still, it empowered cuts in the payments to veterans. These
latter reductions required great courage, for the
basic demands of the veterans, ever since the time
of the Grand Army of the Republic, were traditionally sacred. But the salary cuts and the dislike
of offending the veterans were not the only reason
for the sullenness of many Congressmen who voted
for the bill, or for the open mutiny of nearly a third
of the Democratic majority which voted against it.
There was presented, at once, a political dilemma
that could not be resolved.

Economy and Federal thrift were popular cries
among the alarmed conservatives of the East. The
smash of 1929 and the continuing depression were,
for this school, the inevitable wages of financial sin.
But such was not the view of the debtors of the
South and West, or of men and women with no passion for financial orthodoxy and formal solvency.
And while the new President had been elected by
so widespread a majority that he was not the representative of any section, he had been nominated
by the same sectional combination that had preferred Bryan to a sound Cleveland Democrat in
1896, and Wilson to Champ Clark in 1912; the
same groups that in the North had voted for the
elder La Follette in 1924 rather than for the Demo-

cratic candidate, John W. Davis. In 1932, Roosevelt had carried 282 counties that no Democrat had ever carried before, but of these only 42 had not been carried by Theodore Roosevelt in 1912 or by Robert La Follette in 1924. Passage of the economy bill was a defeat for the coalition that thought it had won at Chicago.

The Cabinet, to some degree, illustrated the coalition character of the Administration in its first months. In many ways Roosevelt defied the old rules of Cabinet-making. Sectionalism was recognized to a minimal degree. Himself from New York, the President appointed three other New Yorkers: the Secretary of the Treasury, William H. Woodin; the Postmaster-General, James A. Farley; and the Secretary of Labor, Miss Frances Perkins. Congress provided two Southern Senators in the new Secretary of State, Cordell Hull of Tennessee, and the Secretary of the Navy, Claude A. Swanson of Virginia. The West was represented by the Secretary of War, George H. Dern of Utah, and both the West and the South by Daniel C. Roper of South Carolina and California, who took the Commerce Department. New England provided Homer Cummings of Connecticut, and that important bloc, the Progressive Republicans, was represented by the Secretary of Agriculture, Henry A. Wallace of Iowa, and Harold L. Ickes of Illinois. Wallace was the third in an important dynasty of agricultural leaders in the Middle West, and his nomination required no explanation. But Ickes was so little known that a New York *Times* correspondent had to tell his readers how the name was pronounced. Within a few weeks, the American people needed little information about the new Secretary of the Interior that he could not be relied on to supply himself.

Woodin was a slightly unorthodox, public-spirited, and liberal businessman; Hull represented the basic ideas of Woodrow Wilson; Miss Perkins was the spokesman of that increasingly important class, the trained social workers and administrators. But important party sections were not represented at all. The "Al Smith" Democrats were ignored; some indeed held that they were insulted by the nomination of Roper, close ally of Senator McAdoo. Organized labor was irritated by losing its presumptive right to see one of its own men head the Department of Labor. It was not an all-star Cabinet; it was not even a politically well-balanced Cabinet. And it was evident that, whatever its strength, it was not going to be the only instrument of executive government. The new Director of the Budget, Lewis Douglas, was at least as weighty a spokesman of financial orthodoxy as Secretary Woodin; a new Assistant Secretary of State, Raymond Moley, was, many thought, likely to be more important than Hull. And these were only some of the more conspicuous of the driving young men who now poured into Washington; a group which included Rexford Guy Tugwell, Dean Acheson, Adolf Berle, and Charles W. Taussig. Some of the rapidly changing members of the "Brain Trust" were abler and more efficient than others. But as a group the younger "New Dealers" were to the public the most interesting, unusual, and baffling figures among the new rulers of the nation. They were, it was believed, the "kitchen cabinet" of the new Jackson; and though this was not true, they did help to fix the principles of a great deal of the new legislation.

The first weeks of the Administration were marked by endless energy and bold improvisation. The President and his aides were in the position of the little Dutch boy in the familiar story, but the American dike had broken in many places and there were hardly enough thumbs or even fingers to stop all the leaks.

Thus, it was soon found impossible to go back to the gold standard or any approximation to it. The sole question was whether inflation should be Presidential or Congressional in origin and direction. So one campaign promise was scrapped at once. It had to be, since one breaking point was the burden of debt, much of it contracted at prices far above the price level of 1932, or for farm debt, above the price level of 1927. Farm debt alone accounted for $12,000,000,000 and it could not be paid. A month after the inauguration, a judge in normally peaceful Iowa was hanged by the neck until he was nearly dead by embattled farmers who resented his foreclosure orders. The $2,000,000,000 of Federal money advanced to Land Banks to refinance the farm debt was a high but necessary premium against rural disorders. The $200,000,000 advanced to the Home Owners Loan Corporation and the guarantee of interest on $2,000,000,000 bonds was a hasty method of shoring up the collapsing structure of real estate debt. In the three-year period during which it made loans, the HOLC gave more than a million homeowners advances aggregating over three billions.

One of the most desperate problems of the collapse had been the appearance of nomadic groups of boys and girls, discontented and demoralized. The Civilian Conservation Corps was therefore started to deal with them. It dealt, in fact, only with the male victims of the catastrophe. Hastily organized under War Department direction, it was attacked as being militarist, while its primary job of reforesting and forest improvement was derided as a Presidential hobby. But by August, 250,000 young men (some old enough to have served in the war of 1917–18) were in camps, working, being fed, and remitting a great part of their $30 a month to dependents. Soon the CCC was the least criticized and most admired of the experiments.

Relief was an urgent problem. Since as the Administration had promised that no one should starve, the Federal Emergency Relief Administration was at once given $500,000,000 to advance to the states, not as loans but as a gift. Half of it, however, was to be "matched" by three state dollars for one Federal.

The old controversy over the use of the Federal plant at Muscle Shoals was suddenly transformed by the President's request for authority and funds to establish a Tennessee Valley Authority, while a National Industrial Relief Administration and an Agricultural Adjustment Administration were both set up. The Reconstruction Finance Corporation was continued with greatly enlarged powers. FERA, CCC, NRA, AAA, TVA, HOLC, the list of what were to be called "alphabetical agencies," was not complete; but the country was in no mood to be too critical. Action had been promised, action had been given. True, the budget, balanced under the Economy Act, was being unbalanced under many of the new agency policies, but the "regular" budget was separated, statistically, from the "emergency" budget and it was still possible to hope that the emergency—and the deficit—would be brief.

The effect of the sudden spurt of energy was immediately felt. There was a rapid upswing in prices, in business, and then in employment. To the optimistic, the patient was well on the way to recovery; and conservative men quickly developed what was to be a familiar antithesis between "recovery," which was at hand, and "reform," which was no doubt desirable—but should be postponed until the patient could stand the shock.

Even the most conservative, however, recognized that one urgent piece of legislation was a new banking law. The defects of American banking were in humiliating contrast with the general efficiency of the Canadian system. Senator Glass of Virginia, with the authority of a former Secretary of the Treasury and an author of the Federal Reserve System, was for drastic measures against the "little corner grocerymen who run banks." He wanted all banks integrated into the Federal Reserve System. He battled on the floor of the Senate the rising hope of the rural radicals, Senator Long of Louisiana, who defended the "State banks at the forks of the creeks of this country." The final Glass-Steagall Act of June 1, 1933, represented an uneasy compromise between the views of Glass and the much less conservative opinions of Representative Steagall and of that great body of American opinion which was profoundly suspicious of all banking orthodoxy.

The great novelty of the Glass-Steagall Act was

the creation of a Federal corporation to insure small bank deposits. There were strong theoretical objections to such a course; the well-managed banks were made to pay for the badly managed banks over whose policies they had no control. State schemes of this type had been widely tried and had failed. But it was necessary to restore faith in banking. The Act, too, forced a separation of deposit from investment banking, an overdue reform made imperative by the revelations of the current investigation of various large banking houses. Some of these institutions had used depositors' funds in very risky promotions. The Federal Reserve Board was given broad powers in curbing speculative credit expansion by member banks. But although no open system of Federal control of credit was enacted, even at the moment when the low public standing of bankers was one of the current ribald jokes all over the nation, the Glass-Steagall Act, together with the control over the dollar given to President Roosevelt, ended the old autonomy of the American credit structure, and, largely unnoticed, began an extraordinary extension of the directing and regulating powers of the Treasury Department.

If the banks needed moral as well as financial rehabilitation, so did the stock markets and the whole system of selling securities. Perhaps the exchanges needed it most, but a choice had to be made and an act popularly known as the "Truth-in-Securities" Act was passed, based on the maxim "let the seller beware" and putting the policing of the vendors of securities under the Federal Trade Commission. Hastily drafted and representing various compromises, the act was nevertheless important in the principle on which it rested, and for the foundations laid for the work of the future Securities and Exchange Commission. This body, created by act of June 6, 1934, had the duty of licensing and regulating stock exchanges to prevent the flow of too much of the nation's credit into security trading and manipulation of the market.

The public was less impressed by such legislation than by two conspicuous examples of the new spirit now ruling in Washington. Negotiations were at once begun for the establishment of diplomatic relations with the Soviet Union and, on November 16, 1933, letters were exchanged between a special Russian Ambassador, Maxim Litvinov, and President Roosevelt, noting that such relations were a fact. There were still apprehensive critics, and the American public meant to keep a watchful eye on Russia to see whether the Comintern attempted any subversive plottings or propaganda. Time proved that the watch was needed.

In the meantime most Americans were more interested in another achievement of the new Administration, the hasty legalizing of beer with an alcoholic content of 3.2 per cent. At the same time, the law governing the issue of medicinal alcohol (which had threatened to make America a nation of hypochondriacs) was liberalized, while the work of repealing the Eighteenth Amendment was rushed on with commendable speed. Promises were secured against the return of the saloon, and taverns and bars replaced speakeasies in all but the few remaining dry states.

The internal conflicts of the Administration were projected on the international screen by the breakdown of the London Economic Conference. This great international meeting had been planned when there was still reasonable hope of salvaging the old order of international trade. Actually, however, by the time the conference was scheduled to meet in the early summer of 1933, the agenda drawn up at Geneva was already obsolete. The shadow of war was already being cast if the shadow was no bigger than a man's hand. It was not the plans of the new regime in Germany that seemed most relevant, however, but the plans of the new regime in America.

And those plans were highly inconsistent. On the one hand, the chief of the American delegation, Secretary Hull, was a model of fiscal and economic orthodoxy. He wanted an end to tariff and currency wars, an end to unbalanced budgets. On the other hand, the new Administration was com-

mitted to a different view of the crisis and its
cure. The policy just put in hand made the raising
of the American price level its first objective. As
Raymond Moley, exponent of this doctrine in the
inner councils of the Administration, was to put it
later in a letter to the President: "There are . . .
extreme views with respect to our foreign policy,
the one advocating utter isolation, the other, complete entanglement. If I were to describe your following realistically, I should say that, on the whole,
your most loyal followers lean toward the first
point of view." Undoubtedly a great section of
New Deal supporters wanted little truck with
Europe, the home of bankers and war. Nor had
they any taste for financial orthodoxy. In the field
of currency they had achieved part of their program before the conference met. The United States
was not only "off gold," but was increasingly un-
certain of ever going back; and if she did so, nobody could guess when or at what level. This uncertainty had an immediate effect on the countries
clinging to the gold standard. France was the chief
nation of the "gold bloc," but it was Holland and
Switzerland which felt the worst pressure.

A further complication was the question of war
debts. In the previous summer, at Lausanne, German reparations had been wiped out except for a
token payment, a policy strongly endorsed by the
Hoover Administration. To the peoples of France,

Britain, and other nations it seemed that war debts should go the way of reparations, but this argument had no value in American eyes. There was as complete an opposition of opinion between the point of view of the British or French man in the street and his American opposite number as between a representative citizen of South Carolina and Massachusetts in 1861—or an Iowa farmer and a New York banker in 1933. Some early adjustment of the debt, Europeans argued, was a necessary part of the total world settlement on which so much was asserted to depend. Various formulas and solutions were discussed in Washington and in London, but no American Administration could propose a settlement that any European Government could, in its turn, get accepted.

War debts further increased the irritation of the average American with the outside world. It was no happy augury that in opening the conference, Prime Minister MacDonald felt forced to say that "Lausanne has to be completed." This seemed to justify the suspicions of that vigilant isolationist, Senator Hiram Johnson of California, who had refused to be one of the delegation. However, his point of view was well represented by another progressive Republican, Senator Couzens of Michigan, who in all his opinions was at the opposite pole from the Secretary of State. The other Senatorial delegate, Key Pittman of Nevada, was mainly concerned to "do something for silver," while the able ex-Governor Cox of Ohio, the President's running mate in 1920, was nearly as orthodox as the Secretary of State.

These divisions in the delegation were no diplomatic secret, since delegates resented any attempt to curb their rights of free and unlimited utterance. By the time the conference was under way, it was realized that the United States would not reduce tariffs or agree to a tariff truce (which indeed would have been difficult in face of the price-raising devices of the argricultural and industrial control machinery being set up for the domestic market). The main question was whether the United States would agree to limit the devaluation of the dollar, and consent to the linking of the pound and dollar to the only important gold currency remaining, the French franc. If this was impossible, the gold countries and Britain wanted the variations of the dollar to be limited as much as possible. But the countries still formally or really on gold must be reassured. So a late arrival from the United States was told; for the President had dispatched to London Assistant Secretary Moley, supposedly in much closer contact with Roosevelt than were any of the delegates.

Moley made some gestures toward playing down his own role, but it could not be played down. He could see that no nation except Sweden, and she only to a limited degree, approved of the American policy of raising price levels by currency manipulation as the way to recovery. The Secretary of the Treasury announced that rumors of stabilization agreements were false; the dollar oscillated and the pressure on the gold currencies continued. The President was first at Campobello Island and then on a cruiser, while, in London, the apparent division of authority in the American delegation was reaching the proportions of a scandal. Drafts were prepared and amended. The final formula was vague enough. Moley thought at the time that "it expressed no more than a detached though sympathetic interest in the gold standard," and he was confident that the President would accept it. He was wrong, well as he knew the President's mind.

The President's message, when it came, was described by the startled spectators as a "bombshell," a description accepted by its author. It rejected even the most limited and apparently innocuous limitation of complete freedom of action in the matter of currency; it denounced the "old fetishes of so-called international bankers"; it came out for national currencies with a "continuing purchasing power which does not greatly vary in terms of the commodities and need of modern civilization." The conference was dead.

The President dismissed the outcry as "petulant." It may have seemed so to that majority of the American people which approved the Presidential policy of seeking American recovery first. But to Secretary Hull, those who thought with him, and American conservatives in general, the "bombshell" was a revelation and a blow. With the collapse of the conference and the obvious failure of the simultaneous Disarmament Conference, the last chance of avoiding by cooperative action a great world crisis, with grave danger of war, was gone. Probably there was little chance anyway; Germany was now in the hands of as resolute and skillful a leader as was the United States. But whatever chance had existed was dead.

Just how soon the gold standard was abandoned is a matter of controversy. One competent observer held that the decisive step was taken as early as March 10, 1933, when the President forbade the export of gold or gold certificates except under Treasury license. Nor could banks deal freely in foreign exchange except as authorized by the Secretary of the Treasury. A more obvious departure from the gold standard was the order of April 5, which required all persons who owned gold in the form of bullion, coin, or certificates to deliver it to the Government in exchange for other forms of money; while on April 19, gold exports were again forbidden, and a more rigorous control of all exchange transactions was imposed. In his press conference, the President justified and explained his last drastic step. "For the last year, the dollar has been shooting up and we decided to quit competition. The general effect probably will be an increase in commodity prices. . . . It puts us on a par with other nations." Then, in a famous metaphor, the President declared that "here is a team that has a perfectly definite objective, which is to make a touchdown, so far as commodity prices go."

Despite the President's assertion that "one of the things we hope to do is to get the world back as a whole on some form of the gold standard," despite fine words, the American currency was to be controlled (or manipulated, as hostile observers preferred to put it) to produce a rise in the American price level. Some form of the old radical panaceas was sure to be used; perhaps all of them would be tried.

The heirs of the Greenback leaders and of Bryan were quick to take the hint. Senator Thomas of Oklahoma at once had the Agricultural Adjustment Bill amended to give all forms of currency the status of legal tender, and to permit expansion of the currency by Federal Reserve purchases of Treasury bills or other Federal obligations up to $3,000,000,000—all this above the sums they might already hold. If the Federal Reserve Board would not act, the Secretary of the Treasury could issue the $3,000,000,000 in greenbacks, subject to the mild limitation that he had to withdraw 4 per cent a year from circulation. A natural corollary was the formal abolition, by the joint resolution of June 5, of all clauses which required the payment in gold of any past or future debt, whether Governmental or private. This voidance of gold clauses applied to a vast mass of private obligations as well as to almost all the outstanding national debt of $22,000,000,000. The Thomas Amendment meanwhile empowered the President to reduce the gold content of the dollar by 50 per cent, and to coin silver at a ratio to gold fixed by himself.

The degree of possible Federal control of the currency was increased by the Glass-Steagall Act, which added to the powers of the Federal Reserve Board by forcing member banks to limit brokers' loans and other speculative uses of deposits. This was a necessary reform, as was the separation of security affiliates from normal banking business. But both reforms enhanced the degree of Governmental control of banking practice. American banks and bankers in 1933 were in no position to resist, nor had they any reason to expect any popular support should they be tempted to try. The Glass-Steagall Act also expanded the Federal Reserve System to include savings bank memberships. A further extension of Government control of banking was achieved by the Banking Act of 1935, which, if it did not formally set up a Government-controlled central bank, as was the wish of Henry Morgenthau, Jr., the new Secretary of the Treasury, gave complete authority to the President, since he was authorized to appoint the whole of the new Board of Governors which replaced the old Federal Reserve Board. The new Board was given enlarged powers over the Reserve Banks; powers in the opinion of Marriner Eccles, Chairman of the Board, adequate for the "adaptation of monetary administration to present-day conditions and needs."

Those powers were now, in effect, lodged in the Treasury, to which the varied experiments in currency control that marked the first Roosevelt Administration involved in fact, if not in form, the transfer of the central banking functions of the Federal Reserve System.

The first and most notorious of these experiments was the application of the gold theories of Professor George Warren. He held that there was a close relationship between the price of gold and the value of commodities. To devalue the dollar increased the dollar value of existing American gold stocks and so raised prices. In his fourth fireside chat (October 22, 1933), the President announced the new policy.

Six days later the RFC began buying gold at

prices well above the world market, gradually raising the rate until in mid-January of 1934 it reached $34.45 an ounce. Since gold had previously been worth $20.67 an ounce, the dollar had in effect been devalued by about 40 per cent.

Then a new page was turned by the Gold Reserve Act of January 30, 1934. This authorized the President to fix the gold content of the dollar at between 50 and 60 per cent of its former weight. Of the profit which the Treasury would make through the revaluation of its gold stocks, two billion dollars was to be used as a stabilization fund to keep the dollar in reasonable balance with foreign currencies. All the gold owned by the Federal Reserve Banks was to be handed over to the Treasury and paid for with dollar certificates. Gold coin was removed from the monetary system. Two days after this sweeping measure became law, the President revalued the dollar at a rate that kept just inside the maximum legal devaluation of 60 per cent, and gold was now bought at a rate ($35 an ounce) that reflected almost exactly the devaluation. Nearly $3,000,000,000 profit resulted from these measures. Although the formal purpose of the Stabilization Fund was to control the external value of the dollar, it put great internal inflationary powers in the hands of its administrators; they had to get dollars to sell abroad and to get the dollars they had to deposit gold with the Federal Reserve System, adding to the banking reserves in an inflationary sense.

One result of this policy was a drain of European gold into the United States. A permanent and increasing favorable balance of trade existed on the American side, and especially after the armament race had begun in Europe, an increasing demand for goods that dollars or gold could buy in America, with no corresponding increase in American demand for European goods. Each new crisis that racked Europe caused a further movement of gold to America, until the great gold hoard buried at Fort Knox in Kentucky became a symbol of fantastic times. For as the influx continued, the Treasury cut off the new gold from the general currency system by purchasing it direct and allotting it to an "inactive account"; it was sterilized. This hedging against inflation seemed less prudent in the recession of 1937–38, and by the spring of 1938 sterilization was abandoned.

The moment it was seen that the new Administration was sympathetic to an expansion of the currency, it was certain that spokesmen for silver, the traditional monetary friend of the farmer, would be active. An amendment to the Agricultural Adjustment Act authorized the Treasury to fix a ratio between gold and silver and to coin both metals to an unlimited extent at that ratio. Foreign Governments were offered the temptation of paying their debts in silver, at 50 cents an ounce, to a maximum of $200,000,000—a temptation that failed to seduce in competition with the even simpler attractions of not paying at all. Friends of silver, represented by Senator Pittman of Nevada, induced the silver-producing (and consuming) countries represented at the London Economic Conference to agree on a control system which left the main burden of absorbing 70 per cent of the annual production on the American Treasury. The silver was bought at a good deal above its normal market price and still further increased Treasury control over the currency.

In December, 1933, the Treasury began to buy newly mined silver at a price that was profitable both to the silver producers and to the Treasury, which took half the bullion as "seigniorage." The Treasury was then authorized to issue silver certificates against the bullion brought to the mint, a concession that did not satisfy such silverites as Representative Dies of Texas. Pittman again stepped into the breach with legislation, enacted June 19, 1934, that declared it the policy of the United States to raise the proportion of silver in American monetary stocks to one-fourth of the total. The Treasury was directed to buy the white metal until this proportion was reached, or the price rose above $1.293 an ounce. This was yet another addition to the power of the Treasury over the currency, since both the speed of purchase and the rate were within Administrative discretion. The price of silver began to rise in a fashion gratifying to silver producers, and disastrous to China and India. Indeed, China was driven off silver, paradoxical result of a policy destined to rehabilitate silver as a rival to gold. As soon as the silver agreement of 1933 expired, the Treasury began to cut its prices for foreign silver and succeeded in buying it at little more than half the price of domestic silver.

In 1939, the mask was dropped. The new Silver Purchase Act provided for the purchase of all new domestically mined silver at a rate nearly twice the world price. Silver was no longer bought for the formal purpose of "increasing and stabilizing domestic prices." Catering to this sectional interest meant the accumulation of great silver stocks to add to the problem of the gold stocks. None of the critics or defenders of the silver program could have foreseen that, within a few years, $400,000,000 of the accumulated metal would be used in the machinery that produced the atomic bomb.

In his press conference on the day that the message was sent to Congress asking for legislative authority to devalue the dollar (January 15, 1934), the President had declared his own view of the proper location of control over the currency. "The issuance of money or currency or any medium of exchange is solely a Government prerogative." This was good Jacksonian doctrine, and Andrew Jackson was the President's political patron saint. True, General Jackson might have been horrified at the abandonment of "hard money," but the centralization of currency control in the Treasury marked a transfer of power that surpassed in completeness the victory over the Bank of the United States and in effectiveness the establishment of the Independent Treasuries. That gain for Federal authority was permanent.

It was perhaps the only tangible gain, for both fears and hopes had been falsified in the long course of monetary experiment. The Warren theory did not produce that desirable rise in commodity prices which it promised. Agricultural prices in fact fell. The abundance of cheap money did not wipe out unemployment or stimulate investment. On the other hand, there was no inflation, no flight from the dollar, no loss of world confidence in American currency. Experts who had been irritated by the amateurish character of much of the Administration's activity were false prophets of doom, as their opponents were of automatic well-being. The silver schemes were a complete failure; they cost the American taxpayer heavily; and they did great damage to the economic stability of China and Mexico, which had to adopt protective measures. It was proved again, if it needed proof, how feeble were economic laws and business prudence against the claims of a commodity that permanently commanded an eighth of the membership of the Senate of the United States.

CHAPTER IV

THE LIGHT THAT FAILED: NRA

WITHIN two or three years of the end of the great experiment of the "National Recovery Administration," its objects, achievements, and failures were seen through a haze of incredulity. Men who had been at the heart of the fight found it difficult to remember the spirit in which they had plunged into the battle; enemies of the experiment forgot the early days when they had been half-believers, and its symbol, the "Blue Eagle," seemed in retrospect almost as mythical a bird as the phoenix.

Yet there was no clearer proof of the depth and range of the "American jitters" than the NRA. It was designed to meet a continuing emergency whose demoralizing character was such that any remedy was better than none, as long as the remedy was visible, dramatic, and novel.

The absence of what came to be called social services further increased the pressure on the Government to do something drastic. Another winter like 1932–33 would carry most of the American local and state governments beyond their resources. Collections for "community chests" had reached an all-time high in 1932, but the results were bitterly inadequate. It was against such a background that the National Industrial Recovery Act (NRA) became law on June 16, 1933. But there was more immediate pressure than the general anxiety to do *something*. For radicals had introduced in Congress the Black-Connery bill that provided for a national thirty-hour week to spread employment—or, as the critics thought, to spread underemployment and to paralyze, by uniform legalization of a policy of despair, any chance of general recovery.

It was under this threat of rash and disastrous legislation that the Roosevelt Administration acted. There were plans in plenty; there was energy in abundance; and the job of coordinating the plans and utilizing the energy was turned over to General Hugh Johnson, who had behind him a varied and, on the whole, a successful career. He was a West Pointer who had been admitted to the bar while still in the army. He had then held important administrative posts in the war in 1917–18; he had, as head of the Moline Plow Company, learned at first hand what the agricultural depression meant for producers of capital goods for farmers; he had been the principal adviser of Bernard Baruch in various public undertakings. Of energy, originality, charm, and power of leadership, General Johnson had an ample stock. His command of rhetoric, sacred and profane, was soon to be a national asset. Unfortunately, he also possessed some handicapping traits—frequent moodiness, opinionated stubbornness, harsh abruptness, and a tendency to make snap judgments.

The new legislation had an interesting background. In the days of Presidents Coolidge and Hoover, trade associations had made a marvelous growth in numbers and power. When depression came, with general price-slashing and much cut-throat competition, leaders of industry proposed that these trade associations be used to stabilize production and prices, and to prevent "unfair" marketing practices. This would require a suspension of the anti-trust laws. At the same time, leaders of labor were also calling for some broad stabilizing legislation. They wanted laws to provide more employment, to halt the prevalent wage-cutting, and in general to create greater purchasing power for labor. Various schemes for fixing maximum hours and minimum wages took shape. Naturally, Roosevelt and his advisers quickly thought of combining the demands of business and labor.

The objects of the National Industrial Recovery Act were wide enough. In the preamble a "national emergency productive of widespread unemployment and disorganization of industry" was declared to exist. Congress stated that it intended to remedy that situation by the following measures:

promoting the organization of industry for the purpose of cooperative action among trade groups, to induce and maintain united action of labor and management under adequate governmental sanctions and supervision, to eliminate unfair competitive practices, to promote the fullest possible utilization of the present productive capacity of industries, to avoid undue restriction of production (except as may be temporarily required), to increase the consumption of industrial and agricultural products by increasing purchasing power, to reduce and relieve unemployment, to improve standards of labor and otherwise to rehabilitate industry and to conserve natural resources.

A very wide commission, indeed, was given to the Administrator by the Act, but from the beginning his powers were more limited than the preamble suggested. For the job of raising agriculture from the depths was, in practice, the business of the Department of Agriculture and its Agricultural Adjustment Administration (AAA). More important, the great program of public works that was to raise purchasing power was entrusted to a separate organization, the Public Works Administration (PWA). What was left to the National Recovery Administration (NRA) was the fostering of the "united action of labor and management under adequate governmental sanctions and supervision." That was the core of the problem of organization as seen by General Johnson. His experience in the late war had convinced him that, given a tangible object, businessmen could be made to work together for a common purpose; then it had been victory, now it was recovery. And in his original plans, "business" meant big business: the basic, highly unified, highly disciplined industries, like steel, automobiles, and machinery.

The instruments of recovery, the "codes of fair competition," to be approved or, if an industry did not provide one, to be imposed by the President, were to be limited in number and comparatively simple in content. Since the codes would put a bottom under wages and hours and thus end the suicidal competition which was slashing the standards of labor, they would not only win popular approval from the workers, but eliminate the marginal units of production whose only method of survival was wage cuts and the "stretch-out." The codes would, in this view, be a continuation of the necessary but drastic process of eliminating the incompetent units of American industry.

But there was no political chance that such a drastic medicine would be swallowed by the struggling businessman, or even by his badly paid workers whose jobs would be eliminated, if only for a short time, by such a policy. And, within a few weeks of the outlining of the scheme, business big and little was swept into the system, and code-making on a totally unforeseen and largely unmanageable scale swamped the infant organization. Instead of a dozen or so codes, there came ultimately to be more than five hundred. More than two hundred were submitted in the single month of July, 1933. They covered some 22 million workers in every conceivable type of business, living under a mass of legislation that, in addition to the five hundred codes, included nearly two hundred supplementary codes, and 11,000 administrative orders.

In the original version of the NIRA, Section 5 was so broadly drafted that its enactment would have been a real revolution in American law. But in the Senate vigilant defenders of the old bias against "combinations in restraint of trade" managed to amend it to forbid monopolies and to favor "protecting the vocation of manual labor and selling or trading the products thereof." But if the proposed Recovery Act had any meaning, it permitted combinations in restraint of trade, leaving the courts to decide whether the restraint was "reasonable" and whether a Presidential certificate of compliance was adequate proof of reasonableness

The chief sponsor of the bill in the upper chamber, Senator Wagner of New York, refused to admit that the projected act abolished the anti-trust laws. Senator Wagner explicitly denied that the new order was based on the German cartel system, but admitted that it involved "a rationalization of competition." In such a vague atmosphere of verbal agreement it was easy and unimportant to accept the Borah amendment against monopolistic practices, and not be startled by the frank declaration of the President of the United States Chamber of Commerce, H. I. Harriman, that one purpose, and a most important purpose, of the bill was to make possible the establishment of a "fair price" (combined with "fair wages" and "a fair dividend"). Combination in restraint of trade was one thing; combination or cooperation to prevent disastrous competition was another.

The Federal Trade Commission, in the boom years, had begun to consult the leaders in certain industries about practices that were both illegal and disliked, and to build up rules of accepted trade practice that were to be treated as a *"prima facie* law merchant." The Commission, in cooperation with trade associations, thus began to exercise a selective jurisdiction; what both condemned would be prosecuted, and by implication what was not condemned by this new "law merchant" would be immune from prosecution. Hoover, as Secretary of Commerce, had labored to encourage the formation of strong trade associations. "Trade-Practice Conferences" became popular, as a kind of organization for regularizing dispensations from the antitrust laws, as well as courts of commercial conscience. When in 1930 the Department of Justice

announced its disagreement with this view, the
business community showed genuine anger and disillusionment. But the lesson was not forgotten; the
trade associations had acquired the habit of thinking of themselves as legislators. The depression, of
course, immediately intensified the pressure to end
"ruinous competition," and by the summer of 1932,
the necessities of the case had made business acceptance of Government partnership essential. Government oversight of trade rules was to be accepted
in return for the relaxation of the anti-trust laws.
This promised a remedy for a galloping disease,
and it found favor outside the ranks of business.
Every slashing of prices by a competitor which
took away a share of the dwindling business was
no longer a challenge, but a form of piracy. Under the terrible pressure of the depression, the
American businessman turned, unconsciously, to
the medieval idea of the just price and to the business customs of the guild merchant as well as of a
new "law merchant."

If price-fixing was the main bait which the NRA
offered to businessmen, the Recovery Act also appealed to men who were alarmed over the growth
of competitive practices that "cut into profits" and
made competition more rigorous and often "unfair."
A manufacturer who supplied one retailer with a
"demonstrator" who acted as an unpaid addition
to the retailer's sales force and did not supply this

service (or bribe) to a competing retailer might give a decisive lift to the favored customer. This, too, could be done by misleading invoices to get behind a formally fixed price list. Outlawing such practices appealed to businessmen ready to believe that some of the economic troubles of the times had come from a spread of unethical practices.

The resulting programs of reform, as they were embodied in codes, might often seem naive to the hard-boiled believer either in competition or in collectivism. Ranging as they did from a pledge not to receive stolen goods to a refusal to reverse telephone charges, from the denunciation of the practice of first marking up and then cutting down prices to a proscription of the preferential discounts given the great chain stores, these code enactments, if they did nothing more, cast light on the hopes and fears of businessmen. In the desperate years, many an honest businessman must have suffered additional distress from the compulsion to imitate the more nefarious practices of his less scrupulous fellows. If the violence of language with which "unfair competition" was denounced at this time by tens of thousands of believers in "the American system" is to be accounted for, some place must be given to this genuine ethical discomfort.

Meanwhile, the mere threat or promise of the codes led to a rapid increase in production and, to a lesser degree, to a rise in employment designed to take advantage of the period before the wages and hours provisions of the codes in process of negotiation pushed up prices and cut down profits. A brief, law-made boom threatened the negotiation of the codes because the later an industry came under one, the longer it could maneuver and profit by the interregnum. So there was launched the so-called "blanket code" (a name much disliked by General Johnson), or more properly speaking the "President's Re-employment Agreement" (PRA), which was a promise made by individual employers to observe certain minimum conditions of good employment. In evidence of having given this undertaking and as an assertion of a firm determination to abide by these promises, the "Blue Eagle" symbol was to be used by all signers of the agreement (and, later, by members in good standing, of regular code authorities).

The campaign for "selling" the Blue Eagle was launched with the pomp and parade of a Liberty Bond drive; to refuse to sign of the PRA was to defy an aroused and hopeful public opinion. The enthusiasm of a religious crusade spread across the nation. Even more exhilarating was the sense of duty well done and of future benefits assured that accompanied the signing of the early codes. Many business leaders could have joined the President of the National Retail Council in saying they felt, when they signed, "as the Barons at Runnymede must have felt when King John signed the Magna Charta, or as our patriot fathers must have felt when they had affixed their signatures to the great Declaration."

The first code, covering the cotton textile industry, was announced by the President on July 9, 1933. Providing for a forty-hour work week and minimum hourly wages of $12 to $13, it was greeted as ushering in a bright new era. Roosevelt was particularly pleased that it abolished child labor.

Not all businessmen, however, showed enthusiasm; for it was soon discovered that even inside a fairly homogeneous "industry" there were marked conflicts of interest. Hence arose bitter fights, like that in the field of graphic arts between printers who were members of the "Typothetae" and printers who were also publishers of small-town newspapers. The allocation of production quotas was one cause of conflict. Another was the risk that the wage-and-hour standards could be met only by the prosperous units. The question whether it was ethical to clean a suit in New York for less than seventy-five cents was only a sample of the difficulties encountered, especially in the service industries. And the watchers who patrolled the garment districts with fields glasses, to see if a revealing gleam of light showed a breach of the ban on night work, illustrated in their often fruitless vigil the difficulty of enforcing uniform discipline on any industry made up of many small, weak, and highly competitive units.

It was discovered, too, that businessmen often knew little about the general structure of their business, and that important decisions had to be made hastily, on a highly empirical basis. Some codes were "vertical," covering the whole range of processing of a given raw material; thus the lumber code comprehended everything from "felling of trees in Oregon to making of baskets in Jersey City." Others dealt with only one stage in the manufacturing and marketing of some raw material.

The role of the trade associations also presented difficulties. It was laid down in the basic act that "trade or industrial associations or groups" should have the initiative in proposing codes, provided they were "truly representative." There *were* trade associations of that kind, but there were fewer than had been thought. Some trade associations were important, well run, but not representative of the whole industry. Others were simply hasty inventions of promoters who saw in these provisions of NIRA a new field of business to exploit. Still other trade associations were genuine but new and weak. And all represented private interests. True, codemaking was not, on paper, left entirely to the trade associations. Not only did the NRA have a general supervisory power and a right of veto, but representatives of labor and of consumers were placed on the code-making bodies. But it was soon evident that labor representatives were strong only in the degree to which labor was already strong in the business under discussion. And the consumers' representatives were the gallant spokesmen of a highly unorganized mass, the lobbyists of the least-feared pressure group. Labor more and more pinned its hopes on an extension of unionism, and the representatives of the consumers were reduced to protests and inquiries. The Consumers Board appointed by NRA had, in one week, to deal with 73 codes, ranging from funeral service to suspender and belt manufacturing. The codes were written by "industries," a term whose ambiguity was made painfully evident in the winter of 1933–34.

Another problem that involved the NRA administration in endless trouble was that of the classification of industries and the segregation of units entitled to separate codes. It was easy to think and talk of great economic groups like "steel," "automobiles," "woolen textiles," and perhaps not to be very far wrong in thinking that, under these titles, stood identifiable groups of business enterprises similar enough in structure and in problems to be dealt with as units. But it was soon discovered that the typical American business was not so easily classified; that there were scores and hundreds of groups of producers with plausible claims to be separated from other groups of producers.

There thus came into existence codes ranging from the "animal soft hair industry" code, which covered 45 workers, to the retail trade code covering 3,500,000. Even the general classification of industries into 17 categories did not begin to solve the problem. The categories were themselves too wide. Thus "Miscellaneous Industrial" included "cinders, ashes, and scavenger trade (largely trucking)," the "retail jewelry trade," the "retail trade," and "construction." "Miscellaneous Commercial and Professional" included "air transport" and the "laundry trade." Compared with this, "Transportation Equipment," which brought together "automobile manufacturing" and "funeral vehicles," was a model of rationality or at any rate of plausibility.

The likelihood of integrating such diverse units into a general scheme did not seem high, and as trade recession, price rises, labor troubles, and other reminders that recovery was still a problem pressed on the Administration and on NRA, the necessity for speed led to pressure politics by applicants for codes, and made difficult the harmonizing of one code with another. The NRA Legal Division did attempt to keep a general check on the process, and what over-all view *was* achieved was the result of these efforts. But despite the issue of a "model" code, the new "law merchant" seemed likely to lack the generality of law and to be at best in the stage of accumulating cases from which a future Mansfield would make a system.

Yet the making of codes went on even when the faith that most needed restoring was that of many of the code-makers. A Washington paper listed the day's activities like a sports bulletin. "Code Hearings" ranged from the "Folding Box Authority, Mayflower Hotel," through "Motion Picture Laboratories" and "Fly Swatter Manufacturing Industry" (both at the Willard), through "Men's Neckwear" (at the Raleigh) to "Whlse Cop. Brass, Bronze, and Rel.Al." (at the Carlton). Code hearings were public and educational; they seldom represented the real battlefields; the decisive battles were fought inside the industries and were settled by harassed code officials driven to take any formal solution, rather than none, of jurisdictional problems that seemed insoluble.

The odd or downright absurd character of some of the shot-gun marriages and Reno divorces of types of industry gave new ammunition to the increasing group of critics who were working on the hypothesis that ridicule kills in the United States as well as France. Sometimes it was the title of the "industry" that caused laughter and skepticism. The outside world was amused or irritated by the discovery that there were three industries connected with mops: "Wet Mop," "Dry Mop," and "Mop-stick." After that, the reasonableness of a special code for so easily definable an industry as the "Armored-cars operators" was freely conceded.

Other difficulties arose from the fact that a given business unit, under one management and with one common financial structure, might be subject to more than one code in actual operation. Sometimes identical products were under more than one code, rubber balls falling under both the athletic-goods and toy codes. It was all very well for a manufacturer to undertake to obey the rules of the code to which his business belonged, but to what code did he owe allegiance? Often he did not know. The administration of codes cost money, and not merely did employers dislike assessments, but they detested the multiplication of assessments. As the code authorities grew in power, the lesser trade associations lost their utility and dallied with the idea of compulsory membership, a suggestion that seemed to many harassed businessmen a threat to legalize racketeering.

For the businessman *was* harassed. He had more and more paper work to do, not through anybody's fault, but because of the nature of the controls set up or attempted under the codes. Statistics were called for that only the most highly organized corporations could provide, and not always even they. A business might, in an extreme case, have to introduce fourteen systems of cost-accounting, and have to obey the rules of twenty-five different trade-practice agreements. In short, many of the codes were quickly found to be unadministrable. This was a result of the abandonment of the original limited, and possibly practicable, design of regulating only a few basic industries.

General Johnson was not responsible for the original error, and he gallantly refused to admit defeat. He was indefatigable in word and act. He was tireless in Washington, tireless in his brisk raids over the whole field. From the beginning the theory and probable practice of the NRA had been criticized by many economists. Critics who were not totally skeptical asked for a little more thought and consistency. They asked for a policy that, when it was belatedly adopted, was described by General Johnson as sitting "in purple silence—like Buddha on a lotus flower in serene and effortless contemplation of its composite navel."

No one could accuse the General of sitting on a lotus flower or exhibiting purple silence. He kept on claiming for the credit of NRA the four million persons who he asserted had been reemployed in 1933. He also claimed that, but for NRA, there would have been a downward movement of employment and income. To doubt or deny this was to be a pundit and a kind of national saboteur.

Yet more and more people did deny this. The rise in production and employment that had preceded the coming into effect of NRA stopped with its enactment. The discounting of its effect on prices was over. What was left was the higher prices. That rise angered the still vast body of unemployed and the vast body of persons whose pay had not been raised.

These malcontents tended to concentrate their fire on the aid which, it was alleged, NRA was giving to monopoly. The outcry grew so strong that the President was forced to take action or at least to take notice, and in January, 1934, appeals from code decisions were permitted to the Department of Justice or to the Federal Trade Commission. Pressure was not abated and an independent inquiry that spring under Clarence Darrow barely headed off a Senate investigation. The Senate might have been safer, for the Darrow reports were highly condemnatory. He and his committee ignored much evidence pointing to the protection of small businesses by the codes and fixed their attention on instances of oppression. Small business, Darrow concluded, was certain to fare ill under capitalism and could prosper only in a Socialist regime. It was unfortunate that a more judicious report was not submitted. General Johnson shrugged this one off as Socialist or Communist propaganda. But he did take some remedial action, for the attempt to insist on codes in the service industries was abandoned.

Enforcement was the most obvious, as it was to prove the fatal, weakness of NRA. The President's last weapon, the imposition of a licensing system, was never used. The acceptance of the law, or "compliance," became the greatest headache. The "blanket code" was not enforceable by anything but public opinion and the sanction based on it, the removal of the Blue Eagle. But it was one thing to organize mass demonstrations in favor of NRA; it was another to keep the signers of the agreement to their word. It was another thing, too, to enforce the legal powers given by the statute to the NRA. General Johnson seemed to believe that sermons and harangues would do half the work and that dread of public hostility would do the rest. He described the loss of the Blue Eagle, in one of his most famous utterances, as the breaking of "the bright sword of the offender's commercial honor in the eyes of his neighbors." But the businessmen drummed out of the industrial army by being stripped of the Blue Eagle often seemed none the worse for it.

The victims were nearly all small men, harassed, perplexed, and frequently caught doing what their customers wanted. Why should small shopkeepers be held up to public scorn when the greatest of all American industrialists, Henry Ford, refused to accept the NRA? In vain, General Johnson explained that he had never said that he would "crack down" on Henry Ford. The public thought he had and thought he should.

By the summer of 1934, the whole machine was becoming stalled. Difficulties increased. It was necessary, for example, to admit that allowances had to be made for the lower standard of living and wages in the South, but disconcerting to find that the South was defined in ten different geographical ways in the codes and orders. Labor was beginning to wonder what it was getting, if anything, from its right to collective bargaining. The small businessman was now convinced that he gained nothing worth the trouble imposed on him in the name of "industrial self-government." The practice of arbitrary "selective justice" was perhaps necessary and natural, but it terribly weakened the moral hold of the system. And, with the decline of popular faith, "compliance" worked under the handicaps that had proved fatal to prohibition.

In September, 1934, General Johnson finally resigned. He was replaced by a Board, with Donald Richberg as chairman; but despite firm declarations of belief in the utility of NRA by the President, it was seen by many close to him as an incubus. Concession after concession was made to the critics; the facilities given for monopolies were taken away; prices rose and employment did not.

Roosevelt asked for a two-year extension of the Act. But neither labor nor capital was showing much interest in continuance of the experiment when its life was suddenly ended by the Supreme Court.

From the beginning, lawyers and administrators had felt doubts about the constitutionality of NIRA. Dr. Alexander Sachs, one of General Johnson's close collaborators, had expressed his skepticism while the bill was on its way through Congress, stressing especially the "unspecified, endlessly discretionary delegation of power by Congress to the Executive." It was on this point that the Supreme Court especially concentrated its fire in the decisive case of *Schechter Poultry Corporation v. United States*. The Court finding on May 27, 1935, was unanimous. It rejected the argument that a grave national crisis created constitutional authority; it rejected the view that there was no distinction between direct and indirect effects on interstate commerce; and it insisted that, in giving unlimited discretion to the President to approve codes, Congress had far overstepped the bounds of permissive delegation of legislative powers.

The legal killing of NRA was received with more verbal than real indignation. Widespread relief was felt inside as well as outside Administration circles. The labor provisions were soon salvaged by more effective legislation than had been provided by 7-A; the controls of wages and hours and limitations on child labor were salvaged, too, by fresh legislation; but the whole idea of "industrial self-government" was extinct, not much regretted either by the 22,000,000 workers or by the 5,000,000 employers who had tried to live under the codes.

A final verdict on NRA will forever remain impossible. Involved in the judgment are too many intangibles. Foremost among these is the question of the degree to which recovery in 1933 had ceased to be a merely economic problem and had become one of the stability of the social order, in which the ending of panic and the creation of faith were the essential conditions of escape from irreparable disaster—or from far more drastic and revolutionary solutions. More positively, NRA can be credited with breaking down the legal and political barriers to Federal action in the field of child labor, wages and hours regulation, and other later achievements of the New Deal. For good or ill, its work was not entirely "interrèd with its bones." Later "fair trade" laws in the states owed some of their popularity to the precedents set in the codes, and some economists believe that the courts in upholding such legislation have been supporting monopoly as much as the codes did. Yet the memory of the great experiment was not always hostile or contemptuous. A traveler in the South, years after the Supreme Court decision, noted that many mill workers looked back to the Blue Eagle as fondly as many brokers remembered Hoover prosperity. "But we done right well," they would say, "under the NRA. Twelve dollars a week!"

Perhaps the most sober judgment was that of a committee of the House of Representatives in 1937. The NRA, it stated, was an experiment to ascertain how far proposals by industry would uncover policies usefully related to causes of depression and would develop means of resolving conflicts of group interest. So regarded, the experiment yielded some results, though not final solutions of the problems raised. The assets and liabilities of NRA were always confused and confusing; but perhaps the whole experiment can best be charged up in the nation's accounts to education in the limited capacity of good will, economic empiricism, and advertising techniques to solve deep-rooted maladjustments.

CHAPTER V

THE NEEDY AND THE INSECURE

WHEN the depression of 1929 was more than ten years in the past, James Daniel O'Brien of Brooklyn lost his last job and went "on relief." That cut him off from his family in Massachusetts and cut his children off from their grandparents, because, so investigators from the *Ladies' Home Journal* learned: " 'They just have their own ideas. They can't understand how anybody can be on relief.' " That such ideas could keep their force, after ten years of mass unemployment, gives some indication of the strength with which the American people must have held them in 1929.

A good deal of self-deception attended this attitude even in the boom days. Manifest involuntary unemployment on a serious scale existed in stagnant industrial areas like Lowell or Manchester; permanent underemployment was visible in great coal fields. And while there were communities like "Middletown" (Muncie, Indiana) where private charity, organized on a semi-compulsory basis, provided for most of the destitute, in general it was already true that the needs of the poorest Americans were for the most part met by cities and counties out of the taxes—as far as they were met; for they were often not met and still more often met badly. The governmental areas were too small; pools of destitution existed next to prosperous areas, and the depressed cities or counties could not call on the resources of their richer neighbors. State law was often harsh and antiquated; the "poor farm" was a name of horror to its possible guests, and too often a source of profit to a political nominee who received the right to exploit it for services to his party.

America had often known temporary breakdowns in general prosperity, but it took years of mass unemployment to teach the American people that poverty was no proof of sin and that private charity was no longer even a pretense at being enough.

Before the end of the Hoover Administration, the old doctrine that the Federal Government had nothing to do with relief had been covertly if not openly abandoned. The "Emergency Relief and Reconstruction Act" of 1932 made possible both direct loans to the states and the direct employment of workers on Federal jobs like road building. Just as the Federal Government had been forced to help the states, most states were forced to accept relief responsibilities in the face of the financial and administrative collapse of cities and counties.

It was inevitable that the new Administration should do more than Hoover's in accepting Federal responsibility for distress. But, from the beginning, the Roosevelt Administration tried to limit its relief grants to helping the unemployed, not to helping the poor as such. The Federal Emergency Relief Act set up a relief administration which under Harry Hopkins controlled grants to the states but, except in rare cases (unlike the later WPA), did not directly administer them. Another organization, the Civil Works Administration, also under Hopkins, had a brief life in 1933–34 when it was expected to serve as a kind of "shot-in-the-arm" to a languid economy. At a cost of nearly a billion dollars, Hopkins put some four million men to work by January of 1934; but his costly experiment ended in the spring. Although relief under FERA and CWA was supposed to be given to the "unemployed" or to alleviate distress "arising from unemployment," it was in fact often given to persons who might have been classified as "unemployable." Most of it amounted to nothing more than subsistence doles, giving little permanent benefit to the economy. From 1933 to 1935, many workers in the relief field hoped that the Federal Government would accept its responsibility for providing long-term forms of work-relief instead of leaving it to states, cities and counties, most of which were no better prepared to carry the burden under Roosevelt than they had proved to be under Hoover.

By 1935 the mind of the Administration was made up. Federal help would be confined to employables who would be hired under a carefully governed plan, while unemployables would be handed back to the states and local authorities for care. A comprehensive Works Progress Administration was set up by executive orders beginning in May, 1935, under the experienced Harry Hopkins; and its aims were well defined by its first Assistant Administrator, Corrington Gill. It was to provide "an army of workers . . . demonstrating their employability by actually working on projects under the works program, and carefully selected foremen who have been employed to see that they do efficient work." The workers thus enrolled were only a tenth of all gainful workers, but they were half of the total unemployed; nearly five million workers and more than three million families were declared eligible. At no time did the WPA promise to care for all of these. Even the President's original aim of two and a half million jobs included, in practice, boys in the Civilian Conservation Corps. Only in 1939 were nearly three million men employed on WPA projects. But until 1941, year in, year out, nearly two million Americans were found working on WPA projects, saved from poverty and mere relief; given constructive work to do, not the FERA dole that Roosevelt had finally condemned as "a narcotic, a subtle destroyer of the human spirit."

Relief, as such, was not the business of the WPA. It was admitted that "relief workers are not, to be sure, the cream of the labor supply," but they were in general representative workers. *Fortune* in a survey made in 1937 denied the general allegation that "the reliefers are bums," yet WPA and other forms of relief started with two strikes against them. Despite vigorous attempts to make work on WPA not relief of distress but employment paid for at its economic worth to the community, it was impossible to divorce it entirely from general relief problems. And the tradition of waste and politics in public works cast its shadow over WPA achievements.

The WPA did itself some harm by seeming to put too much trust in "planning," whereas under the limitations imposed by Congress, its permanently "emergency" character made real planning impossible. Its labor force was not recruited according to the needs of the projects, but according to the funds voted by Congress.

Again, WPA was excluded from various useful fields of employment by its basic undertaking not to compete with private business. Fidelity to this undertaking was insured by the vigilance with which the Congressional representatives of business watched the projects. WPA was in consequence largely confined to such public works as roads, bridges, public buildings, sewers, sidewalks, recreation grounds, dams, and swimming pools, and to made-jobs of kinds condemned by the critics as "leaf-raking." Even in the field of public works, WPA was subject to harassing restrictions. It was an obvious economy to buy rather than to rent road-building and other machinery, but such a policy was bitterly opposed by the highly vocal representatives of private contracting interests in Congress. Indeed, the embattled contractors finally obtained a nominal prohibition of the use of any WPA funds for buildings costing over $52,000; but in practice this counted for little. Thousands of roads, dams, bridges, schools, and university buildings cost larger sums.

Public works well worth undertaking and made desirable by the existence of pools of employable workers were sometimes left unattempted because no local sponsor could be found. Some local governments were also accused of refusing Federal help just before election times, for if the WPA rolls were full on election day, the gratitude of the workers would probably go to the Administration in Washington. On the other hand, the alleged political abuse of WPA by the national Administration was a genuine grievance of Republicans and dissident Democrats. Critics pointed with suspicion to the rise in WPA enrollment just before the election in 1936; they made far more specific allegations of political pressure in the election of 1938, especially in the primary fights. In Kentucky, where the President was supporting Senator Barkley in a doubtful battle with Governor Chandler, it was freely asserted that WPA workers were marshaled behind the White House favorite. One class of WPA officials, the supervisors, was continually and plausibly under fire for being chosen on a political basis. Since the recruitment of new workers and the retention of the old was in great part in their hands, they had abundant temptation to play politics, and some succumbed.

In other ways, WPA was involved in bitter quarrels because its work bit so deeply into American life. A controversy arose over wage differentials between North and South. The WPA administrators would have preferred uniformity, but refused to let their system be a guinea pig. It was comparatively easy to find jobs and useful jobs for laborers, but there were hundreds of thousands of white collar workers who made poor roadmakers and at the same time lost competence in their old crafts. Retraining was not always easy and was often opposed by union leaders as a danger to the craft structure. The literate could be employed in libraries, for example (sometimes at higher wages than thrifty municipalities paid junior members of the regular staff). Hundreds were enrolled in literary projects, above all on the admirable series of state and city guides. Even this valuable project had its critics. Some citizens of Massachusetts saw no reason why public money should be spent on a guide that insisted on dragging the skeletons of Sacco and Vanzetti from the cupboard. Some citizens of New Orleans found the ironical treatment of the difference between the law and the practice of gambling in the Crescent City impertinent. But the guides were so good that they met less carping than other cultural projects.

No modern government had ever been a patron of the pictorial arts on the scale that the United States became under the lead of WPA. Post offices all over the land were covered with frescoes. Most of them were competent and some extremely good, but they were often startlingly modernistic to small communities for which art was still a laborious way of getting the results of photography.

It was the theater projects, however, that received the most bitter criticism. Over great areas the living theater was dead, slain by the movies. There was no urgent need, many thought, to revive it. Moreover, the plays produced by the WPA theater project were often regarded as modern and "subversive" (that is, radical), when they were

not downright propaganda for the Administration
—as was any play that represented America as a
country plagued by poverty and ignorance. Charges
were made that the theater projects suffered from
internal politics and that in New York it was more
important to be a good Communist than a good
actor. Suspicions were easily aroused, especially in
Congressmen from evangelical districts of the
South who had been brought up to regard the
playhouse as a device of the devil and were horrified by rumors that in some plays white and colored performers acted together. Perhaps if some
Congressmen had been more literate they would
have known that Congreve was not a Communist
subverter of the American way of life, but it is also
possible that had they known more about Congreve
they would not have liked him.

By 1939, the patience of Congress was exhausted.
Despite the President's protest that Congress was
singling out "a special group of professional people
for a denial of work in their own professions," the
Act creating the successor to WPA, the Emergency
Relief Administration Act of 1939, barred theater
projects. The role of the United States Government as a patron of the public art once so highly
appreciated and subsidized in the republic of
Athens was over. The permanent results of the
program are hard to assess, but it did save some
talents from sterility, it did encourage some useful

theatrical and musical experiments, and it introduced performances by living actors to regions that had almost forgotten the art since the last stock company had left the local opera houses.

The full achievement of the WPA was impressive and was obtained at a cost which the nation could well afford to pay. Many a city, many a university, many a rural community, received permanently valuable additions to their resources and amenities from Hopkins's organization. Heads of the WPA boasted that, down to the autumn of 1937, it had erected 11,000 public buildings and repaired some 30,000 more; it had constructed 43,000 miles of road and repaired another 146,000; and it had covered much of the country with useful works ranging from athletic fields to levees. It had planted more than 9 million trees, and renovated nearly 30 million library books. It had put women to work on sewing projects, doctors in useful clinics, and architects in drafting offices. One of its component elements, the National Youth Administration, had helped a multitude of hard-pressed high school and college students to keep on with their education. Finding them part-time employment, it had supplied the margin which made continued study possible. As time gave citizens perspective, the jokes about "boon-doggling" were forgotten, and the immense value of the WPA in alleviating misery, maintaining self-respect, and

converting the energies of idle men into works of
lasting benefit, was appreciated at its true worth.

With the ending of FERA, the withdrawal of
the Federal Government from direct relief was an
essential condition to any proper operation of the
general unemployment-abatement policy of the
Roosevelt Administration. To continue aiding the
states in dealing with normal casualties was held
to remove any stimulus to local improvement in
providing social security. It was not only thought
undesirable that the states and their subdivisions
should thus become parasitic on the Federal Government, but it was held that a general relief policy
underwritten by the Federal Government could
easily be represented as making a work program
unnecessary. If this was right, WPA had every
interest in separating its problems from the old
problem of the aged, the sick, the young, the unemployable. Yet whatever austere theory might
be professed, men would be taken on WPA who
were not its business and whose employability was
far below adequate standards, if the only alternative was to leave them to the mercies of an inadequate relief program. And over great areas, relief
programs were very inadequate indeed.

By the end of 1935, panic was past; and when
relief was turned back to the states, it was turned
back to political units whose habits and institutional resources had not notably changed. It was,

indeed, an evasion to talk of relief being given back to the states. It was often turned back to counties and to cities, many of them at the end of their taxing resources, many unconverted to the view that relief was a problem calling for skilled administration, for objectivity, and for the elimination of politics. Some states accepted full responsibility for those workers classed as "employables." Some states made no distinctions and refused any responsibility. But whatever policy was adopted, few were the instances in which state or local relief was not given on terms that made WPA highly attractive by comparison. Thus was created a new underprivileged class, that of "employable workers" who failed to get on WPA and were reduced to relief. It was an inevitable consequence that being on WPA came to be a privilege, and hence time limits were imposed on WPA workers; when the time was up, they suddenly found themselves, for no fault of their own, plunged from the meager solvency of WPA into the near destitution of relief.

Relief standards varied greatly from state to state, and within even rich states, according to the solvency and policies of the local political units. Most cities, great and small, had relief crises as funds ran out, and as changes in WPA policy had their inevitable repercussions on the total relief situation. In poor states, especially in the

South, not only were relief rolls cut and relief standards wretchedly low, but administration was amateurish and politics-ridden. Inevitably, the main sufferers were the Negroes in the South; their economic situation was the worst, and they did not possess any effective means of political pressure such as could, at times, be used with effect by the masses in the great cities of the North.

With the pressure of relief loads falling heavily on inelastic tax revenues, themselves the result in many states of obsolete tax laws, it was natural that localities should try to keep to a minimum the share of their inadequate revenues that went to strangers. States felt the same way, and, in the highly nomadic society of the twentieth-century republic, laws of "settlement" were enacted that in their severity would have startled eighteenth-century England and provoked anew the censures which Adam Smith had passed in 1776. Some states raised to three years the period of residence that qualified for relief; others made it terribly easy to lose the legal qualification that alone gave a right to appeal for aid. For a time, transients were helped in Federal camps, but in general, so far as the local law went, the American who left his home town to look for a job was taking a very serious risk indeed. The natural result was that the mobility of labor was lessened and the stagnant pools of unemployment remained full. Rather, they would have remained full if Americans had taken the law as seriously as other peoples might have done. Mobility was not destroyed; it was simply seriously penalized. So, too, were the poorest communities, whose relief burden was highest and who were not able to share their troubles with their more prosperous neighbors in their own states.

Although it was on WPA that the Roosevelt Administration placed its hopes both of relieving distress and of priming the pump of the national economy, the needs of other classes than the unemployed were too urgent to be ignored. And these needs were summed up in a phrase that was also a program, "social security."

When President Roosevelt signed the Social Security Act on August 14, 1935, he declared that "today a hope of many years' standing is in large part fulfilled," and he thanked Congress, the executive departments, and others for their share in "this sound, needed and patriotic legislation." The statute embodied a momentous change in the American psychology. Once such "socialistic" legislation had been regarded as proper enough for Europe, but unnecessary and improper for the New World. That the law was now indispensable most citizens—since the cruel lessons of the depression— had come to agree. That the law was wholly sound was widely doubted at the time, and subsequent legislation, silently changing much of the basic Act, suggested that the doubts were legitimate. Its main objects, however—the coordination of Federal and state action on old age and unemployment insurance, and the grant of continuing assistance to the states in public health work, vocational rehabilitation, and aid to children, widows, and the blind— were eminently commendable.

The Social Security Act had great dramatic as well as practical importance, since it marked so striking an innovation in American legislation, so notable a change in the relations between the Federal Government and the states. No shibboleth had been more sincerely mouthed in the years before and during the depression than denunciations of anything like the British "dole." But men came to revise their attitude toward the "dole." The years of mass unemployment, loss of savings, and failure of private pension schemes ate away the moral and emotional basis of the once universal belief. Its intellectual basis was undermined too. It was not evident that the disastrous effects of Federal relief were as great as the physical and moral losses accompanying years of unemployment, making life for the individual and his dependents a bitter struggle for mere survival. Proud independence did not flourish in the bread line, or family feeling under the legal coercion that bound in common want the members of a legal group, those who had some work and wages and those who had none.

But it was not only this change in the climate of informed opinion that made possible the passing of the Act. The increasing pressure of uninformed opinion, inside and outside Congress, also counted for much.

The limited scope of recovery had put an end to the hope that "business," left to itself, would reduce the problems of poverty to proportions manageable by the traditional means. That realization had fostered all kinds of radical movements, from the "share the wealth" of Huey Long of Louisiana to the "End Poverty in California," the EPIC movement led by Upton Sinclair. But the two most effective sources of political pressure came from the Townsendites and from the odd aggregation of movements and individuals supporting the proposals of Representative Lundeen of Minnesota.

The Townsend scheme bore the marks of its birth in California. Not only was the political climate of that commonwealth traditionally favorable to panaceas, but Dr. Townsend's remedy appealed to a very important group, the old. Into the Golden State there had poured, during the golden years, hundreds of thousands of refugees from the climate and toil of the Middle West. Some had few resources; most had saved, they thought, enough for a life of frugal comfort in the cheap and easy climate. The depression wiped out savings and reduced to angry misery hundreds of thousands of men and women who knew they had earned a peaceful old age. Dr. Townsend had the answer.

He appealed to two different groups of the discontented. First of all, to the aged he promised $200 a month, much more than most of them had counted on in the days of their solvency. Then, since the beneficiaries were to retire from all work and spend their allowance within the month in which they received it, the scheme had some appeal to younger people who were unemployed and to believers in the virtues of accelerating the circulation of money. It also attracted the attention of politicians who knew the value of so big a voting block as the aged and who hoped that general support for the plan would not involve any concrete responsibility for putting it into operation or meeting the cost. That cost, economists calculated, would be formidable. Paul Douglas estimated that half the then national income would have to be turned over to beneficiaries of the scheme, that is, to 8 per cent of the population. The exponents of the scheme proposed to finance it by a 2 per cent tax on transactions that, skeptics calculated, would produce an adequate· revenue only as a consequence of a rise in prices which would reduce the real income of the worker at $16 a week by at least a third—in order to pay $50 a week to the aged. That this scheme should have had so powerful an appeal as to frighten many prudent politicians into verbal support was proof enough that something had to be done.

What the solution was to be was not clear. People manifested a sturdy refusal to learn from any experience paid for outside the United States. Since the British system was associated with the "dole," some more American scheme was sought. It was at first found in Wisconsin, which had enacted a pioneer unemployment law, in which its spokesmen took great pride. President Roosevelt had appointed in June, 1934, a Committee on Economic Security under Secretary Frances Perkins. It had a number of expert advisory groups, and the comprehensive plan of joint Federal-State action which they reported owed much to Wisconsin ideas.

Yet the Wisconsin scheme was not regarded with approval by the experts who had overcome any reluctance to learn from foreign countries. It permitted the creation of pockets in the general state scheme; industries or single plants were allowed to set up their own plans. Only employers contributed to the scheme and it was largely controlled by them. This was "the American plan," as contrasted with the British scheme, in which all payments were pooled, in which workers also paid, and in which control was left to the Government. Behind the defense of the American plan lay a belief that employers had a special duty to their unemployed, that an unemployment tax was a kind of penalty for neglecting them, and that those employers who kept up a demand for labor deserved a merit rating as a reward.

The Social Security Act, as passed in 1935, covered unemployment insurance, old-age pensions, public aid to uninsured and needy aged people, care of the blind, provision for dependent children, and the expansion of existing services in the public health field and in maternal and child care. Indeed, it was almost a blanket scheme. For the aged, the program was to be administered by the national Goverment alone. All employers and workers in the country, save certain exempted groups (small businesses with eight or less employees, farms, domestic service, seamen, and so on), were to pay a payroll tax. This was to begin at 1 per cent of the wage of each worker, and rise to 3 per cent in 1949. From the receipts a great reserve was to be built up in the national Treasury; and out of it, beginning in 1942, superannuated workers were to be paid pensions of $10 to $85 a month, according to their wage scale and the length of time they had been paying into the fund.

The scheme for unemployment insurance, meanwhile, was to be a Federal-state scheme. The national Government was to levy an unemployment tax which would start at 1 per cent of the wage of the worker and rise in 1938 to 3 per cent. Again certain exemptions were made to prevent hardship. Whenever a state plan for aiding the unemployed was approved by the Social Security Board, the state would receive 90 per cent of the tax levied within its borders, the other 10 per cent being kept for grants to assist in administrative costs. Thus the states really managed the work; the Federal Government simply kept the right to approve or disapprove any plan presented. Before the end of 1937, all the states had passed satisfactory unemployment insurance laws.

The new breakwater against unemployment was built at an unlucky time. Its benefits came into operation only in 1938, just as a heavy business recession suddenly increased the load. The state offices administering the system were new to the task, were sometimes politically minded, and were everywhere faced with the results of the inadequacy of the benefits. Even in New York, with a high level of administrative competence, the delays were irritating and were made an important campaign issue by the Republican candidate Thomas Dewey in the gubernatorial election of that year.

More serious was the discovery that the new system would cover only a small part of the unemployed for a short time. The best that a fairly well-paid worker in a state with a good scheme could hope for averaged less than $100 for about ten weeks in a year. In their zeal for actuarial purity, the drafters of the law had ignored the danger of illusory benefits. To give anything like adequate benefits, the payroll tax would have to be rather more than 5 per cent, instead of the average of 2.7 per cent. That, in turn, meant that the employees would have to be called on to pay a share of the tax. There had been and were good arguments for associating the workers with the scheme by making them pay part of the cost of greater benefits. But these were outweighed by the greater political risks of such a system. True, the Republican attack on the Social Security Act in the campaign of 1936, where in some states attacks on the alleged threat to the worker's pay envelopes had been inserted in the envelopes themselves, seemed to have backfired; but 1936 had not been a normal year.

The problems of the aged were not likely to be forgotten by an Administration and a Congress under the pressure of the Townsendites. Social security obviously included security from the nightmare of the poor farm or of the burden placed on children who, for good reasons, might find the support of infirm parents beyond their meager resources, or even simply on children who had more of the spirit of King Lear's elder daughters than popular American folklore suggested as likely.

The old-age insurance scheme, like the unemployment insurance scheme, was based on principles appropriate to a private insurance company's business. Too little account was taken of the fact that the scheme was compulsory, that it was universal, and that its solvency was inseparable from the solvency of the United States. Within the first three years more than forty million workers applied for old-age accounts. Insurance taxes were computed and reserves built up that, had the scheme continued unaltered, would by 1980 have created a reserve of $47,000,000,000. That is, the aged would by then have been owed the entire national debt of 1938, the year when benefits were to begin. This would have been at least as deflationary as the payroll tax for unemployment insurance. Such actuarial purity involved forcing elderly people to contribute to a scheme that could give them only illusory benefits. These arguments led to a practical abandonment, in 1939, of the project of piling up reserves. They led, also, to a recasting of the benefits which now gave the old substantial rewards for their compulsory contribution. But since the Federal Government still did not make any contribution to the funds, these uncovenanted benefits were paid for by the young, who received less than actuarial justice called for, while the aged received more.

No insurance scheme, however generous, could earn that name and do much good to masses of aged poor whose earning days were past and whose

former contributions to the wealth of the United
States were beyond accountancy. For them, the
Federal Government abandoned its austere role as
mere controller and collector and made a positive
contribution. By a system of "grants-in-aid," state
schemes of assistance for the aged were financed,
in part, by Federal money. The administration of
this scheme naturally produced difficulties. Since
each state (under general control) could make its
own rules and regulations, there were temptations
to pad the rolls; young Oklahoma turned out to
have a surprising number of aged residents, and
politics and favoritism were not unknown elsewhere. But the Social Security Board did impose
increasing regularity, and while some Federal
money may have been wasted, the amended system, by 1940, had earned the praise of such former
critics as Dr. Abraham Epstein.

One other class of beneficiaries under the new
dispensation was the large group of children and
mothers whose normal support had been removed
by death or desertion. The "widow's pension" was
a method of public relief dating back to 1911 in
some states; by 1933 it existed in most of the country and had been extended to cover the numerous
family groups deprived of the male breadwinner
by other means than death. But the generalization
of the system uncovered startling discrepancies in
the amounts paid to the beneficiaries. These ranged

from $69 a month in Massachusetts to $11 a month in Mississippi and $4.33 in Arkansas. The South was not the only region that doled out its aid with caution; Kansas provided an average of only $14 and New Hampshire less than $20 a month. Inside states, too, where the counties were the effective units, there were astonishing discrepancies; some Illinois counties paid but $2 or $3 a month per child, other counties from $16 to $22.

It was not only the great discrepancies in payments, but the great masses of children left unaided, that made the schemes look better on state statute books than in operation. In 1935, some 7,400,000 children under sixteen years of age were receiving relief, and it was estimated that there were more than 350,000 families with no male breadwinner; but only 110,000 families and only 280,000 children were benefiting in any form and on any scale from family pensions. In more than half the counties of the United States there were no beneficiaries at all.

Federal aid was specially needed by orphaned or deserted children. The Social Security Act did undertake to provide grants-in-aid for state schemes for dependent children, but these grants were much less generous than those offered for old-age pensioners (who, after all, were voters). Federal grants ceased whenever state payments reached $18 for the first child or $12 for the succeeding children.

But (an important innovation) the grants were conditional on a uniform system administered by the *state*; they could not be earned by counties, and states were thus given an incentive to take over an important duty that hitherto had been left to local units. More grants-in-aid were made for child welfare, for crippled children, and for maternal welfare; and although it still made a great difference what part of the United States children or mothers or widows lived in, it now mattered less in what county they lived. The doctrine laid down by the Supreme Court in the case of *Massachusetts v. Mellon* was now given general effect. It was for the United States to determine how it would use its revenue to promote the welfare of great classes of handicapped human beings, and to do so was no wrong to a taxpayer or no wrong for which the courts would give a remedy.

Those sections of the American people so fortunate as to escape the necessity of going on relief, or the strain of desperately avoiding it, naturally but erroneously came to see the problem largely as one of parasites on the public purse, who preferred not to work. They believed that if relief were cut, the former recipients would be forced to take jobs at an economic wage. It was perceived that, in some places and at some times, relief payments were in excess of the wage rates of available jobs. Farmers, at harvest time, looked with dislike on any alternative means of support that kept down the supply of temporary labor. In the South, some feared that the Negro population would "get above itself" were it paid or given pensions or other forms of relief on anything like a Northern scale.

The administrators of relief knew how far from the truth these fears generally were. But they also knew how essential it was to lessen the hostility of the taxpayers to the continuance of the relief programs. So, at harvest times, relief was often cut and, under exterior pressure, men were from time to time cut off the relief rolls, either to make room for others or to test their desire for private employment. In general, jobs in private employment paid better than under the most favorable relief conditions. But it was soon evident that whatever the will to work of the relief recipients, they might stand all day idle in the market place because no man had hired them.

To be cut off relief, in 1936, was less serious than to be cut off in 1937 (when the recession was imminent), or than in 1938 or 1939. When WPA dropped nearly 800,000 workers in 1939 because they had been 18 months on its rolls, a test made three months later showed that only 12.7 per cent had got jobs and half of those received less wages than the WPA had paid. The 87 per cent still unemployed simply fell back on local relief, on savings, or on begging and borrowing. The effect of being dropped from WPA was striking; the medium income in Boston of those employed was $16 a week, the medium income of those not employed by WPA or by private employers was under $7; and a quarter of the unemployed had no income at all as winter set in.

A portion of the workers who left and returned to the relief rolls were part of the permanent reserve of labor, only called on at times of high production. But many of the more or less permanent clients of the relief organizations, state and Federal, were skilled workers who before the depression had a record of steady employment, who had saved enough to acquire a house, some insurance, a car, a telephone; the two last were generally gone, while the house and the insurance were heavily mortgaged but desperately clung to. Age was the greatest single handicap. The middle-aged worker saw his chances of permanent employment dwindle with each year. He might have just confidence that he had not lost his skill or his capacity for work, but despite appeals and even legislation, the givers of private employment preferred to take no chances and to use younger men. The middle-aged "reliefer" was no longer a full producer, pulling his weight and duly rewarded; he was now merely the head of a unit, "the relief family," with no permanent hope of security or dignity. For him the promise of American life was bitterly unfulfilled.

CHAPTER VI

SOME EMERGENCY PROBLEMS

ONE part of the National Industrial Recovery Act had set up a Federal Emergency Administration of Public Works, all of whose powers were to be exercised by an Emergency Administrator. It was the not unreasonable expectation of General Hugh Johnson that operations under all parts of the Act should be conducted by himself, so that unity of command would be achieved under one officer. But the President had no great belief in such unity, and the task of supervising emergency public works was conferred on the Secretary of the Interior, Harold Ickes.

Ickes had been one of the dark-horse nominations in the new Cabinet. He was a Chicago lawyer who had specialized in fighting vigorous if unsuccessful campaigns against the hosts of unrighteousness in Chicago and Cook County. He had been a Progressive in 1912 and an independent Republican later. When the characteristics of the new Secretary began to be understood, this personal history was an added grievance for the practicing Democratic politicians, who found in his irregular political background an explanation of his refusal to see the political necessity of courses of action that did not come up to his standard of administrative fitness.

As a critical admirer put it later, Ickes was "born wired for sound." His tongue was a weapon of offense that he did not let suffer from disuse, and although he boasted that he was a "curmudgeon," Secretary Ickes had no reluctance to find himself called just and honest.

The $3,300,000,000 voted for public works under the Recovery Act called both for justice and for honesty in its custodian. Inevitably, the vastness of the sum (by the standards of 1933) attracted the hopeful, the enterprising, the foolish, and, it is safe to assume, the corrupt. Secretary Ickes certainly assumed it. Langdon Post, a zealous New Dealer, attributed to Ickes' Chicago experience his "lack of faith in human nature, his fear of graft and corruption." These traits led to excessive centralization, and to a system of checking and counter-checking that imposed delay at a time when the rest of the Administration was acting on the motto that speed was the essence, and indeed almost the whole, of the task of recovery. As one of the reasons for the public works program was the need for stimulating the construction industries, perhaps the hardest-hit sector of the whole American economy, delays at Washington were considered by some as a kind of treason and by others as a manifestation of a "meddlesome Matty" temperament, out of place in the brave new world.

The administrator of PWA, as the Public Works Administration was universally known, was nevertheless unshakable. He was willing to delegate a little; roads were turned over to the Department of Agriculture, which had great experience in rural road problems and was now prepared to deal with urban roads, too. The Navy and Army were left to spend their own share in direct construction. Battleships, even if useless (as most New Dealers apart from the President thought them), employed a very high proportion of labor in their building. If Army housing was so bad that it needed to be taken in hand on a big scale, this also employed labor—even though it distressed members of the Cabinet like Miss Perkins, to whom expenditure on the armed forces seemed specially wasteful. By Lewis Douglas, Director of the Budget, the whole policy of great public works was distrusted, in so far as it involved pork-barrel or nonproductive projects; but he was fighting a losing battle.

The planning of public works in a fashion that would cushion the effects of falling demand in a depression period was no New Deal innovation. As early as 1930, the Hoover Administration had planned a program that would be less of an improvisation than the old style of Federal public works appropriations. And moving from the accepted conception of Federal public works, in 1932 the "Emergency Relief and Reconstruction Act" authorized the RFC to lend $1,500,000,000 to state and local authorities for local public works. But the conditions were onerous; the projects had to be self-liquidating, and little advantage was taken of the offer. Federal public works, on the other hand, had been pushed ahead.

The great new Government office buildings of Washington were one evidence of this. Another was the far-reaching power and flood-control system on the Colorado River, whose most ambitious monument, the great dam, had its name rather ungraciously changed by the new Secretary of the Interior from Hoover Dam to Boulder Dam. What was newer was the degree to which the PWA was used to increase demand for building and other types of construction labor; the degree to which its standards of wages and hours were used to prop up labor standards; its preference for union members to support the closed shop, or at least to weaken the open shop; and the solicitude of Congress for the needs of veterans, which resulted in complicated scales of priorities in the hiring of the labor force.

Of profound institutional importance was the

degree to which Federal financing of local projects approved by the PWA ate away the foundations of the old divisions between state and Federal spheres of action and led to direct contact between the Federal Government and local governmental units. The states were of necessity often by-passed —of necessity, for many states had tied their hands by constitutional limitations on their borrowing power, or had no adequate plans for public works that PWA would pass.

Most states behaved reasonably. Some, like Virginia, enacted "bond codes" that made it easier for political subdivisions to conform to PWA requirements. Other states, like Colorado, New York, and New Jersey, in their anxiety to meet the needs of the case, legislated more enthusiastically than wisely, and created new legal snarls. It was not always possible, politically or constitutionally, to amend or abolish legal limitations on local borrowing powers. There developed from this situation a fine new crop of legal fictions. Thus although Detroit could not borrow any more, Wayne County could, and was then able to lease the incinerator built by borrowed funds to the city. More common was the issue of "revenue" bonds, to be amortized with interest by the strict application of the revenues rising from the improvements; these were legally not "additions to indebtedness" within the meaning of constitutional law. Another device, older than PWA, was the creation of "authorities," corporations created for specific purposes and empowered to borrow. A variant on this device was the creation of the "self-sustaining state agency," which got Kansas out of the constitutional straitjacket that had made the creation of an adequate road system impossible. Last and boldest evasion of all, the right to borrow in times of great peril, provided for in most state constitutions, was used by the State of Washington, which issued bonds in 1933 "to suppress an insurrection"; there was no insurrection, but a stitch in time saves nine, and there might have been one had the bond issue not been made.

PWA was not merely sympathetic but helpful to states entangled in their own constitutions; legal advice and model bills were lavishly provided to help them in escaping from the labyrinth of local law. Only two states refused to amend their laws to suit the views of the dispensers of Federal bounty. In 1935, this legislative function was transferred to the "National Emergency Council," which was to act as a general clearing house for all state and Federal legislative cooperation. Not all Federal requests for legislation were consistent, and even the most docile state legislature might hesitate when asked to enact two conflicting model statutes. Again, this form of Federal persuasion was attacked as undermining the independence of

the states, and again, state submission to the out-
rage cast a light on the realities of state and Federal power.

In other ways, PWA showed unexpected ten-
derness for state susceptibilities. The "regional
men," the field agents of PWA, were active in getting projects proposed and in stimulating a demand
for PWA grants; but there was no other compulsion. If the wage standards imposed by PWA
seemed demoralizing to the local rulers, the remedy
was simple. As a Maryland city was told in 1938
they could refuse the grant—and see it go to another city.

More valid criticisms were that the various state
authorities were "borrowing machines," and that
state and city debt was in fact increased far beyond the breaking-point. But the insolvency of so
many governmental units in 1933, combined in
many instances with the archaic character of the
tax system, made some relief inevitable. PWA got
local government units gently out of shackles that
otherwise might have had to be burst.

Ickes certainly maintained a noisy guard over
Federal funds. His war to force the City of Chicago to pay the Sanitary District the money it
owed, and incidentally to force the meat-packers
to pay their due share of the cost of sewers, was
his most epic battle. It was Chicago, too, that
Ickes used for his classic example of what hap-

pened when inspection of public works built in
part with Federal funds was left to local officials
who "would no more think of arguing with a con-
tractor than with their alderman." Not only did
he insist on using his own inspectors, but he had
the Federal inspectors inspected, too, and some
critics thought the morale of PWA suffered. Later,
certain lessons of the first years were applied; there
was less centralization, less time-consuming vigilance; Federal standards were better understood,
and state, city, and Federal officials had learned to
work together. It was also an emollient fact that
PWA had been forced to depart a little from its
purist attitude, and to plan with a little more regard for the employment needs of the time. It was
not a relief organization like its rival, WPA, but
it did take note of relief needs. Especially did it do
so after the hasty founding of the Civil Works
Administration in 1934, a device adopted, so many
thought, because PWA was not spending its money
fast enough. Indeed, in 1935 there was a momen-
tary possibility that it would be abolished altogether, and that the double job of providing public
works and furnishing employment and economic
stimulus to a still depressed industry would be
turned over exclusively to the new Works Progress
Administration. That danger was avoided, but possibly the lesson implicit in the threat was learned.
Yet the vigilance of Ickes was probably well

worth while. Never in American history has so much money been spent with so little graft or even rumor of graft. There was some defective construction and some waste of funds. But on the whole, the billions poured out by PWA were not wasted, and by 1938 they were being expended with almost as much speed as if no questions had been asked, no precautions taken.

Projects ranging all the way from great bridges, sanitary improvements, schools, and hospitals down to privy-building schemes had contributed tangible and permanent improvements to American life. It was estimated, too, that for every worker employed on PWA, two and a half persons were employed in private industry; and the new standard of probity and efficiency did something to destroy American skepticism about the possibility of a great scheme of public improvements without corruption, waste, and politics.

Another emergency problem was presented by the questions of Federal personnel, civil service standards, and the use of patronage for party services. If Ickes was a novelty in politics, so were many other newcomers to Washington, for the comparatively small and changing group of "Brain Trusters" round the President were only the general staff of the "New Dealers" who poured into Washington. It was not the mere changing of an Administration that flooded the capital with aspirants for office. It was the opportunity suddenly offered to thousands of American men and women to serve their country in a crisis, in an epoch in which faith had been steadily draining away and which had suddenly been restored. The capital city, lately so full of pessimism, the home of discredited politicians and officials, became overnight the center of national hope. Old residents were reminded of the war years, and the Administration was able to call on the spirit of sacrifice of thousands of competent Americans. It was unjust to the outgoing Administration to assert that it had exhibited no faith in experts. The outgoing President was probably a better judge of what constituted an expert than was Roosevelt. But the Hoover experts were for the most part mere consultants; now there was a chance for action, a chance to experiment, to rescue a stricken nation, to escape from the frustrations of mere study. The seal of the United States bore the legend, "Novus Ordo saeclorum." The new order of the ages had come:

> Bliss was it in that dawn to be alive,
> But to be young was very heaven.

It was also bliss, or at least highly advantageous, to be a good Democrat.

Three weeks before the inauguration of the new President, the Chairman of the National Committee (already slated to be Postmaster-General) addressed the Miami "Roosevelt-for-President" club. "Naturally," said James Farley, "we feel that Democratic government can be best given if in the positions of trust are placed unselfish men and women who have the faith in our principles so necessary to insure their execution speedily and efficiently. These men and women shall be selected with the greatest care. They shall be placed in their positions because of party loyalty and qualifications for the jobs they are to fill." For Farley there was no doubt of the order of importance; party loyalty came first and there was every reason to believe that there were competent Democrats for nearly all posts. His candor bred criticism, but that was taken philosophically.

Mr. Farley was handicapped, of course, by the existing civil service laws which covered most minor offices. But the sudden growth of New Deal agencies outside the classified service was an opportunity that was not wholly missed. Even had there been any intention of turning over the new jobs to the Civil Service Commission, the economy policy of the Hoover Administration had kept down fresh appointments, and the existing "lists of eligibles" were out of date. The Commission "couldn't provide even adequate stenographers," a New Deal appointee complained. But no number of jobs at the free disposal of the Postmaster-

General would have been adequate. It was not only
that the Democrats had been twelve years out of
office, but even minor jobs had an abnormal attrac-
tion in the eyes of men and women driven desperate by the terrible depression years. Farley had to
weigh the claims of Senators and Congressmen, of
National Committeemen and city bosses. So had
his Cabinet colleagues, and the Postmaster-General relieved them of some of their troubles by
suggesting the appointment in their departments
of "agents of clearance," who took over the burden
of weighing political claims. Even the Department
of Agriculture, probably the best staffed and least
politically run, had its patronage expert.

The New Deal had called to Washington hundreds of zealous and competent but politically
naive experts, anxious only to give public service
in a great crisis but often ignorant not only of the
need for "political clearance," but of the very
names of the local Democratic politicians who
could provide it. Usually, the defect was easily
remedied. The politician was mollified by a formal
reference and a confession of ignorance. On the
whole, the amount of spoils politics was less than
the public supposed.

Democratic politicians who knew the rules well
enough were not surprised, though they were not
pleased, when they discovered that the Postmaster-
General's wonderful memory and admirable sense

of system did not fail him in the matter of reward-
ing the early laborers in the vineyard. Despite
scriptural precedent, the eleventh-hour recruits
had to wait for their reward till that more deserv-
ing class, who could claim to benefit by the magic
formula "F.R.B.C." (For Roosevelt before Chicago), had been satisfied. Especially in the President's and the Postmaster-General's own state, it
was firmly noted and long remembered that the
machines in all the New York boroughs except the
Bronx had been against the Governor of New York
till he was the candidate—and not enthusiastic
even then.

Nothing could have seemed more proper, and
not many things safer, than an attempt by the new
Democratic administration to secure control of the
municipal government of New York City. New
York was the President's state, and the state of
the head of the Democratic party organization. But
the metropolis was in the hands of Tammany Hall
and of former supporters of ex-Governor Smith, or
at any rate of politicians suspicious of such Democrats as Roosevelt and Farley. And this semi-
hostile organization was threatened by a revolt of
the traditional type, based on the moral indignation and economic discontent of the more prosperous elements, worried about taxes, deficits, and the
low level of administration. More important still,
the mass of poor voters had learned during the

depression years how limited and inadequate were
the resources and imagination of the Hall, how far
beyond the powers of even the most famous of
machines were the problems of the modern trade
cycle. And if the replacement of Mayor Walker by
Mayor O'Brien had made the City Hall less offensive to the serious-minded, O'Brien was no soul-
stirring executive or candidate.

The attack on Tammany was the work of a
"Fusion" ticket. The Republicans, allied with various types of independent Democrats and plain independents, put in nomination Fiorello H. La
Guardia, an ex-Republican Congressman of radical
views. He was of partly Jewish and partly Italian
origin, in New York a happy combination for a
politician. A ticket giving recognition to the various
groups behind the fusion movement was ingeni-
ously constructed, and there was little doubt that
it would defeat the regular Tammany ticket.

But if little love was lost between Tammany and
the White House (or the office of the Postmaster-
General), there were obvious political objections to
letting the mayoralty of New York pass into independent hands. There was at hand in Joseph
McKee, former president of the Board of Alder-
men, a Democrat with proved drawing power who
was not saddled with the sins of the Walker
and O'Brien administrations. With McKee, both
Farley and the rising ambitious boss of the Bronx,

Edward Flynn, could, it was hoped, seize control of the metropolis, unseat the sullen braves of Tammany Hall, and keep New York safe in "regular" hands.

These dreams of empire were destined to remain dreams. For in Fiorello La Guardia the fusion elements had got hold of a candidate who was as remarkable a campaigner in his own field as was the President in the nation. He won and won handsomely. The New York voters, more or less consciously, made the same kind of protest in 1933 that had been made in 1932 in the nation. They wanted a change, and a mere shift from one kind of Democrat to another was not enough. The defeated strategists were philosophical about it all. They had known, like Browning's Cardinal, "four and twenty leaders of revolt"; no reform administration ever succeeded itself; 1937 would set all right. And Edward Flynn of the Bronx was secure in his own bailiwick, destined for more public roles in future. But the election had long-term importance all the same. Despite his Republican origin and Republican support, La Guardia had run his campaign on a much more New Deal platform than had either O'Brien or McKee. His success seemed to show that there was a great group of New Deal voters not tied by any real loyalty to the local Democratic party, and that this independent support for the Administration in national affairs might be organ-

ized locally into a powerful independent voting
bloc. Farley had something to worry about, after
all.

Still another emergency problem was furnished
by the plight of the railroads. Three-quarters of
the Class I railroads had failed in 1932 to earn their
fixed charges by $250,000,000, and over 40,000
miles of railroad were in the hands of receivers or
in process of reorganization. Even this desperate
situation had been kept from being worse only by
the fall in the cost of coal, lowering of wages, cutting of services, and most ominous of all, the suspension of essential maintenance. "De-maintenance," by the standards of the diminished traffic
in 1932, was around $300,000,000, and by the
standards of the years 1927–31 was around
$600,000,000. And there was no hope of any real
alteration in this disastrous situation, by normal
methods. Help had been forthcoming, but on an
inadequate scale. Limited rate increases had been
permitted in 1931. These had produced about
$75,000,000, and the RFC had advanced $337,000,-
000, of which $200,000,000 had gone in various
forms of debt payment.

Bad as was their situation, the railroads were
subjected to strong attack for their refusal to adjust freight rates to the declining level of prices and
business activity. Actually freight rates on staple
products were materially lower than in previous

decades. The critics also asserted that the railroads would *gain* by a reduction in rates—gain by the general improvement in business that would result, gain by recovering some of the traffic lost to trucks and water transport. Whether this was true or not, the complainants did not really care. Their object was to secure a general rate reduction in place of those partial reductions which had been given chiefly at points where competitive methods of transport were most seriously eating into railroad revenue. Such reductions threw the burden of keeping up railroad revenue on those branches of industry and agriculture where, so far, competition was not effective.

The ICC refused the application for rate reduction, but a minority opinion stressed the worthlessness of mere rate maintenance for the salvation of the railroads. No traffic was "tied to the rails," and rate maintenance merely insured that rival forms of transportation would be attracted into more and more sections of the railroads' "normal" field. Revenues would rise with an improvement in general business; but the basic problem remained. And that basic problem concerned many more persons than the railroad stockholders, managers, or employees. "De-maintenance" was a serious matter for the steel industry, as was reduction of services for the coal producers. Solvency of the railroads was important not only for tens of thousands of small investors, but for savings banks and insurance companies. Here was a call to action which the new Administration could not afford to ignore.

The New Deal railroad policy was designed partly to stave off a disastrous bankruptcy of the whole system and partly to reform the main financial abuses. Legislation was passed which defined the duty of the ICC primarily in terms of providing not a fair return for investors, but an adequate service for shippers. The ICC was given far more effective control over that large part of the railroad system that was in or might pass into the hands of receivers. Receivers' fees were reduced, and their schemes of reorganization subjected to more direct oversight. The famous Section 77 was designed to make reorganization easier and less disastrous to stockholders.

In the early days of the Administration, it was not merely the accounting and financing problems of the railroads that were dealt with. A Federal Coordinator was appointed, and he was the famous dissenting member of the ICC, Joseph Eastman. Since he had publicly disapproved of the way the railroads had been run, he was deemed to have a better idea of how they should be saved. Although Eastman was able to make useful reforms, a thorough reorganization of the railroad system would have meant facing the fact that a great deal of its equipment was obsolete and should be scrapped, that many lines were superfluous, and—here was the political rub—that many of its employees were superfluous too. But no form of reorganization was permitted which cut down the number of employees as of May, 1933. The Railroad Retirement Act of 1934 (declared unconstitutional in 1935), by making it easier to get rid of veteran employees on a pension basis, met a small part of the problem and was finally enacted in 1937 in a form that passed the courts. But although the railroads did not secure the right to cut the cost of employment to match the demand for railroad services, the number of railroad employees steadily fell; since what was protected was the vested interest of the existing employees, not the right to enter railroad service. The railroads, like their customers the farmers, continued to suffer until war came from an overexpansion of facilities that could be more easily diagnosed than cured.

As late as 1931, the ICC had optimistically decided that the railroads had little to fear from motor transport over long distances or for bulk transportation. By 1933, it knew better. Yet road haulers were exempt from Federal regulation. Moreover, the Supreme Court in *Buck v. Kuykendall* and *Bush Co. v. Maloy* had effectually excluded the states from regulation of motor carriers in interstate commerce. Both the ICC and the Federal Coordinator of Transportation favored the

extension of ICC control to motor carriers. This
was effected in 1935 over the opposition of truck-
owners, the automobile manufacturing industry,
and organized shippers.

The ICC was given powers in this new field
roughly equivalent to those it possessed in that of
rail transportation. But with an unwonted tender-
ness for states' rights, Congress forbade the ICC to
supervise interstate motor transportation on any of
the grounds that had permitted it to supervise
interstate railroad business. Another important
difference in its effective powers arose from the
nature of the business. Railroads were few in number, easily identifiable, and easily located. But it
was hard to identify an interstate motor-trans-
portation business. For newcomers, it was practicable if not easy to lay down conditions of service
before licensing, but what of the existing businesses? They were protected by a so-called "grand-
father clause" preserving the rights of those in the
business in 1935. When the Act came into force,
80,000 applicants asserted that they had been in
business in 1935, and 40,000 of these claims were
contested by railroads, other carriers, and state
commissions.

Of less immediate importance was the extension
of the power of the ICC to cover the rates and services of air-mail carriers. Here the ICC was not
given a general control of air transportation but

only of that part of it subsidized by the Federal mail contracts. The way was open for a more general Federal power over the newest method of moving men and things. By the "Civil Aeronautics Authority Act" of 1938, Congress took the last logical step in extending Federal power over the whole field of aviation, setting up a new body to exercise that power.

Even the most determined defender of states' rights could not deny the necessity of some Federal control over communications by telegraph, wire, telephone, and radio. The Federal Communications Commission was created in 1934 with a general power of inspection and control over these mediums of transmitting news and opinion. It was in the field of radio control that Federal action was most necessary. Even an apologist for *laissez-faire* did not relish an air crowded with unintelligible competing radio programs, and the allocation of wave lengths had necessarily to be entrusted to the administrative discretion of the FCC.

CHAPTER VII

BANKRUPT FARMERS AND THE AAA

THE census of 1930 revealed one new and momentous fact. For the first time since the coming of the
white man to North America, the area of forest had
increased in the United States. The forest was now
encroaching on the clearing, and the desert was
encroaching on the sown. This was a shock for a
nation that had both been taught and had spon-
taneously believed with the King of Brobdingnag:
"Whoever could make two Ears of Corn, or two
Blades of Grass to grow upon a Spot of Ground
where only one grew before, would deserve better
of Mankind, and do more essential Service to his
Country, than the whole Race of Politicians put
together."

The shock to the traditional faith of the American farmer, and indeed of the American people,
was one of the permanently disturbing factors of
the period between the two great world wars. Alone
among the great sectional interests, the American
farmer looked backward, not forward, to a golden

age, to the years before the war of 1914, when what
he produced was bought at "fair" prices and when
his share in the national income seemed equitable
in retrospect, if it had not at the time.

Almost every change in world trade, technology,
and legislation seemed to work against the interests of the farmer. The technical improvements in
the methods of agriculture were very striking, and
the American farmer, in the two generations before
the great collapse, increased his output to a degree
comparable though not equal to the increase in
industrial output. This increase was accompanied
by a steady drift from the rural regions into the
cities, an internal emigration that concealed the
degree to which the agricultural needs of America
were being met with a smaller proportion of the
national labor force. Yet over a great part of rural
America, especially in the South, a stagnant pool of
population accumulated for which there was no
adequate economic demand. The new tractors and
combines not only cut down the labor force needed;
they cut down the animal force needed, too. The
gasoline-driven engines that replaced the horses and
mules did not need the crops that, in the past, had
been raised to feed the motive power of the millions
of American farms. The American rural community now produced its own motive power in de-
creasing degree, and had to pay for the substitute.
The individual farmer might gain, but the com-

munity had an extra charge to meet and the farmer with little capital was more and more handicapped.

The need for capital was exhibited in a great growth of farm debt, which doubled between 1910 and 1920, and in an increase of farm tenancy, especially in the corn and wheat belts of the Middle West. That burden of debt represented, in part, a natural increase in capital investment; it also represented an overoptimistic discounting of the "inevitable" rise of American land values. But the assumptions on which the rise had been predicated were no longer universally true.

The competitive position of the American farmer in the world market was being more and more adversely affected. He had to face the competition of Canada, Australia, and Argentina. The virgin lands of the Canadian prairie provinces depressed the land values of their American neighbors as the Western states had depressed the land values of rural New England a century earlier. It was not only the great cereal exporting regions that were hit. American pork, whose export had been the stand-by of so many thousands of farmers, had to face novel competition. The tropical and semitropical countries now provided, in their exports of cottonseed oil, palm oil, and peanuts, a substitute for pork. Indeed, feeding corn to pigs to produce pork was simply a more roundabout way of producing the result that, in tropical Africa, was achieved by one operation.

To these permanent new handicaps of the American farmer, some temporary "political" disadvantages could be added. The artificial prices during World War I encouraged the extension of arable culture into marginal lands of the High Plains as it encouraged rash speculation in land values—speculation paid for in 1920, when farm income fell from $17,000,000,000 to $10,000,000,000. European customers were not only impoverished by the war, but were tempted to protect their own agriculture by high tariffs, while their power to buy American products was cut down by American tariff and immigration policy. Moreover, changes in the world's eating habits imposed a new strain of adjustment on the conservative producer of pork, corn, wheat. In time, no doubt, the American farm economy could adjust itself to the demand for more vegetables, fruit, and milk, but the adjustment was painful for farmers whose capital resources and credit had been dissipated by rash speculation.

All these handicaps were accentuated in the South. For cotton growers the export market was of overwhelming importance, and new sources of supply, not only in Egypt and India but in Arizona and California, meant increasing competition for the worn-out fields of Georgia. Changes in fashion

and the coming of artificial silk hurt the cotton producer even more than changes in diet hurt the
wheat and pork producer. And it was in the South
that the menace of a technological revolution
loomed most grimly. If the long-promised mechanical "cotton-picker" was marketed (and that it
would be few doubted), the South would have a
pool of superfluous labor far more difficult to
assimilate than the similar pool in the North and
West.

Thus it came about that, even in the boom days,
American agriculture was sick. In 1926 its income
was far short of the income of 1919, and its burden
of debt had to be carried on a far smaller share of
the national income than had been calculated on in
the hopeful years. Of course there was still hope, in
some regions at any rate. As late as 1926, it was
thought worth while to extend a railroad in Colorado to tap new farm lands. But shadows covered
more of the agricultural landscape than did the few
bright spots. There was a rapid drift of the more
energetic from the land; there was a practically
complete disappearance of the migratory labor
force, the "Wobblies" of the old radical movements; there was an increasingly bitter sense that
the centuries-old promise of American life was
being betrayed.

This discontent was reflected in politics, though
with less force than might have been expected.

Men made no rush for a panacea like greenbacks or free silver. The farm bloc in Congress was more modest in its aims. It wanted to give to the American farmer an equivalent of the higher prices that the tariff gave to the industrialist. But since so much of the American farm production was exported, this aim involved differential prices; the American consumer would have to pay more than the foreign consumer. No Republican Administration could be induced to accept this principle, and the less drastic method of providing Federal funds to take crop surpluses off the market was tried instead. But Hoover's Farm Board was unfortunate in the time of its birth and operation. The hoped-for epoch of rising prices, during which it could unload its holdings, never came, and the existence of huge carry-overs of wheat only depressed the world price, already pushed downwards by the weakness of the Canadian wheat pool.

By 1932, American agriculture was in worse shape than American industry, and the traditionally Republican farmer of the Middle West was ready to try any remedy. The Democratic candidate outlined his program at Topeka. The producer of staples must be given an "equivalent to the benefit given by the tariff to industrial products." How it was to be done was only sketched. Legislation must call for cooperation from the farmers; it must not further alienate European

customers by dumping; it must not take the form
of a direct subsidy from the Treasury.

The new Secretary of Agriculture had left the
Republican party in 1928 because he was convinced that it would do nothing for the farmer. But
Henry Wallace had too keen a sense of political
realities to think that, despite the sentiments expressed in the Topeka speech, there was any chance
that the American tariff would be so reduced as to
restore to the American farmer his European
market. "America must choose," and a choice of
high tariffs meant that special measures must be
taken to deal with those sectors of the American
rural economy which could not sell abroad because
their customers could not buy. The experience of
the Farm Board had been conclusive. Any attempt
to keep up prices without controlling production
was self-defeating, since any rise or even stabilization of prices brought more of the commodity into
the market. Of course, a rigorous refusal to interfere
at all would, in time, squeeze out all the weaker
producers. But the social and political cost of that
drastic method of cure would be beyond the resources of the American community as it was in
1933. The billion-dollar drop in farm debt represented not more prosperity, but the elimination of
thousands of miserable mortgagees. Rural credit
was ruined; bank failures were endemic in rural
America before the disease spread to the cities.

Quick, drastic, empirical remedies were called for.

The Agricultural Adjustment Act of 1933 was justified in its preamble as an emergency measure, the emergency lying in the disparity between agricultural and industrial prices. Agricultural returns were to be raised to a "level that will give agricultural commodities a purchasing power with respect to articles farmers buy, equivalent to the purchasing power of agricultural commodities in the base period August 1909–July 1914." (For tobacco, the base period was 1919–29.) The consumer was to pay the difference to the farmer through the mechanism of a tax collected at the first stage of processing. But the proceeds of this tax were not to be turned back to the farmers unconditionally. They had the free choice of going their own way under the old system, or getting payments in return for agreeing to control production on staples—cattle, corn, cotton, dairy products, hogs, potatoes, rice, wheat, sugar, tobacco, flax, rye, and others. The Agricultural Adjustment Administration, set up by Secretary Wallace with George N. Peck as head, was not prepared to underwrite any flood of crops poured into the market.

Some such control of production, as a necessary part of any effective scheme for supporting prices, had long been advocated. So, too, had the principle of having two prices, one for the competitive world market, one for the protected domestic market, a differentiation that might mean the subsidizing of foreign markets at the expense of domestic customers. This part of the AAA program was only in a loose sense an "emergency" measure, for the underlying conditions that made the scheme advisable were not likely to disappear overnight.

But the new Secretary of Agriculture was forced into the adoption of real emergency measures as unwelcome to the administrators as they were to the farmers and to the public. Wallace believed in curbing production; Peck did not. Faced with a threatened glut of pigs, the Secretary in the spring of 1933 bought both young pigs and sows to keep them off a future market. The farmers proved willing to sell their young pigs to be turned into fertilizer, but much more reluctant to surrender their sows. It was therefore over the fate of the young pigs that so much genuine and so much artificial concern was expressed. It was true that the killing of the young pigs only anticipated their fate by a few months; they were not, in any case, being raised as pets. But the deliberate interference with the processes of nature that fattened pigs for market was a real shock. Even more of a shock was the ploughing-under of more than ten million acres of cotton. It was too late to prevent the planting of the cotton, no crop was more a victim of excessive carry-overs, and the only remedy seemed to be the deliberate destruction of a great part of the growing crop. Secretary Wallace rented land from more than a million Southern farmers, requiring them to carry out his program. This was a blow to deeply engrained rural habits. It was said that mules deliberately stepped over the growing plants, as they had been trained to do, and that one Negro farmer found a way out of the distasteful task by offering to plough up his neighbor's cotton while the neighbor ploughed up his. The plough-up, which eliminated (experts computed) 4,400,000 bales, was followed by a rise in the price of cotton. But the willful destruction of wealth left a bad taste, and years afterwards was a constant occasion of reproaches to New Deal planners who could, it was asserted, organize the destruction of wealth but not its creation.

Payments for acres not planted, for pigs and cotton destroyed, brought money into the pockets of the farm community and eased the crisis that not only threatened all sections of rural society with ruin but had also wiped out the profits of the mail-order houses and threatened the stability of insurance companies holding great areas of unsellable agricultural land.

What the candidate had promised the Administration had carried out, for the complicated schemes of the AAA were in fact largely administered by the farmers themselves. Farmers did not need to cooperate, but it paid them to do so. A great and successful experiment in democracy got under way. When Peck resigned late in 1933, Chester A. Davis took his place. By accepting the offers of the AAA, farmers joined self-governing groups that estimated the past yield of farms, carried out the necessary bookkeeping, and explained to the six million independent farmers the means and aims of the new policy. Even the mere mechanical clerical work presented no light problem. In the first year of the AAA, the contracts made for the four major controlled crops (cotton, wheat, corn-hogs, and tobacco), were nearly two million. When the farmers were well-educated, self-reliant, and accustomed to cooperative effort, the job was simpler. But when they were ignorant, economically weak, loosely attached to the land, the administration of the AAA was very difficult indeed. In some fields, application of the Act did not seem wise; adjustment programs were never carried out for cattle and dairy products or for flax.

It was in the South that the difficulties were greatest. There a European expert, Dr. Gunnar Myrdal, thought that the combination of world agricultural trends and Federal agricultural policy "threatened the rural Negro population with disaster." The situation was, indeed, grave. For the AAA payments made in the first year often went to the landlord, partly as rent and partly in the

liquidation of past debts. In so far as it was true
that the landlord in the early years of the AAA
could secure the cash payments for himself, he had
an economic interest in keeping the tenants on the
old system. But with improved administration, the
cash payments went straight to the tenants; an
average rise of payments from $11 to $27 per
family between 1934 and 1937 (shown in one selective survey) made a great difference to the economic status of the croppers, since the average cash
income of the tenants was only $300. The AAA
tried to force landlords to keep the same number
of tenants, but it could not really force them to
keep the same tenants. It was often to the interest
of the landlord to replace tenants having a claim
to cash payments under AAA by wage laborers
who had not. And in the general administration of
AAA, Negro farmers were as handicapped by illi-
teracy, political impotence, and the Southern social
structure as in other departments of life.

Then AAA further turned the scales against the
Negro by encouraging mechanization, the deadly
enemy of the poorly skilled Negro labor force in
the South. And there was no alternative work at a
time of general unemployment. The AAA payments
to the planters were both relatively and absolutely
a good deal higher than those to the desperately
poor tenants, white or black. The Farm Security
Administration which *did* help the poorer economic

strata was regarded with suspicion as "relief,"
while much higher AAA payments to planters were
"business." It was the Hoover philosophy of the
RFC applied in the South by the dominant planter-
politician caste. Farm security, the establishment
of a stable and self-sufficient rural population, was
not in the interest of wealthy landowners whom the
existing system suited and who were able to impose
much of its cost on the Federal Government. This
was an unconscious revenge for Reconstruction.
Yet AAA, silently and with little overt protest,
opened a way into the citadel of Southern race
superiority, for in the elaborate mechanism of
democratic choice, the self-administration of the
crop reduction schemes, Negroes could vote; often
they voted in a higher proportion than their white
neighbors of equal economic status. They might not
reach positions of authority, but for the first time
since the end of Reconstruction they were exercis-
ing quasi-political rights. Moreover, some of the
tenant-farmers and share-croppers pushed off the
plantations by crop restrictions broke over the
color line by forming a bi-racial Southern Tenant
Farmers' Union.

The great droughts of 1934 and 1936 underlined
one difficulty in agricultural planning, the refusal
of nature to fit its pattern to that of men. The
droughts upset the price policies of the Department
of Agriculture, sometimes to the extent of making

them ludicrous. They did more; they brought home
to the American people the grim fact that the land
was wasting and blowing away. And it was not
merely in the worn-out cotton lands of the South,
the deep gullies in the red soil, the dams with silted-
up lakes behind them, the coffee-colored rivers
carrying the precious soil down to the Gulf of
Mexico, that the work of erosion could be seen. In
Missouri it was terrifying; even in fertile northern
Ohio it would have been terrifying, if natural
American optimism had not concealed the ugly
truth from the average farmer and city dweller. Of
the four hundred and fifteen million acres of arable
land, one calculation estimated that seventy-five
million acres ought to be withdrawn from agriculture "as being incapable of supporting those who
work them." No wonder the author of this pessimistic judgment called his book *Deserts on the
March*.

But what was to be done with the dwellers on
the land that could not support them? The depression of 1929 and the retarded recovery of 1933 and
onwards had slowed up the generations-old movement of the rural population into the cities. Indeed,
there was a small reflux as recent immigrants to the
towns went back to their rural kinsfolk to escape
the hopelessness of unemployment and relief. But
it was the absence of opportunities in the cities, less
than any tenacious affection for the land, that kept

millions fighting desperately in the marginal farms. Had the movement to the cities continued at its old rate, there would have been one-fifth fewer farm dwellers by 1939. As it was, 32,000,000 people were trying to live on a farm income that would have gone round handsomely—if there had been only 26,000,000 people on the farms.

Hundreds of thousands of Southern farms were barely subsistence farms, worked on a "peasant" basis (using peasant in its derogatory American, not its west European sense). Hundreds of thousands of farms did not even provide a subsistence livelihood, where human and soil wastage went together and where the human product was swept North into rural and urban communities that saw in these prematurely aged, illiterate, incompetent people some of the social wreckage of the American agricultural system in its Southern version. It was not very easy to know what to do with these casualties of economic war. Attempts were made to encourage rural industries in derelict farming and mining communities. But these experiments were not carried out on a sufficient scale, or with enough realistic prudence, to provide an example of what could be done with the most depressed elements of the rural population. Even if all the criticism of subsidized communities like Arthurdale was unfair, Congress would not pay for many Arthurdales.

More hopeful was the provision in the Bank-head-Jones Act of funds to enable tenants to buy or lease farms. But the sum provided ($50,000,000 a year) was very inadequate for the scale of the problem, and the absence of compulsory powers of
· purchase further limited the effectiveness of the act. No American legislature was prepared to imitate such drastic schemes of compulsory land purchase as the British Parliament had enacted in Ireland. Even had Congress been willing and able to carry out, in the South and other regions of rural impoverishment, a great program of compulsory purchase and settlement, it would not have met all the needs of the time. Many tenants, share-croppers, and mere hired hands had not the minimum of knowledge and capital required for a successful peasant proprietor. And the economic forces that sucked the poorest dwellers on these lands into the Northern or even the Southern cities were not necessarily working against the public weal.

It was, however, another type of migration that attracted public attention to the plight of the rural poor. It was perhaps because it was only a generation since Oklahoma had been settled that the flight from the "Sooner" state to distant California attracted attention. Westward poured tens of thousands of "Okies" (and "Arkies"), men, women and children, miserably poor, driven out by dust storms and low prices and seeking employment on the great farms of California, in what were critically called "factories in the field."

They presented serious problems for a state that had already its own problem of surplus labor. The newcomers were white and yet were destined to compete with Mexicans, Filipinos, and Japanese in what was significantly called "stoop labor." They were often inefficient and ill-trained in the techniques of modern life. They added to the relief burdens as well as to the labor force—and those who paid for relief were not necessarily identical with those who benefited by cheap labor. The Federal and then the state government took in hand the problems of providing camps for transients and the protection of the interests of the migrants. But the American people, who read not the sober academic treatises, but a powerful propagandist novel, *The Grapes of Wrath*, were disturbed by this horrifying parody of the traditional westward course of empire.

Significant, too, of the end of an era was the withdrawal in 1935 of 165,000,000 acres of public lands, the last remnants of the immense public domain, now to be operated on a conservation basis for the benefit of all rather than the profit of a few. The Taylor Act, which provided for the organization of most of the public lands into grazing districts, was a landmark indeed.

The first AAA program, for all its limitations, did

effect a temporary shoring-up of the collapsing
rural structure. It was highly valued by much of
the agricultural population. Hence it was that the
bitterly contested Supreme Court decision of January 6, 1936, which invalidated the original Act,
placed farmers, the Administration, and Congress
in an awkward legal position. In this so-called
Hoosac Mills Case the judges voted six to three
that the processing tax was unconstitutional. Not
only was the Federal Government morally committed to millions of farmers; it was an election
year, and literally something *had* to be done. The
Supreme Court forced on Congress the necessity of
a bold exercise in legal fictions. A minor purpose of
the original Act was made an ostensibly major object of a new law. The Soil Conservation and
Domestic Allotment Act was rushed through Congress, and signed by Roosevelt on February 29,
1936.

Under this new law, farmers who carried out certain types of soil improvement, thus withdrawing
land and crops from the market, were rewarded or
compensated by direct grants. The processing tax
was abandoned and the processors were left with
their windfall gains. Half a billion dollars was made
available at the discretion of the Secretary, and
Wallace and his advisers set about planning a second AAA that would be both more constitutional
and less of a collection of expedients than the

hasty, crisis-born original scheme had inevitably been. The new program would cut down various overproduced crops and increase the attention paid to soil-restoring plants—to clover, alfalfa, soybeans, and cow-peas. The farmers applauded the alacrity with which the Government had filled the breach. They knew that the agricultural policy of the Administration had prevented a desperate position from becoming catastrophic; and whereas there had been a widespread belief after the NRA decision that a return to "freedom" would improve the position of business, there was no such confidence in the healing power of liberty applied to agriculture. That great national industry was too sick to be left alone and not quite sick enough to be ready for truly desperate remedies.

From the condemnation of the first AAA in 1935 until the adoption of a "permanent" or second AAA policy in 1938, the Department of Agriculture and the farming community felt their way. The grant of $500,000,000 to the Department to aid the farmers by using the Soil Erosion Act of 1935 and the Soil Conservation and Domestic Allotment Act of February 29, 1936, was designed to raise farm prices to the level of the golden era of 1909–14 and to insure "parity" for the farmer. The farmer would be encouraged by acreage payments to reduce his production of surplus cotton, wheat, corn, and other soil-depleting staples, and to plant soil-saving and soil-building crops on the land thus kept from adding to the surplus. What Secretary Wallace later called "the quietness and strength of grass" was to be called in to heal the wounds inflicted by the mining methods traditional to American farming. Those mining methods were now regarded with a less tolerant eye, as men began to realize that, with only 4 per cent or 5 per cent of the world's good agricultural land, the United States was land poor, and a good deal poorer than such competing rural economies as the British dominions and Argentina.

The second AAA law, enacted February 16, 1938, avoided the political aggressiveness of the first; it passed much of the responsibility for distributing payments to the states, and rather cautiously approached the problem of making the national agricultural policy broader and firmer. A mere reduction program was inadequate for the semi-arid areas of the Great Plains states, and, to reorganize their defective agriculture, Government land purchases and an extension of cooperative grazing were required. In other regions, the farmers had to be treated with tact and induced to work together, a job not made any easier as prosperity slowly returned. The rights of minorities had to be preserved, quotas could not be imposed unless approved by a two-thirds majority of the farmers involved. Farmers, too, had to be asked to assess the production potentialities of their neighbors, for the natural pessimism of the farmer vanished when it was a question of estimating what crops he *could* have raised but didn't. The Department was, in fact, trying to get away from "bases" to "goals," from rearranging the existing farm pattern to reconstructing the American rural economy.

The chief novelty of the new AAA was this insistence on control rather than on mere restriction and destruction. The aim of the new departure was the creation of an "ever-normal granary." Droughts and other natural catastrophes had made plain the unstable character of American agricultural production under the formal rigidity of the acreage figures. The quotas allotted to farmers who agreed to cooperate in return for parity payments were an attempt to adjust production to the market while coaxing the farm community into less soil-wasting methods of husbandry, but no Federal planning could guarantee that there should not be fat and lean years, or that cotton would be scarce in the years that wheat or corn was. That meant that crop shortages and crop "hangovers" had to be provided for. So a system of loans on crops not immediately marketed was created, and the Federal Government found itself again subject to the usual pressures. If Federal payments made up only 15 per cent of parity, there was a temptation to lend on the unmarketed crop enough to make up 85 per cent—regardless of the world price of the crop. There was also pressure not to unload the crop at the best moment for the insurer, since that might depress the current price. The difficulties that had beset the Farm Board of the pre-New Deal years were not abolished.

Crop loans were of little avail to a farmer who had lost all his crop, so an experimental system of insurance against drought, insect plagues, and floods was started with wheat as the guinea pig. A Federal Crop Insurance Corporation was set up; and premiums could be paid in wheat. Presently the system was extended to other basic crops. It was found that the actuarial estimation of probable losses was hard to make and that, humanly enough, farmers who owned more than one farm heavily insured the bad risks and took a chance on the good ones. The Government found itself, therefore, insuring too high a proportion of the marginal farm lands. By the time that war had temporarily solved most of the financial problems of the American farmer, it was still doubtful whether crop insurance could be made self-supporting.

Surpluses in the "ever-normal granary" were increased by good crop years and by the decline in world purchases, as European nations bought elsewhere for price or political reasons. It was obvious that waiting for the day when the outside world would take the surpluses off American hands was an evasion of the problem, that the farmer's main market was in America. Subsidies to send cotton to Europe or wheat to China were no real answer, nor could the most ingenious marketing agreements hide the fact that, for different reasons, millions of Americans as well as tens of millions of Europeans could not buy. Cheap milk could be supplied in schools, apples bought for relief purposes, but the most ingenious detour round the basic problem was the issuance of "food stamps."

The Surplus Marketing Administration was set up to transfer the price-destroying surpluses of the farms to the underfed unemployed of the cities. If the food purchases of these millions could be raised by a moderate amount, they would provide the farmers with an additional two billion dollar market at home. The simplest way was to raise the national income from the $46,000,000 of 1933 to twice that amount, but while waiting for that desirable consummation, unorthodox ways of getting food to the needy were in order. A food-stamp plan first tried at Rochester, N. Y., in the spring of 1939 demonstrated what might be done.

The official in charge of this job was one of the most enterprising officials of the "Second New Deal," Milo Perkins. He came to the Department after a successful business career, and was warmly welcomed by Wallace for more reasons than one, but above all because his attack on the problem was not restrictive. Agricultural surpluses which had come into the Government's hands had been issued to families from the beginning of the New Deal. But this had been done spasmodically and outside the usual channels of commerce. The food-stamp plan used the corner groceryman, and thus avoided antagonizing the small businessman. It avoided, too, the resentment caused by relief workers' dictation (as it was seen by the recipients of relief). The mother of a family on relief, by buying a dollar's worth of orange stamps a week for each member of the family, could spend the equivalent value at any store in the scheme. For each dollar of orange stamps she received fifty cents worth of blue stamps with which she could get surplus foods allotted by the Department of Agriculture, which thus raised the expenditure on each meal from five cents per head to seven and a half—and made the production of foodstuffs less frustrating.

The scheme, from its small beginnings, had by the middle of 1941 been extended to 363 areas covering more than half the population of the country, and directly affecting 4,000,000 people. A limited experiment had been made in the creation of a "cotton-stamp plan," which permitted low-income purchasers of a dollar's worth of cotton textiles to get another dollar's worth of "any product made entirely from American cotton and manufactured in this country." A real test of the cotton-stamp plan was prevented by the war boom, but the food-stamp plan was perhaps the most ingenious single administrative invention of the second New Deal.

In the long decline of the farmer's share in the national income, the only break had been in the war years; so it was to be again. But on the eve of the Second World War, the American farm problem had responded to palliatives and drugs, although the fundamental ills affecting the system were still operative. There were too many people on the farms, in effect a labor surplus concealed by archaic methods of production. Even in the most prosperous farm regions, farm tenancy was an established part of the pattern, and the descendant of the pioneers was as often a rent receiver as a tiller of the soil, or even a gentleman cattle-breeder.

The farmer was no longer, statistically, the representative American. The census of 1940 showed the rural population living on farms or in centers of less than 2,500 population as 37.8 per cent. Yet between fifty and sixty million Americans still lived on or near the land. This great mass of Americans might have noted that the census of 1940 showed the farmer receiving 3 per cent less for what he sold than in 1910–14—and paying 123 per cent of the basic prices of that golden age for what he bought. The farmer was still at the little end of the horn of American plenty.

CHAPTER VIII

THE REVOLT OF LABOR

THE condition of millions of American workers was so desperate by 1932–33 that they were ready to clutch at any straw. The news that they could organize, and that the new Administration in Washington wanted them to do so, was a stimulus to action without knowledge.

The labor provisions of the National Recovery Act seemed plain enough, at any rate to the harassed and angry workers. Section 7-A declared that under "every code of fair competition . . . employees shall have the right to organize and bargain collectively through representatives of their own choosing." A supplementary clause provided that no employee should be compelled to join a company union. There was a widespread belief (except among veteran labor leaders of the American Federation of Labor) that unionization would be easy. A Labor Advisory Board was set up to help carry out the law. One of the many signs of new hope was the rapid turning to what was for

167

millions of workers a totally unknown remedy. Another was the sudden rise in the number of strikes. Every month of the new Administration saw more of them, involving more and more strikers. It did not seem absurd for the AFL to profess to look forward to 10,000,000 members, a threefold multiplication of its nominal strength.

It was soon obvious that most employers had no intention of taking 7-A seriously, and the wave of strikes provoked by this discovery and by mere resentment over the long ordeal of the depression threatened to interfere with recovery. The Administration therefore replaced the Advisory Board by a more effective National Labor Board. Created by an Act of August 5, 1933, this was destined to a checkered history. It had three employer and three employee representatives, and, more important, its chairman was Senator Robert Wagner of New York, whose experience in this role was to have great legislative results. The Labor Board heard complaints, conducted elections for collective-bargaining agents, and settled disputes.

Strikes and violence accompanying unorganized mass movements cast an increasingly black shadow, and the AFL found itself riding a tidal wave on a precariously unstable surf board. The long reaction that since 1919 had drained the American labor movement of men, money, and strength was over. The political change was equally notable.

Perhaps its most dramatic illustration was provided by the truck strikes in Minneapolis. For
there, the violence of the first strike was answered
by an unusual exercise of administrative discretion.
Minnesota had an extremely vigorous "Farmer-
Labor" Governor, Floyd Olson, and he called out
the militia—but for a novel purpose. Only trucks
with permits were allowed on the streets, and Governor Olson gave permits only to trucks that were
free from any imputation of being "scab."

In San Francisco the situation was complicated
by the fact that in the fairly recent past the city
had been a union stronghold, in contrast to its
impregnably open shop rival, Los Angeles. But
morale had been weakened by the unsuccessful
strike of 1926 and by schisms in the unions. In the
port, the great grievance was the control by the
employers of the "hiring halls," which had to be
wrested from them if the Longshoremen's Union
was to have effective control of employment. Control by the Industrial Association and allied bodies
imperiled the very existence of unions. The stage
was set for a bitter conflict, and it took the form of
a general strike that for a few days paralyzed the
city. The end of the strike was not an end of the
conflict, but the union leaders could boast that
they had held their own, securing the ground for
further advance (or aggression); and the labor
masses of San Francisco had found a new leader,

the Australian chief of the longshoremen, Harry
Bridges.

The story was different in rural California. Here
the influx of ruined farmers from the plains had
upset the social structure and economic life of one
of the wealthiest farming regions of America. Labor
organization had been practically unknown since
the decline of the IWW, and when the union wave
began to mount, it was the skeleton Communist
organization, the Cannery and Agricultural Workers' Industrial Union, that took over. Around this
nucleus, the strikers rallied, and for a year the great
valley of California was ravaged by labor conflict.
There were some victories for the strikers, but the
absence of a regular union organization was reflected in epidemics of strikes that expressed anger
as much as hope and had little chance of success.
But the employers and their economic allies were
frightened; and, in their fright, they were not particular about their methods. Law and order was
defended by gangs of vigilantes. Wages and work
conditions of the farm labor force showed some improvement; but there was still no effective union
organization of the racially and socially divided
farm workers.

The most dramatic rise and fall of the NRA
unions came in textiles. Membership of the United
Textile Workers rose from 15,000 to 300,000 in the
cotton mills alone. Cotton textiles had been doubly

disorganized by the shift of the industry from North to South and by the bankruptcies and re-organizations that accompanied this change of base. In the South, the mill workers were recruited from a population unused to town life, suspicious of strangers, and linked to their employers by many emotional and religious ties.

But the depression had hit the textile mills very badly, and if fewer mills simply shut down in the South, wages were very low: $11 per week, just over half the national average for manufacturing workers. News of the NRA put hope into the workers and heartened the union organizers. The great textile strike that began on September 1, 1934, was the most important and significant of all the NRA strikes. It covered the whole area from Massachusetts to Alabama. It illustrated the impotence of the codes to deal with such conflicts, for the basic claim was for union recognition. The scale of the strike illustrated, too, the hopes, fears, angers of the workers. So did the new technique of "flying squadrons," motorized pickets which rushed reinforcements to towns and villages where the local pickets were too weak or too terrified to shut down the mills. Equally significant was the reply of the employers or of some of them. The strikers were denounced as anarchists, troublers of the public peace; the militia was called out, and on at least one occasion, well-armed "loyal workers" stormed the picket line, killing six of the human obstacles between them and the right to work without union interference.

The strike failed; true, the board appointed to settle it, presided over by John G. Winant, admitted the truth of many of the charges brought by the workers. But the union ranks melted away and the moral victory was no compensation for the sense of failure, the feeling that rights under NRA had little meaning unless supported by the workers' power or the power of the Government.

The strikes, too, demonstrated the fact that the country was still far from having a unified working class, conscious of its own solidarity and convinced that it had nothing to lose but its chains. There were still conflicts of race, color, religion, and sectional interest. Men learned that to unionize the South it was best to send in exclusively white, Gentile, Protestant organizers. It was learned, too, that in New England it was a mistake to run the new unions entirely with a Jewish general staff. "They don't seem to realize we are Christians," one aggrieved worker was to say a few years later. Finally, organizers learned to avoid the red label. In the yeasty movements of 1933–34, the Communists played a part out of all proportion to their numbers if not their zeal. But all the zeal in the world could not alter the fact that the American worker was not ready to be led on to the Revolution, and the possessing classes were not in the least defeatist.

The greatest single union in the American Federation of Labor, the United Mine Workers of America, was as sick as the coal industry. Even in the boom year, 1929, the United Mine Workers had only 84,000 members out of a mining personnel of 522,000. And there were many, inside the union and out, who put a great deal of the blame on the leader of the miners, John L. Lewis. He was dictatorial inside the union; opponents were abused as Communists and carrion, and were not always lucky enough to escape with merely verbal chastisement. Inside the American Federation of Labor, Lewis was one of the most powerful and adroit manipulators. He had done much to make William Green, his lieutenant in the United Mine Workers, the head of the AFL, and William Green was believed to give satisfaction to Lewis. The United Mine Workers fought a series of losing battles, giving way on wages, accepting breaches of agreements, and totally failing to hold its own, much less expand the unionized areas. Attempted revolts inside the union were crushed. There were rival unions, the Communist-dominated National Miners Union and the Progressive Mine Workers of America, but they were feeble.

To the United Mine Workers, NRA was a godsend. Within a year, the 80,000 members had risen to near 400,000; vast new areas were unionized and far better terms had been secured from the owners than could have been hoped for in 1932. The leader of the miners was now the most formidable figure inside the AFL, and his conversion to the principles of "industrial unionism" was an event of the greatest moment.

There were plausible reasons why the leader of the miners should support the new departure. The failure to unionize steel meant that the "captive" mines, owned by the steel companies, were not unionized or, where unionized, were under constant attack from owners anxious lest the idea of unionization should spread from the mines to the mills. But there was more behind the change than that. The year 1933 had brought a new air into the stuffy conference rooms of the old unions. And, as head of the greatest industrial union in the AFL, Lewis was prepared to listen to the advocates of a new policy.

The AFL was basically a federation of craft unions, though it had a few industrial unions like those of the miners, the barbers, the bricklayers, and the masons and plasterers. Its fundamental purpose was to regulate what Selig Perlman has called "the job empire." Its powers were used to make peace between competitors for disputed areas of the job empire. Some of those disputes had gone on for many years, and in the critical conference of

1934 more time was spent trying to patch up the old feud between the carpenters and the sheet metal workers over the installation of "metal trim" than on the new radical policy proposed by John L. Lewis.

The position of the AFL was less absurd than it was made to seem. Every effort to organize the great mass-production industries had failed. The rulers of the AFL denied that they were opposed to organization of the mass industries. But it must be done in due form. "Federal unions" would be chartered and given direction and help from headquarters. But the federal union was, at best, unorganized territory compared with the craft unions —the sovereign states of the AFL. And the federal unions were assembly points for future members of craft unions, a kind of Ellis Island where the immigrants into the AFL were to be kept until the crafts had decided into what pen they were to be driven. Neither steel nor automobile workers could be organized in this spirit.

So thought Lewis; so also thought David Dubinsky of the Ladies' Garment Workers and Sidney Hillman of the Amalgamated Clothing Workers, both powerful unions with a record of caring for what was to be called "social significance." But President Green did not agree, nor did his two lieutenants, William Hutcheson and Matthew Woll. They represented the conservative view that labor would advance further and faster in the long run through strong craft unions unimpeded by alliance with inchoate masses of unskilled or semi-skilled workers.

As this clash of views developed, the Wagner-Connery Act of July 5, 1935, altered the whole labor situation. This far-reaching law was necessitated by the annulment of the NRA. It reenacted the general labor-organization guarantees of Section 7-A. It also created a permanent and independent National Labor Relations Board of three men, empowered to investigate complaints and to issue "cease and desist" orders to halt unfair practices in areas involving interstate commerce. What were unfair practices? They included any attempt to interfere with collective bargaining; any refusal to bargain collectively; any attempt to discharge or penalize an employee who testified before the NLRB; any exercise of undue influence over labor unions through financial or other support; and any discrimination against union members. Within two years some five thousand instances of alleged unfair practice were brought before the NLRB. Time was to prove the law Constitutional, for in 1937 the Supreme Court upheld it in several cases. Plainly, labor now had more sweeping Government protection than ever before. The National Association of Manufacturers and other business organizations protested vigorously that the law was partial and unfair; but under it the growth of unions went on apace. By the time the Second World War began, no fewer than eleven million workers belonged to some union organization. The old-style company union meanwhile tended to disappear, for within four years the NLRB ordered about 350 such unions dissolved. Business had long been a giant in the United States; now labor was becoming a giant too.

As labor thus received its charter for a mighty new growth, the question of the form of that growth became urgent. The huge mass-production industries—steel, automobiles, rubber, machinery—must now be added to the domain of organized labor; and how could it be done except by broad industrial unions? The scheme of setting up locals tied to the AFL had been tried under NRA in the mass-production industries and had proved inadequate. In motor plants, in rubber factories, and above all in the major steel mills which the Amalgamated Association, an AFL union, had left untouched, workers were crying for organization and leadership.

The battle between John L. Lewis and his aides on one side, and William Green and his lieutenants on the other, came into the open at the Atlantic City convention in 1935. The leader of the attack on the AFL conservatives was a figure made to delight cartoonists. Formidable in mere bulk, Lewis had glowering brows and a battleship chin that were becoming familiar to all Americans. So, too, was his Welsh eloquence. "The craft unions of this country," he shouted, "may be able to stand upon their own feet and like mighty oaks stand before the gale, defy the lightning; yet the day may come when these organizations may not be able to withstand the lightning and the gale. Now, prepare yourself by making a contribution to your less fortunate brethren, heed this cry from Macedonia that comes from the hearts of men."

The craft unions rallied to defeat the appeal; and the AFL convention saw what had been unknown for a generation, a fist fight on the floor between Lewis and Hutcheson. But Lewis did not have the votes. His victory in physical battle did not alter the fact that the AFL flatly refused to try to organize steel, automobiles, and rubber in the only way they could be organized—in industrial unions. It adopted a report clinging to craft unionism. Some maneuvering for position followed; diplomatic exchanges took place. But the breach was total, and an organizational split was now inevitable.

In November, the first step toward schism was taken. At a convention in Washington, the "Committee for Industrial Organizations" was set up by eight AFL unions. These were the Miners, the Amalgamated Clothing Workers, the Ladies' Garment Workers, the Typographical Union, the United Textile Union, the Oil Field, Gas Well and Refining Workers, the United Hatters, and the Mine, Mill and Smelter Workers. Like most rebels, the new committee was at first anxious to profess loyalty to the rulers whom it was, in fact, defying. It was above all anxious to avoid the imputation of being guilty of the most damnable of sins, "dual unionism." It talked of "educational and advisory" work. But it meant to go the whole road. The unions of the CIO refused to give up their plans of using all their power to organize steel and the other basic industries, disregarding in the process the interests of such craft unions as might get in the way.

From the point of view of the AFL executive, this was treason. The rebels were warned; they ignored the warning; they were suspended, in September, 1936; but apart from protesting against the tyranny and illegality of the suspension, the CIO went on. They had undertaken a more dangerous task than defying the AFL. There was something symbolic in the removal of the headquarters of the Miners from Indianapolis to Washington, near the President who was soon to have a contribution of $500,000 of Miners' funds to secure his reelection. There was meaning, too, in the acceptance of Lewis's leadership by former rebels in his own union, like John Brophy. They were now more than willing to follow him, since he was going the way they wanted him to go.

The union leaders who were committed to the forward policy showed courage in attacking the enemy at his traditionally strongest point, the steel industry. It was not like the automobile industry, a field of action which the unions had never entered; it was one from which they had been expelled. By the standards of the time, the iron industry had been a union stronghold; and although, as steel replaced iron, the unions did not keep up with the growth of the industry, it nevertheless took more than twenty years to kill them. It was the anti-union policy of the mammoth United States Steel that, from 1901 on, set the pace. By 1910, the "Amalgamated" (The Amalgamated Association of Iron, Steel, and Tin Workers), the AFL charter union, had about 10,000 members out of a possible half million, and they were confined to minor and decaying plants. In 1919, William Z. Foster tried to unionize steel by a great but unsuccessful strike, tepidly supported by the AFL and warmly aided with great gifts of money by the Amalgamated Clothing Workers and the International Ladies' Garment Workers. The lesson was learned by the workers and by the AFL: steel could not be unionized.

The years between the end of the strike and the coming of the depression saw marked improvements in hours and conditions of labor, as well as in welfare work. They saw, too, the creation in Bethlehem and other plants of "employee representation plans," commonly called "ERP," and still more commonly "company unions." But the rulers of the steel empire, in general, did not think it necessary to make even this concession. In company towns like Alequippa and Homestead, the control by the local government of all forms of local economic life, of the press, and to some extent of the churches, was so complete that organized resistance to the will of the steel companies was barely a dream. Even when the industry was booming, it was especially subject to fluctuations in demand. Moreover, the amount of employment it offered was shrinking in relation to output, as new technical devices, above all the continuous-strip system, replaced by means of semi-automatic processes the skill and physical strength which were the only salable assets of tens of thousands of workers.

The depression made terrible inroads on the well-being of the steel workers and dampened any lingering sparks of revolt. But the coming of NRA made a sudden change. In steel, the guarantee of the right of collective bargaining rendered unionization a live issue. But the steel codes did not, in fact, do more than make a formal bow to an abstract right. Workers who had rushed to join

Amalgamated were soon disillusioned. The rulers of the moribund union had the temperament of Austrian generals; they did not expect to win and their lack of faith was visible to the new recruits. The Communists were active in the promotion of a rival body, the Steel and Metal Workers' Industrial Union, but despite the zeal of its leaders, it made little headway. To be "red" was a terrible handicap in the steel regions, and, following the change in party tactics decided in 1934, the Communists gave up the creation of rival unions and took up the policy of "boring from within." But in steel there was little worth boring into.

From a totally unexpected source came the first effective organization of the steel workers: from the steel companies themselves. NRA had been only a threat, but it *had* been a threat to the anti-union policy and it was a threat that might be renewed. So as a homeopathic remedy, the few ERP unions were suddenly multiplied, until all the major and most of the minor companies had their own unions. To make them effective lightning rods, they must be similar to independent unions. Thus, in giving these ERP unions a sufficiently plausible appearance of power and in making them effective aids to personnel management, the steel companies not only provided the mechanism for electing plant leaders, but also unwittingly trained them in union strategy and tactics and put important patronage in their hands. All was well as long as the leaders remained loyal, but many company union officials, freely elected by their fellows, developed new loyalties and ambitions. Rapidly becoming more than mere plant spokesmen, they began to create a federation of plant locals for some of the most important companies and to push reasonably effective Trojan horses inside the steel citadel, thereby constituting a far greater menace to the established order than Amalgamated.

The men who had undertaken to organize steel were not steel men—which accounted in part for their courage. For it was the high command of the United Mine Workers who had committed themselves to this doubtful battle. Failing to carry with them the rulers of the AFL, the leaders of the United Mine Workers offered the leaders of the Amalgamated $500,000—on conditions. The formal union rights would be preserved, the recruits directed into the empty ranks of Amalgamated, but the control of the campaign was to be exclusively in the hands of the "Steel Workers Organizing Committee," the SWOC that was born on June 16, 1936.

The marshal sent into the field by John L. Lewis was the second in command of the Mine Workers, the Scottish-born Philip Murray, and he and his colleagues took over the job on a scale and with methods unknown to the leadership of the Amal-

gamated. The Committee for Industrial Organization, in effect, bought the franchise to organize
steel and thus avoided the imputation of the sin
of "dual unionism." Success would not necessarily
save the CIO, but failure would definitely kill it
and discredit the ambitions of its chief.

The steel companies awaited the attack with
confidence, but also with an uneasy sense that
something was new in the situation. "I don't know
how well they are doing their organizing job," said
a spokesman for one of the companies, "and neither
does Phil Murray; no one will know till there's
a show-down." The show-down took place under
very different political conditions from those that
had prevailed in 1919. There was now a Democratic Governor in Pennsylvania as well as a
Democratic President in Washington; it was a
Presidential year, with much of the financial and
more of the voting strength of the Democrats coming from labor. A turning point in the campaign
was the candid announcement by Lieutenant-Gov-
ernor Kennedy of Pennsylvania, himself a leader
of the miners, that strikers would be given relief
and a hint that administrative discretion would be
exercised in their favor. "The great thing today,"
said a veteran labor reporter, "is that the steel
workers think the cops are going to be on their
side." It *was* a great thing in a region where, not
long before, the Secretary of Labor had been able

to speak, in one town, only from the steps of the Post Office—Federal property and thus immune from the local police.

The sudden appearance of some of the leaders of the company unions on the payroll of the SWOC was a blow to the morale of those workers, who were still, from loyalty or fear, taking their lead from their employers. And when concessions were made to the company unions, the credit was chalked up to the pressure of the SWOC; when they were refused, the company unions were exposed, so it was asserted, as frauds.

Behind the recruiting and the propaganda loomed the threat of the strike. When the election returns were in, justifying the political judgment of John L. Lewis, the time was ripe. Wage concessions were made, but too late, and the labor world waited for the explosion. When it came, it was not in steel but in the motor industry; and before putting all to the touch the steel workers waited to see whether the CIO could fight General Motors and Chrysler. Victory in Detroit gave the necessary faith, and, before that faith could be tested, victory was won in steel without fighting. The behemoth of the industry, United States Steel, suddenly broke the front of the resisters. After secret negotiations between John L. Lewis and Myron Taylor, the SWOC contract was accepted and the fact announced to an astonished mass of workers and to a largely infuriated group of employers on March 2, 1937. After a brief but very successful strike, Jones & Laughlin signed, too. The campaign seemed to have been won without a battle.

Why had the employers, or the most important of them, suddenly surrendered? The election results showed that any hopes of a political reaction were vain. Worse might befall. The orders coming into the steel industry were largely from the United States Government, which insisted on the Walsh-Healy Act with its provision for fair labor standards. Other Governments then steadily rearming had no interest in the union controversy, but a great interest in smooth production.

It was natural to assume that the surrender by United States Steel, like the victory over Jones & Laughlin, signified the end of the campaign. This was an error. The rulers of companies classed as "Little Steel" were rugged individualists who saw in Myron Taylor not a leader to be followed but a traitor to execrated. They decided to stand firm. And the CIO fought before it was ready, before it had even a nominal majority in some plants. Possibly the local leaders, all miners, took for granted the automatic solidarity of their own craft; there, once a strike was launched, you could count on the cohesion of the whole mining community. But the steel plants now attacked were not natural social units like the mining villages. They were not concentrated in socially homogeneous villages, but lay in cities over a wide range from Pennsylvania to Illinois. Where a nucleus of cohesion existed, it was not necessarily friendly to the union. Frequently the small businessmen of the small town were more concerned over the possible alienation of the steel companies than of their immediate customers.

It might have been wiser to wait, but the temptation to move forward upon what seemed the flowing tide was too great; the strike was called. It mattered little that the immediate issue was whether or not Republic would sign a contract, or whether or not the lock-out at Massillon, Ohio, would be followed by a strike; the battle was on. Republic organized sympathy for the "right to work," and slowly but inexorably the early enthusiasm of the workers for strike action was worn down. One most effective method of mobilizing sympathy against the strikers was the threat to move the plant. It evoked both anger and passion; the workers, under the lead of outside agitators, were menacing the whole economic life of the community; they were traitors to their home town. A century-old American tradition of local loyalty was called in against the new solidarity of the workers with each other. The strike failed.

But before it failed, the usual violence had occurred, and the result was not an unmixed victory for the companies. For at Massillon there were two

deaths, both strikers; at South Chicago, there were
ten, all strikers. In neither instance were any serious casualties suffered by the defenders of law and
order. The country was horrified by plain evidence
of ruthless and unnecessary violence by the police.
There were news reels and photographs; the dead
bodies, the merciless clubbing of the pickets by the
Chicago police, were seen by millions. This had
something of the same effect as the photograph of
"loyal Ford workers" beating up, in a fit of "spontaneous" indignation, Richard Frankensteen, the
CIO organizer. The handcuffs visible in the hip
pocket of one of the company agents undid much
of the good will won for the Ford Company by
publicity experts. Both the Little Steel companies
and the Ford plants had won a respite, not a final
victory.

In Detroit, the clash between the new industry
and the new unionism assumed a classical form. In
the great mass-production plants of Ford, General
Motors, and Chrysler, the old craft divisions had
least meaning, and the unity and uniformity imposed by the assembly line seemed to create a situation in which the industrial union was the inevitable
method of organizing labor. But in this new industry, apart from the relatively small group of highly
skilled workers, there was no tradition of unionism
or of solidarity. The automobile industry was a
boom industry and Detroit had some of the in-

stability of a mining camp. Only 1 per cent of the workers were natives of the city. They hailed from everywhere, from all parts of Europe, from most parts of America. Imbedded in the heart of Detroit was the almost exclusively Polish city of Hamtramck; but there were scores of thousands of workers of native American stock, from the deeply depressed mining and lumber areas of northern Michigan, from the eroded cotton fields and hill regions of the South. Black and white, Catholic and Protestant, the Detroit proletariat was divided, rootless, depressed. Its only focus of unity was the plant.

In Detroit, as elsewhere, NRA brought a brief and transient epidemic of unionization. It was largely toward the unionization of the automobile industry that the compromise resolution of the AFL convention of 1934 was directed. But the weaknesses of the traditional approach were especially visible in the great mass-production industry. The workers were bewildered by rival industrial claimants. There was the Automobile Industrial Workers Association, patronized by the local clerical demagogue, the Reverend Charles Coughlin of the Shrine of the Little Flower. There was Communist activity, and there was the official AFL union, the Automobile Workers of America, under a regular AFL organizer, Francis J. Dillon. Under NRA, a special board had been set up to deal with union problems in the motor industry, and the election (for delegates, not for given organizations) was a victory for the employers and for the company unions they had created. By the summer of 1935, the "federal unions" sponsored by the AFL had, even on their own showing, only 35,000 members. The first union offensive, run in the old way, had failed.

It was the CIO secession that revived unionism in Detroit. Dillon was overthrown and replaced by Homer Martin, an ex-minister whose evangelical eloquence was a real asset. Another was provided by the internal disharmonies of the industry. In Detroit unrest was endemic. It was symptomatic that the great automobile plants were among the biggest customers of the agencies that hired out detectives to bore into unions and provided strike-breakers, better known as "finks," who defended the right of the workers to ignore the picket line at a fixed rate of compensation *per diem*.

By December, 1936, the United Automobile Workers were ready for an attack, and they chose General Motors. The management refused to talk with anyone professing to represent all the workers. It was a deadlock that on December 28, 1936, was most dramatically broken—and not at the expense of General Motors. That day occurred the "sit-down" in a Fisher Body plant at Cleveland. (Later there were as many claimants for the honor of this invention as there were for the birthplace of Homer or of the Republican party.) Fisher was again struck, at Flint, and the standard rumor that the company was going to move the plant to Pontiac and Atlanta backfired. The workers in Flint replied by more sit-downs and the strike spread all over the Fisher empire as far away as Georgia.

The employers, the Government, Federal and local, and the CIO were about equally embarrassed. The Roosevelt Administration in Washington, like Governor Murphy in Lansing, knew how much it owed labor for cash and votes. But Lewis himself was in no easy spot. The main effort and most of the resources of the CIO were already committed to the battle with steel. Could the infant organization fight two such campaigns at the same time? It was very doubtful. Yet to let the workers fight without help and direction would be to repeat the mistake of the AFL. The battle must be joined, and John Brophy was sent to Detroit to play the role that Philip Murray was playing in Pittsburgh.

Flint was the Lexington of the new quasi-revolution; the sit-down method was imitated in all kinds of industry. For a time sit-downs were a curious mixture of a semi-revolutionary technique and a fad like midget golf. The rubber plants at Akron, Ohio, witnessed one of the most prolonged and stubborn of the sit-down movements, which won the workers important concessions.

The advantages of the stay-in strike from the point of view of the union were immense, especially in winter. Instead of the cold, boring job of manning the picket line, the workers were under cover, in their normal environment, held together by the only discipline they knew, that of the plant. Moreover, the employers, instead of having to bring workers or "finks" through the picket line, had the much more serious job of forcing their way into the plants. Instead of maneuvering to keep their plants open, they were tempted to shut them before a sit-down could develop. In a small plant, and in a state like Connecticut with a highly developed system both of law and of union bargaining, the sit-down could be firmly repressed, but in Michigan, with its vast, amorphous, excitable body of workers, it was difficult to break up mass pickets and still more difficult to recapture the plants. The strikers could possibly be frozen or starved into submission, but heated demands that the law must be enforced though the heavens fell were ignored by the unions, by Governor Murphy, and in effect by the employers. True, General Motors got an injunction ordering the workers out of a plant. It was soon made widely public that the enjoining judge was a big stockholder. General Motors got its legal victory but Judge Black could not enforce it.

The sit-down wave was so universal that it presented the states and Federal Government with a problem that could hardly be solved in terms of formal law. Despite the ingenious efforts of some eminent lawyers to show that the sit-down was not illegal, it was plainly contrary to property rights as hitherto interpreted; it was a breach of the law as the public understood the law. The workers replied that the employers themselves had defied the Wagner Act and did not come into court with clean hands.

But it may be doubted whether the letter or spirit of the law interested the contestants very much. It was a trial of nerve and strength. Flint was the testing ground, not only of the power of the companies, but of the effectiveness of that mobilization of the smaller businessmen that was effective in the strike against Little Steel. The trial of strength proved that in Michigan the time was not yet ripe for pressure of this kind to be effective, at any rate so long as Governor Murphy did not put the state police and militia at the disposal of the employers. The CIO leaders did not rely solely on their own strength. They reminded the President that the main stockholders in General Motors, the Du Ponts, were conspicuous "economic royalists," deeply involved in the recent campaign to overthrow the Roosevelt Administration. Finally General Motors gave in; like United States Steel, they recognized the union as bargaining agent but only for its own members, a limitation that salved the honor of the company. CIO had won another astounding victory.

It took the biggest of all sit-downs, forty thousand workers occupying the plants, to induce Walter Chrysler to give way—but he did. Of the big three in the automobile business, only one remained and he, symbolically, was the most important. Henry Ford held out and was to continue to hold out for years to come. The industry was not wholly unionized, but Ford was losing ground to General Motors, losing ground in production and design; and it was suggested that his refusal to deal with the unions was only one sign of the stubborn conservatism that made Detroit say that Ford was slipping. Among the critics of the settlements was William Green; John L. Lewis had settled for far too little. But the public thought that, with standard AFL leadership, there would have been no settlement at all.

Other AFL criticisms had more merit. The victorious Automobile Workers were suddenly perplexed by internal quarrels that had nothing to do with their immediate interest but a great deal to do with the fight between the orthodox (Stalinite) and heretical (Lovestonite) sects of the American Communists. Inside the plants, union discipline was at first very weak. The mechanisms of democratic control of locals of the colossal size necessitated by the scale of the industry did not work with anything like perfection. The CIO leadership was from the top. The motor union was not run so exclusively by viceroys from the United Mine Workers as was the steel union, but both were in a kind of colonial status for the time being. Collection of dues was difficult and the AFL was scornful of the CIO claims to numbers, claims not substantiated by statistics or independent revenues. The management complained that its new desire to work with the union was often frustrated by the inability of the union leaders to deliver the goods. But the feeling of labor and left-wing elements, in general, was better expressed by an amended version of a famous American song:

> Old John Lewis had a farm,
>   CI, CIO!
> Here a picket, there a picket,
> Everywhere around a picket,
>   CI, CIO.

For the moment, John L. Lewis ranked high in the list of famous Americans, whether as an object of admiration and love, or of detestation and fear. The CIO had established itself as a great permanent force in American life. Powerful in the rubber, steel, automobile, and electrical industries, it had also unionized large bodies of employees in the textile field, organized many office workers and

shop clerks, and made its Newspaper Guild a powerful body in journalism. Jurisdictionally, labor was
split into two great bodies. But when its basic rights
were threatened, the CIO and AFL were usually
found standing together.

CHAPTER IX

THE SECOND ROOSEVELT LANDSLIDE

FEW Presidential years have opened under less auspicious circumstances for the "outs" than 1936. Indeed, there was much to be said for reserving the strength of the Republican party for another four years, for determining to make a campaign for the record, rather than waste assets and prestige on a doomed effort for victory. It might be wise to be content with a protest vote and keep the not very abundant powder dry for 1940.

Against these prudential considerations, powerful forces fought. Already the opposition to the Roosevelt Administration had taken on a bitterness and passion that were novel in modern American politics. The Liberty League, formed in 1934 by conservatives in both parties, and amply financed by the Du Ponts and others, displayed a savage temper. Something of the panic and anger aroused by the Bryan campaign of forty years before was visible among politicians and businessmen. They wanted a new McKinley and a new

Mark Hanna, perhaps more the Mark Hanna than the McKinley. Over a large section of the business world, there was no thought of prudence, of waiting for 1940. It was now or never.

More important still was the attitude of the professional politicians, of the thousands of party workers who were still suffering from the shock of 1932 and of 1934; especially that of 1934, for the defeat of 1932 had been discounted. No party could buck bad times, especially such very bad times. The only thing to do was to retire to the storm cellars of opposition and wait. They had waited, and 1934 had come, a far more formidable phenomenon than 1932. For the Roosevelt Administration had gained, not lost. The blow was felt not only in Congress but in state Capitols, in city halls, even in county seats. So severe had been the bloodletting that it was not certain the party could survive or that the demoralized (and unemployed) party regulars could hold together at all. In the darkest hours of the Democratic party, it had possessed the solid South and the great northern cities to nourish the *cadres*. But now there was not only a Democrat in the White House, there was a Democrat in the Pennsylvania Capitol. Of the great prizes of politics, only Philadelphia was in non-Democratic hands in the East; only California, by a chapter of local accidents, was held with difficulty in the West. The party regulars

could not wait; they had to fight. And they had
to fight, if not to win, at any rate to make a good
showing; to profit by a candidate who might not
get to the White House but who, in doubtful states,
would carry the ticket into the local strongholds
lost in 1932 and 1934. In this desperate situation,
many of the old rules of availability went by the
board. After the Reign of Terror, a member of
the Convention was asked what he had done during that ordeal. "I survived," was his reply. Such
might have been the reply of the Governor of
Kansas who, in the autumn of 1935, began to
appear as the most formidable competitor for the
Republican nomination. He had survived 1932;
better still, he had survived 1934. And this in a
state which, despite its birth in the Republican
party, had gone Democratic in 1930!

Alfred Mossman Landon had many qualities to
commend him to the Republican party. He was
young as Presidential candidates go, just under
fifty. He was not, in the derogatory sense, a professional politician, but he had a political record—
and a helpful one. He had bolted the Republican
party in 1912 in support of Theodore Roosevelt, a
certificate of liberalism needed in 1936. An independent oil prospector and operator, Landon was a
businessman but not a big businessman; he was a
Westerner born in Pennsylvania. Even the fact
that he had supported the early measures of the

New Deal, and had used language about the crimes of the big bankers and market manipulators that differed from the President's only in rhetorical finish, was no handicap.

Governor Landon had more than mere survival to recommend him. The abandonment of its economy program by the Roosevelt Administration was one of its greatest crimes in the eyes of the opposition and was the most obvious breach of the campaign promises of 1932. For many conservatives, Republicans and Democrats alike, the acceptance of a policy of debt was the great divide. In such a situation it was a good selling point that Governor Landon had balanced his budget. Critics might point out that he had done it only by the aid of lavish Federal grants and that, if the state government of Kansas was not deep in debt, it was because the state constitution cut down to nothing its powers of borrowing. They stressed, too, the fact that lesser governmental units in Kansas were in many cases highly insolvent; that many school districts had got round their financial difficulties by the simple expedient of closing down the schools. But the fact remained that the state was solvent and that Kansas had shown its appreciation by reelecting the man to whom the praise was due.

From the celebration of Kansas Day (January 29, 1935) Governor Landon began to be a figure outside his own state. He attracted the favorable notice of very diverse figures. William Randolph Hearst came out on his side in the fall, and, almost at the opposite pole, Raymond Clapper, columnist of the then New Deal Scripps-Howard chain, moved perhaps by local patriotism (for he, too, was a Kansan), was for a time a Landon man. But it was in his own state and in his own region that Landon's candidacy was really launched. There he got the support of such traditionally important veterans as ex-Vice-President Curtis. A Kansas publisher, Oscar S. Stauffer, took up the work; the national committeeman, John D. M. Hamilton, came over and, most important of all, the rulers of the chief daily of this region decided that in Landon was the instrument not only to defeat the Roosevelt Administration, but to rescue the Republican party from the dead hand of the East that had almost killed it. The party had to go back to the grass roots, back to where it belonged, the plain people of the Middle West.

Such was the gospel of the *Kansas City Star* and the triumvirate who ruled it, Roy Roberts, William Haskell, and Lacey Haines. Such was soon the theme of numerous saviors of the party all over the Mississippi Valley. Politically speaking, Governor Landon was the most available aspirant. By the beginning of 1936, he was clearly in the lead. Inevitably, there developed a "Stop Landon" movement. But there was no other possible candidate with the same claims, or, at least, none whose claims were being pressed. Senator Vandenberg's achievement in getting reelected in Michigan, as well as his record as an effective critic of the Roosevelt Administration, made him a marked man. But Vandenberg made it plain that he did not choose to run. Senator Dickinson of Iowa was one of the loudest critics of the New Deal, but his ambitions were not taken seriously by others. Colonel Frank Knox, publisher of the Chicago *Daily News,* old Rough Rider and Progressive, was entitled to claim the mantle of the elder Roosevelt; Hoover might ask for a vindication by nomination; possibly Senator Borah would request a long-deferred reward. But even before the refusals of Hoover and Vandenberg and the failure of the "Stop Landon" movement to find a plausible alternative, it was certain where the Republican nomination would go, although the prospective nominee was unknown, even by sight, to most of the regular politicians, and had delivered only one speech east of the Mississippi.

The Republican Convention met on June 10 in Cleveland, where only eight years earlier it had acclaimed the rule of Calvin Coolidge. It was noted by the ironically minded that the convention hall was only got ready by the aid of the WPA and that the citizens of Cleveland, hotel proprietors apart, displayed a chilly indifference. Even the sight of a covered wagon drawn by oxen, symbol of the prairie communities which were to rescue American tradition, provoked the jest that, not content with a horse and buggy, the Republican party insisted on something still more archaic.

But the delegates were full of zeal or anger. The great oratorical success of the convention fell to ex-President Hoover. His was a fighting speech against those who "offered the mirage of Utopia to those in distress," but more significant was the warmth of the reception given the formal leader of the party. Some thought, indeed, that if he had not taken himself out of the fight in May, the ex-President would have been the real beneficiary of the anti-Landon efforts. But smoothly managed, the convention moved on to its predestined end.

The platform seemed liberal. Whether it represented a triumph of the progressive elements of the Republican party over the Old Guard or simply an attempt by shrewd political leaders to go the New Deal one better was open to debate. But the candidate insisted, once nominated, on interpreting it. He sent a telegram demanding the earliest possible return to a gold standard, to the indignation of Senator Borah, whose hopes of nomination had gone but who had been placated by vague "soft money" references. Landon, too, came out for a Constitutional amendment, if necessary, to permit legislation on wages and hours that would end the impasse of the recent Supreme Court decision. This energy made a good impression. The convention, after nominating Knox for Vice President, adjourned in a mildly hopeful mood.

It was in a very different atmosphere that the Democrats met in what had been the very heart of unshaken Republicanism, Philadelphia. Never since the great days of Jackson had his party been more united and confident. True, a number of leading Democrats had appealed to the delegates to throw off the yoke of the New Deal. But though the signatories ranged from Al Smith through Bainbridge Colby down to Daniel Cohalan, few expected that the manifesto would have any great general effect and none that it would affect the convention. Democratic headquarters were not worried. Postmaster-General Farley was chairman of the National Committee and head of the New York organization. He had the situation well in hand. Tammany, in bad odor with the Administration and excluded from local patronage by the La Guardia Reform administration in the city, was docile if sulky. There were rumors of revolt in Maryland and of disaffection in Virginia, but Farley did not really care what Senator Glass said on the subject of Patrick Henry. Patrick Henry had been dead a long time.

To the old-fashioned Democrat, the convention

was odd, indeed. To be in power and so confident of keeping it was novelty enough. An observer noted the glee with which every reference to the Republicans as "the minority party" was received. At Cleveland, the delegates had been thrifty eaters and drinkers; not so at Philadelphia. A woman observer who covered both conventions found many more women at Philadelphia—and found them far more metropolitan than their sisters at Cleveland. If the Republican party, as revealed at Cleveland, was middle class, the Democratic party on show at Philadelphia was not so easily placed. There were the veterans of the Deep South and of the great city machines; there were the newly conscious representatives of the industrial masses; but there were also "socialites," new converts to the New Deal. "Duco Democrats" they were sourly styled by the Republicans they had lately left and by the old-line Democrats they had newly joined. No doubts were felt as to the outcome in Philadelphia. The delegates were there to applaud and receive orders. They were told, for instance, to abolish the century-old two-thirds rule that had played so great a part in the history of Democratic conventions. The alteration made it impossible for the South, in 1940, to veto the choice of the North and West. The veterans had just received almost two billion dollars, the bonus which the President wanted to deny them, but they bore him no malice. The Republican candidate was a veteran, but no one thought that would do him much good. Landon had come out for all kinds of unions, including company unions, and though he had hastily amended his first statement, men assumed that he would get few votes from organized labor. Even the Negroes were thought to be wavering in their allegiance to the party of Lincoln, and the seating at Cleveland of a "lily-white" delegation from Florida seemed to show that the Republicans were more anxious to recover their Southern gains of 1928 than to hold the Northern Negroes to the old cause. The Democrats had plenty to make them hopeful and plenty of political reasons to be grateful to Roosevelt.

The climax was the arrival of the President. As he drove to Franklin Field, a poor man on the sidewalk threw his watch into the Presidential car as a thank-offering. The President was received with awe, and for the moment knew the delights and temptations of the *triumphator*. He spoke, adding one more telling phrase to the American political vocabulary. The "economic royalists" were denounced to the delight of the immense crowd. "As he finished," wrote Raymond Clapper, "standing there with his mother and family round him, the strains of 'Auld Lang Syne' floated out over the audience. There was a pause. 'I'd like to hear "Auld Lang Syne" again,' the President said. The audience

joined in. . . . Still a third time it was repeated.
. . . In a moment Roosevelt was gone. The audience stood in its tracks for quite some time, as if still
under the spell, and then quietly began to leave."

The lines were joined, and more important than
any possible defection of ex-Governor Smith was
the increasing probability that Governor Lehman,
greater vote-getter in New York than either Governor Smith or Governor Roosevelt, would agree
to run again, to protect his program of social
legislation, stubbornly held up by the rural majority in the legislature.

John Hamilton, chairman of the Republican
National Committee, announced that "We are going to carry everything from Kansas straight east-
ward. . . . The West is all afire for Landon and
Knox." The West was all afire in another sense;
the sun was beating down pitilessly, ignoring state
lines and the Constitution, drying up rivers, killing crops and cattle. It looked as bad as in 1934.
Memories of the repeated calamities that had embittered the farmer were revived; memories, too,
of bold, if rash and empirical, rescue work. The
President summoned Middle Western Governors
(including the Governor of Kansas) to meet him
to discuss the drought situation at Des Moines on
September 1. At a small party conference of Republican leaders in that region, one bored member
broke in: "We all know Alf isn't going to win. He

isn't even going to carry Kansas. He won't carry a county west of the 100th parallel. Harry Wallace will carry them all."

Amid the encircling gloom that wrapped the Republican campaign, one light shone kindly, the *Literary Digest* poll. Since 1916, this magazine had been sending out test ballots to an increasingly large number of Americans. In 1932 the results seemed again to bear out the claims of the magazine, and where the final result differed from the *Digest* prediction (as in Pennsylvania) critics expressed doubts as to the administrative honesty of the vote-taking. With this background of success, it was no wonder that the increasing confidence of the *Digest* in a Landon victory should have buoyed up Republican hopes. The Institute of Public Opinion, conducted by George Gallup, a statistician associated with the great advertising agency of Young and Rubicam, the Crossley poll conducted by an agency whose normal specialty was the assessment of the popularity of radio programs, and a poll conducted by Elmo Roper for the magazine *Fortune,* all showed an overwhelming victory for Roosevelt

The differences among the prophets had more than a technical interest. The *Digest* method was to send cards to car owners and telephone owners and to assume that American public opinion was still represented by the middle classes, by those to whom "relief" was a burden and a nuisance, and the balancing of the national budget a problem that their own solvency gave them time to wory about. The other polls were based on a "sampling" method, on the creation of a small panel of voters which would allow due weight to the opinion of the rich and the poor, of white and black, of Republican and Democrat, of those whose faith in the old order was unshaken, of those whose hearts had been full of doubt and now found room for some hope. A sample thus constructed gave very different results. So did the poll conducted in Maryland by the Baltimore *Sun* which polled every voter in the state. And so did less organized polls like that conducted in a movie theater in Bridgeport, Connecticut. In that city a voter brought to the microphone had only this to say: "Roosevelt is the only President who has ever cared for people like us."

The class aspect of the campaign was brought out in a score of ways. This year marked the three-hundredth anniversary of the founding of Harvard College. And by what, at another time, would have seemed a happy dispensation of Providence, the President was a Harvard man. (It did not appear in this light to a large body of Harvard alumni.) Of course, the President was invited to the celebration, the greatest academic festivity in American history, but the welcome that Roosevelt received from street crowds in Cambridge and Boston seemed to underline the contrast with the coldness he met inside the Harvard halls.

Never, it seemed to most good party men of the minority party, had an Administration more shamelessly exploited its advantages. Everywhere the President went, Federal improvements were to be inaugurated or pointed to with pride. There were stadiums and dams, there were tunnels under the East River, and a hospital center in Jersey City, where the credit was shared with Mayor Hague, most notorious of city bosses and commander of many thousands of faithful voters. The Republicans, on the other hand, were handicapped by their own internal disunion. In so far as the Landon nomination had been the victory of Western elements who wished to modernize the party, it had irritated standpat Eastern Republicans who had no desire to compromise and who placed their hopes in a simple reaction. Total condemnation of the New Deal relieved tempers, but it was bad politics. The President was able to point out how many New Deal measures had got Republican support in Congress. He was able, too, to tax some of his most vehement opponents with ingratitude.

The President was able to emphasize the difference in the Republican campaign; the emphasis on liberalism in the West, the stress on conservatism in the East. His campaign, he boasted, was the

same in New York and Kansas—so he told an
audience in Landon's own state. It was in the East
that most blunders were made by the Republican
high command. It was a good debating point that
the Democratic platform of 1932, with its promises of rigid economy, had been totally disregarded
by the Administration. But, as Joseph Kennedy,
spokesman for the "Businessmen for Roosevelt"
group, said, the Congressional election of 1934 had
ratified the breach of contract; and in any case,
you vote for a man, not a platform. "A party platform is only one of several factors which fore-
shadow the probable future action of the elected
man"—one of the most elegant variations of the
old maxim that platforms are things to run on,
not to stand on.

Combining the offices of candidate and President, Roosevelt was able to blanket his opponent.
He could promise action, set in motion machinery
for crop insurance, announce a dramatic currency
agreement with Britain and France that seemed to
secure the dollar, both carry the fight to the enemy
and provoke him to lead with his chin. At a meeting in North Carolina (three weeks before the
official opening of the Democratic campaign), the
President displayed his mastery of the ambiguous
art of rhetoric in an appeal that evoked the Bible,
the powerful American tradition of rural virtue,
and the fears of the harassed millions of voters,

not at all sure that they were yet out of the dark wood of the depression:

I am told that this meeting is a Green Pastures Meeting. . . .

He maketh me to lie down in green pastures:
He leadeth me beside the still waters.

. . . Green pastures! Millions of other Americans, with whom I have also been associated of late, live with prayers and hopes either that the floods may be stilled—floods that bring with them destruction and disaster to fields and flocks, to homesteads and cities— or else they look for the Heaven-sent rains that will fill their wells, their ponds and their peaceful streams.

It is not every candidate who can call in the Psalmist to win both North Dakota and Connecticut and profit by drought and flood alike.

Certainly Landon was not such a candidate. His speaking voice was untrained; he often made good points, but seldom a good speech. He had the unnerving experience, borne gallantly, of facing hostile or indifferent crowds in great cities like Los Angeles. He had the depressing knowledge that even in his own state, in urban centers like Wichita, Landon men were scarce among the voting majority. He was not helped by publicity that represented him as a plain, average man. The Republican candidate's features, which in repose at close quarters struck a British newspaper correspondent as those of a shrewd and cultivated French *abbé*, did not in action impress the public. His allies talked too much. In the *New Yorker*, Frank Sullivan noted that the Republican ticket was still the same. "For President, John D. M. Hamilton, for Vice President, Frank Knox, for second Vice President, Alfred M. Landon." It was unjust, but it was not implausible.

Some Republicans continued to hold delusions. That the New York *Times*, the St. Louis *Post-Dispatch*, and the Baltimore *Sun* all turned against their party traditions and the candidate they had supported in 1932 gave them encouragement. Hopes were placed in the defection of Al Smith. More hopes were placed in internal feuds in the Democratic party. Would the Democratic voters of western Massachusetts forgive the victory of Governor Curley in the primary? Could the Democrats of Illinois patch up the bitter feud between Mayor Kelly of Chicago, master of so many myriads of loyal voters, and Governor Horner, who had fought and defeated the great city machine? Would not the Coughlin-Lemke ticket set up by certain radicals take away votes in critical states? Against that, the Democrats could set the support of the new American Labor party in New York, the support of the Farmer-Labor party in Minnesota and the Progressives in Wisconsin, and the personality of such keepers of the left-wing conscience as Senator Norris and Mayor La Guardia.

By the end of the campaign, the issue was not in doubt. The President wrote an election prophecy which he sealed in an envelope. As the event proved, he was pessimistic as to his chances. The figures were almost beyond belief when they were announced. Roosevelt had carried every state except Maine and Vermont. Even Pennsylvania, even Philadelphia, fell into line. His popular majority was nearly ten millions; and with him he swept into office even more marginal Democrats than in 1932. The Democrats won seven seats in the Senate and eleven in the House. Unlike the practically uncontested reelection of Monroe in 1820, this victory was no proof of an era of good feeling; far from it. This was no revolt; it was something like a revolution.

The failure of all the opposition third parties, Socialists, Communists, and the Coughlin-Lemke ticket, was ominous, for it meant that the forces of social discontent had moved into the Democratic camp, or into such allotropic forms of it as the American Labor party. Even the Negroes had abandoned the party of Lincoln. In such centers as Pittsburgh and Chicago they had swelled the Democratic majority, possibly out of proportion to their numbers. The Negro voters now wanted

more than "recognition" for leaders and kind words
for the rank and file. A Democratic Congressman
who had accompanied the President on his New
England tour later confessed he was almost alarmed
by the passionate fervor of the crowds which lined
the roads for scores of miles. A vast wave of hope
and gratitude had swept over the Union, or over
all but one corner. There was real wit shown by
the practical joker who erected a sign on the New
Hampshire-Vermont border: "You are now leaving the United States."

CHAPTER X

THE BATTLE OVER THE SUPREME COURT

As was natural, the Republican platform of 1936 had been full of warnings of danger to the American way of life. The second article of the detailed indictment declared that "the integrity and authority of the Supreme Court have been flouted." Republican leaders might well feel uneasy about the position of the Supreme Court and the danger of its becoming as deeply involved in politics as at the time of the Dred Scott decision. The Court seemed determined to oppose with all its power the long-established trend of Governmental policy and to veto the extension of the social power of the nation and states. It was not merely since the coming of the New Deal that the Court and Congress had been in opposition. As early as 1923, Chief Justice William Howard Taft, speaking with the special authority of an ex-President, had warned his colleagues that "it is not the function of the court to hold Congressional acts invalid simply because they are passed to carry out economic views which the court believes to be unwise or unsound."

By limiting both state and Federal competence in the general field of social legislation, the Court in the ensuing years created what some critics called a "twilight zone," a legal "no man's land" in which neither state nor Union could act. In the flush days of the twenties it was difficult to arouse popular indignation over this judicial barrier to a type of social legislation common to all civilized nations. There was, in fact, more criticism inside the legal profession itself, especially in the great law schools, than among the general public. The extended doctrines used to justify some recent decisions were asserted to go far beyond the simple principle laid down by Marshall. The Court was forgetting the wisdom of its greatest chief, forgetting that it was a Constitution that it was expounding. In this new climate of legal opinion, some of the old reverence for the Supreme Court withered away. One of the most conservative members, so the story ran, demanded of the Dean of a great law school if he taught his young men that the justices of the Supreme Court were fools. "No, we let them find out for themselves."

With the coming of the New Deal, with the flood of bold experimental legislation, the question of the role of the Supreme Court was certain to come on the agenda of politics—unless the Court effaced itself. In the early critical months, the Court fortunately had no chance to say anything, and when it did speak, it gave some support to the experiments. It upheld, narrowly, a Minnesota statute limiting the rights of mortgage-holders, and it dismissed suits seeking to establish the right of holders of securities payable in gold to a price that represented the alleged value of the gold dollar in terms of the new paper dollar. True, the petitioners were denied remedies in terms that were not flattering to the political morality of the Government of the United States. But all was saved but honor, and the Government escaped the terrifying possibility of having its currency policy wrecked by a Court decision.

Although the tendency of the Court had been to limit Governmental authority, it did not stick to that line in all cases and in *Nebbia v. New York* it gave a new and more satisfactory interpretation to the old classification of businesses affected with a public interest. Perhaps, so some New Dealers thought, the Court is obeying Mr. Dooley's law of legal politics and is following the election returns. Justices McReynolds, Sutherland, Van Devanter, and Butler were well known to be ultra-conservative in their economic opinions. Could they possibly be swinging over to the more moderate stand of Chief Justice Hughes and Justice Roberts, if not to the liberal position of Justices Stone, Brandeis, and Cardozo?

The optimists were soon to be disillusioned. In a series of decisions, the Court wrecked a great part of the New Deal program. In the *Schechter* case, it unanimously killed NIRA. True, the Blue Eagle was as sick as the Schechter chicken and there were many who breathed a grateful prayer when the Court relieved the Administration of the incubus. But that was not the reaction of the President, who declared at his press conference that the new interpretation of the commerce clause put the country back to "horse and buggy" days. More serious was the majority decision in *United States v. Butler*. Here the Court not only struck down the AAA, but attacked Congressional prerogatives at their most tender spot, the use of the taxing power. "The tax can only be sustained by ignoring the avowed purpose and operation of the act," said Justice Roberts, and the majority of the Court refused to turn a blind eye to the real object of the processing tax, the "coercion" by Federal payment of American farmers. If the Court was to scrutinize the motives of Congressional legislation (which was otherwise valid) it was engaging in battle on very dangerous ground.

Such was the opinion of the leader of the dissenting minority, Justice Stone. He, too, turned to Marshall and quoted from *McCulloch v. Maryland* the famous definition of what means are Constitutional. Justice Stone did not shrink from calling some consequences of the majority doctrine "absurd," and protested against the assumption that the Court had the exclusive duty and right to guard the nation and the Constitution from legislative follies. The free right of Congress to use the spending power as it thought fit had been established. "The suggestion that it must now be curtailed by judicial fiat hardly rises to the dignity of argument."

The Court did not heed this warning. On May 6, 1935, it struck down the Railroad Retirement Act of 1934 by a narrow interpretation of its relationship to interstate commerce, although Chief Justice Hughes, dissenting, wrote that the decision "is a departure from sound principles." It was obvious that the Court, should it continue in this course, would so restrict the Federal Government as to make a progressive social policy impossible. So it seemed to the framers of the Democratic platform of 1936, who affirmed:

We have sought and will continue to seek to meet these problems through legislation within the Constitution. If these problems cannot be effectively solved by legislation within the Constitution, we shall seek such clarifying amendment as will assure to the legislatures of the several states and to the Congress of the United States, each within its proper jurisdiction, the power to enact those laws which the State and Federal legislatures, within their respective spheres, shall find necessary in order adequately to regulate commerce, protect public health and safety and safeguard economic security. Thus we propose to maintain the letter and spirit of the Constitution.

The Republican platform was less bold in its proposals to deal with what both parties agreed was a serious problem of Constitutional interpretation. The opposition would "support the adoption of State laws and interstate compacts to abolish sweatshops and child labor, and to protect women and children with respect to working hours, minimum wages and working conditions. We believe that this can be done within the Constitution as it now stands."

Unfortunately, the Supreme Court did not agree with the Republican platform makers, for in the case of *Morehead v. New York ex rel. Tipaldo,* with Chief Justice Hughes again dissenting, it supported the New York Court of Appeals in holding a New York minimum wage law invalid. This was especially serious. The Court held that the nation could not pass such laws because this was invading the rights of the states; it held that the states could not do so because that would violate the Fourteenth Amendment. The Court was making the Government helpless! If the Democrats won, some form of clash was inevitable; the question was, what kind? A friendly critic of the New Deal, Charles Taft, warned the Republicans against putting too much hope in slogans about defending the Constitution. The people would not be impressed. If the Administration did try to pass a centralizing amendment, then was the time to act in the state legislatures and the amendment would be defeated. With the recent defeat of the child labor amendment in the state legislatures and with the inevitable delays of the amending process to chill Democratic hearts, it was natural that a way round the barrier should be sought by the President, who had just been given a decisive mandate to carry on the New Deal.

The Court had been warned by a former Republican Attorney-General. It was again warned, though not in such vehement language, by Chief Justice Hughes in the railroad case (*Railroad Retirement Board v. Alton Railroad Co.*) . "The power committed to Congress to govern interstate commerce does not require that its government should be wise, much less perfect." But the irony was wasted. The Court seemed set in its ways. For the Democrats to accept the Court decisions and abandon so much of their policy was politically intolerable. And there was no knowing what the Court would do to other important New Deal statutes, notably the Wagner Labor Act.

The day after the election of 1936, men saw

that the triumph of President Roosevelt was so complete that to a degree probably unprecedented in American history, he could "write his own ticket." What that ticket might contain was a subject of intense speculation. The Congress and President were the first to take office under the Norris Amendment, that is, in January, so that the period of waiting was cut short. On January 6, the President addressed Congress, and he emphasized, by the inflection of his voice, those scattered references that dealt with the role of the Supreme Court. "The judicial branch also is asked by the people to do its part in making democracy successful."

It was possible to think that the President would do no more than call the attention of the Supreme Court judges to their duty as he saw it, and would rely on the impression made by the overwhelming support he had received in the election of 1936. If the Court paid no attention to the election returns, there were other possibilities of action. Justices might be encouraged to retire by a bill that would guarantee them full salaries for life—and resignations would make possible the reconstruction of the Court. Leading Senators were coming out for a Constitutional amendment allotting to the Federal Government some of the powers denied it by recent Court decisions. Other leaders proposed to require seven out of the nine justices to concur before a statute was invalidated. Still others would allow Congress to overrule the Court by special majorities on the analogy of the power to overrule the Presidential veto.

But the President had already decided on a bolder and more personal attack. Keeping his choice a secret from all but a few carefully chosen assistants, he had decided on a series of changes in the whole Federal judicial system and, at the heart of the elaborate draft bill, lay a proposal that would make it possible to tame the Court more effectually than could any amendment.

On February 4, the detailed scheme was communicated to the Congressional leaders expected to push it through, not one of whom up to that time had any knowledge that a plan was under preparation. The bill purported to reform the Federal judicial system. It dealt with the lower courts as well as the high, with judicial organization as well as personnel and powers. But the central purpose was plain enough. It provided that when any judge of any Federal court became seventy years of age, after having served for ten years, and did not retire, the President could appoint "one additional judge to the court to which the former is commissioned." Not more than fifty judges could be appointed under this provision and the total number of Justices of the Supreme Court was not to exceed fifteen. Or, as this the most important provision of all was interpreted, the President might appoint not more than six extra Justices to the Supreme Court of the United States—for six of the nine existing members were above seventy. He could, it was at once affirmed, "pack the Court" and by flooding it with new and trusted nominees break any judicial blockade of his program. This was the President's answer to the Court, his interpretation of the mandate to carry on the New Deal given him by the people of the United States.

On this proposal and its implications Congressional and general attention was immediately focused. The other projected reforms were largely ignored, though some were important and eminently desirable. Thus a notable section of the bill would have put an end to a demoralizing variation in the interpretation of the law between one judicial district and another. At the moment, one lower Federal court might hold a statute unconstitutional and another hold it binding. Legal delays added to the confusion caused by the law's uncertainty, since a final decision by the Supreme Court might not be handed down for many months. Federal justice was not only variable and slow; the use of Federal judicial personnel was often wasteful. Some courts were overburdened, others were underworked; here there was congestion, there anemia. The bill proposed to deal with this situation by creating the office of proctor. The Supreme Court was to appoint an official to organize the distribution of business in the lower Federal courts under the general direction of the Chief Justice, and under his direction assign Federal judges to the courts where they were most needed.

The United States was also to have a right to be heard in all forms of judicial procedure where the Constitutionality of a Federal statute was in question. No longer would it be possible to exclude the United States from litigation to which it was, in reality if not in form, one of the most important parties.

One of the ironies of the great debate that followed was that the leaders were often forced to speak of one thing while meaning another. Nowhere in the original Presidential project was there any detailed or continuous statement of the case against the Court. That all was not well with the Federal judicial system was asserted; that the bill was a cure was claimed; but not for a month after the first shots were fired was the attack from the White House directed on the real target—the imposition by a conservative majority of the Supreme Court of their own political dogmas and prejudices.

In deciding to turn the flank of the Court's position, the President took a great political risk. It was plain from the first that the practical political grievance arose from the fact that there was no necessary harmony between the movement of public opinion and the movement of the minds of the majority of the Court. Senate, House, and President were all kept more or less in line by the electoral system. A complete breach between Congress and Executive could not last indefinitely. But there was no such automatic restoration of concord between the Court and the other two branches. It was a political fact of great importance that the Supreme Court in 1937 contained no member appointed by the President who had been twice overwhelmingly elected by the people. It was a fact of greater importance that its majority represented a political philosophy disowned by the people and was a barrier to a political program wanted by the people.

In the past such a crisis had always ended, sooner or later, in the more or less graceful retreat of the Court. Now there was no visible sign of a retreat and time was running out. Important statutes were coming up before the Court for adjudication; important legislation was being presented to Congress for enactment. It was too much to expect that the people would possess their souls in patience till death or conversion lowered the barrier erected by the Court.

What was at issue was a political problem; the remedy proposed was the historical equivalent of the *lit de justice* with which the sovereign King of France brought his obstructive judges to heel,

or the threatened creation of peers with which the
English House of Lords had been frightened into
docility. But what was formally proposed was a
change in the tenure of judges and in their number,
a change justified by statistical arguments that
were seen to be of doubtful validity.

Yet it was in no very hopeful spirit that the
opponents of the bill began to fight. They were
almost as convinced as the President that he was
bound to win. Had not the Democratic party
an overwhelming majority in both houses? Was
not party discipline vigilantly guarded by the
Postmaster-General and by almost docile chief
lieutenants in each house? Was not the official
opposition reduced to humiliating impotence? The
President's electoral success had bred almost super-
stitious awe in the minds of practical politicians,
and both houses of Congress were full of men who
knew that they had been elected because they had
run on the Roosevelt ticket, not because the voters
had supported them for their own sakes. The very
boldness and ingenuity of the plan dumbfounded
the doubters.

But opposition developed in an unexpected quarter. That conservative Southern Democrats would
be torn between their party loyalty and their devotion to traditional Constitutional pieties had
been expected and was possibly not altogether
regretted at the White House. Far more serious was

the defection of Senator Wheeler of Montana, for he represented Western liberalism in its classical form. He was a hero of the war on the Harding Administration, and by bolting the Democratic ticket in 1924 to run with the elder La Follette he had endeared himself to many independents. He, too, had been a critic of the Court and was prepared to give Congress the right to reverse Court decisions. But he saw in the Administration bill an attempt to destroy the independence of the judiciary and to do it in a disingenuous way. It was surmised by some that Senator Wheeler remembered the days when he had been persecuted by the Department of Justice, which he was investigating, and that he was adverse to leaving uncontrolled power in the hands of any executive, no matter how elevated the character and admirable the program of the President might be. Another veteran liberal, Senator Norris of Nebraska, came around to support of the plan but with manifest misgiving. The younger La Follette supported it, and other Senators of the same general outlook reserved judgment.

But it was soon evident that there would be no simple line-up of conservatives against liberals, a line-up which would have greatly helped the Administration. Some of the opponents of the bill had been sterling New Dealers, and it was especially significant that Senator O'Mahoney of Wyoming came out on the opposition side, since he was not only a representative liberal, but had begun his career in Washington as a protégé of Farley. The deans of the Columbia and Michigan law schools opposed the bill; those of Yale and Northwestern, with E. S. Corwin of Princeton, espoused it.

Within a month of the beginning of the new Administration, the Republicans saw to their incredulous delight the beginnings of a rift in the massed battalions of the enemy. But to make the rift grow, it was essential not to make the contest a continuation of the disastrous electoral campaign of 1936. So the open resistance, the public debate on the bill in Congress, was left to the Democrats. Such redoubtable Republican orators as Senator Borah preserved a difficult silence. For it was in the Senate that the battle was being fought. The Chairman of the House Judiciary Committee, Hatton Sumners of Texas, was a capable opponent of the bill, and it was considered dangerous to let him conduct hearings of draft amendments. Indeed, it was necessary to call in the authority of the White House to keep the bill from being broken up and put before the House in a form that would permit members to vote for the reforms admittedly necessary and yet vote down the "packing" clauses.

In the Senate, the Judiciary Committee was presided over by Senator Ashurst of Arizona who had come out in support of the bill, but the committee had just lost its ablest New Deal member,

Hugo Black of Alabama, who had resigned to become chairman of another committee. It was before a body fairly evenly divided that the first fight would have to be made, and it was evident that the Administration was not going to win easily. That this was realized was made plain to the nation when Roosevelt himself took a hand. On the anniversary of his first inauguration he addressed a great dinner of party workers and exhorted them to bring the whole weight of party pressure behind the bill; and a few days later (March 9), in the first fireside speech of his second term, he appealed to the American people. This speech stated the real issue far more candidly than did the bill itself or the official statements expounding it. It was no longer a matter of technical reforms, one of which happened to affect the Supreme Court. It was a question of the political role of the Court. "In the last four years the sound rule of giving statutes the benefit of all reasonable doubt has been cast aside. The Court has been acting not as a judicial body, but as a policy-making body."

And the proposed reform of the Court would "bring to the decision of social and economic problems younger men who have had personal experience and contact with modern facts." As for the charge that this amounted to packing the Court, "I will appoint Justices who will act as Justices and not as legislators."

Belatedly, the President was trying to undo a tactical mistake. For, to many members of Congress, the most ominous aspect of the original bill had been its disingenuous minimizing of its basic purpose. Few found it easy to believe that its object was to speed up procedure in the Supreme Court or thought it likely that increasing the number of judges would make the Court better able to do its business. The three senior justices, Chief Justice Hughes and Justices Sutherland and Brandeis, were induced to issue a very powerful rebuttal of the official thesis of the Department of Justice. That Justice Brandeis was thus aligned with the opponents of the Bill was a new blow, for he was the "first New Dealer," the keeper of the liberal conscience. His friends, if not he himself, resented the imputation that age, as such, unfitted a man for good service on the Court.

By the time the President spoke, the battle had ceased to be confined to Congress. Spokesmen of both sides appealed to the people. Organizations were founded overnight to fight the bill and "save the Constitution." Legislatures voted resolutions, generally hostile. Liberal Senators, known or suspected to be hostile, were pleaded with by their friends. Long before the parliamentary battle was well under way, prudent politicians were searching for means of compromise. Not since the days of the League of Nations fight in the Senate had there been so general and passionate a debate; not since the Kansas-Nebraska bill had there been such a strain on party unity.

One way out would be open if justices would leave the Court and create the vacancies that nature had failed to provide. So a retirement bill that had languished in the Congressional limbo was suddenly brought out and passed. Under it, a justice could retire on his full salary, preserving his judicial status. It was hoped that more than one of the elderly justices would see the attractions of such a dignified retreat. However, it was not individual justices but the Court as such that retreated. For although the secret had been well kept, the majority in the Court had begun to shift even before the judiciary bill had been produced. Justice Roberts had joined his four "liberal" colleagues, Hughes, Stone, Cardozo, and Brandeis. On March 29, the Court upheld the Washington minimum wage law, not only reversing its decision in the New York case of 1936 but frankly abandoning the famous judgment in the *Adkins* case. From that day, the new majority of the Court began to give the Federal Government the powers it had claimed. It opened the way to further extensions of Federal authority by a wide interpretation of the commerce clause. On April 12, by a five-to-four decision upholding the Wagner Labor Act, it gave a new legal status to those powerful allies of the

Administration, the labor unions, and it made it appear likely that much of the original New Deal legislation could, with minor amendments, be re-enacted. The fear that the Administration would be reduced to impotence was now proved baseless, or so the conservatives and the conciliators asserted. And with each new decision, the number of conciliators or compromisers grew.

The President was not among them. He wanted the whole bill and nothing but the bill. It was not only a matter of prestige and obstinacy. It could be argued that the recent course of the Court had shown how just were the criticisms directed against it. The fact that the reversal of policy was obtained by a majority of one underlined the charge that the members of the Court had extraordinary political powers.

The center of interest shifted from the White House to the room where the Judiciary Committee of the Senate held its public hearings. Before the committee, facing crowds of spectators, week after week, Americans of all views and types testified. Again the Administration miscalculated. It limited its direct testimony to two weeks and then closed its case, while week after week the witnesses coming to oppose the bill gave the country an impression of an overwhelming preponderance of opinion on the side of the opposition. These witnesses did reveal how deeply opinion was moved by threats to the autonomy of the judicial system, how much the American people had come to identify the rule of law with its essential freedoms. And a shadow was cast over the Committee room—a shadow of Europe where those liberties had been lost, where in Germany, even before Hitler came, the essential guarantees of freedom had been abandoned or betrayed. By the time the public testimony had been completed, it was a safe guess that the majority of the Committee would oppose the bill. On June 14 they did so, seven Democrats joining three Republicans to attack the measure, while eight members stood behind it. The majority termed the bill "needless, futile, and utterly dangerous." It was a tremendous blow.

It was on the Senate floor that the fight would have to be carried on, and the leader on the Administration side, Joseph T. Robinson, led his troops into action far more from party loyalty than from burning conviction of the need for the bill. At last, in June, Justice Van Devanter took advantage of the retirement law, and it was known that Senator Robinson had been promised that he would be given the first vacancy on the Court. But that reward was not to be his until the battle was over. The Committee did report—adversely; and the language of the report, in its candor and severity, revealed how deep the gulf between the two sides had become.

As if to heighten the drama of the last act, Robinson was found dead in his apartment, clutching a copy of the *Congressional Record*. Some saw in this the finger of Providence. Others regarded the Senator as a victim of loyalty to the President who had refused all compromise while there was still time to gain a partial victory. That time had passed. There could now be no increase of the number of Supreme Court justices. The technical reforms could go through, but on the main issue the President was beaten. The emasculated law was passed and signed, although the President reiterated his view that the need for dealing with the central problem remained. It was a great defeat, and more than the Court bill had been defeated. The ambitious program of legislation that the President had announced was still in the main a mere program. The fears of Executive encroachment aroused by the Court bill had led Congress to refuse the President adequate powers for the reorganization of the Executive departments. This reasonable request had been bitterly assailed as another step toward dictatorship, and its defeat underlined the extent to which the Court controversy had distorted judgment.

One function the President had the undisputed right to perform. He had to fill the vacancy caused by the retirement of Justice Van Devanter. Acting in a fashion that showed that he was still com-

bative, still reluctant to restore peace by concession, he nominated Senator Hugo Black of Alabama, most radical of Southern Senators. It was
a defiance of conservatism, and it gave the Court
a member poles apart from the erstwhile majority.
It was soon shown that the possibilities of drama
were not exhausted. Senator Black was easily confirmed under the Senatorial tradition by which a
member of the upper chamber is fit for any post.
There were rumors, however, that the nominee had
been a member of the Ku Klux Klan. Apart from
assuring his colleagues that he was not now a member of the Klan, Mr. Black preserved silence on
the charge, but a diligent newspaper produced
proof that it was valid. At last, Justice Black spoke
to the American people, admitting his past membership, but declaring his complete breach with the
Klan and his devotion to the principles of civil
liberty. It was an ironic ending to the great debate.

The exultant Republicans took good note of the
damage done to the dominant party by the long
struggle. The myth of Presidential invincibility
was destroyed and the unity of the dominant party
shown to be a fiction. The Democratic party managers ruefully reviewed the changed positions, and
there was bitter criticism of the President's obstinacy. The once invincible leader had lost his great
battle. It was Waterloo—or so the Republicans and
conservative Democrats hoped.

Their hopes were not destined to be fulfilled. Indeed, it was soon doubtful if the lost battle was as important as it had seemed. Repeated vacancies gave to Roosevelt the chance to nominate every member of the Court but one. In due course, Felix Frankfurter, Stanley Reed, William O. Douglas, Frank Murphy, and Robert H. Jackson were all appointed. That sole survivor of the old Court, Harlan Stone, was to be made Chief Justice when Hughes retired in 1941. The Court, thus reconstituted, gave a most generous interpretation to the powers of Congress. A series of statutes reenacting most of the New Deal was upheld, including the Frazier-Lemke Farm Mortgage Act, important provisions of the Railway Labor Act, and legislation which in effect restored a good deal of the NRA. The Federal Government was not now crippled by legal limitations.

Nor was the new Court either careless of civil liberties or depressingly unanimous. Justice Black, in particular, distinguished himself by the zeal with which he defended the Constitutional rights of the weak. The new Court developed as marked a division into left and right as the old, although the grounds of division were very different. A battle had been lost but a campaign had been won; so Presidential supporters now comforted themselves. A campaign *had* been won, but as the ablest defender of the original plan, Robert H. Jackson, pointed out, fundamental questions had been raised and not answered. Contemplating the final result of the war on the Court, the Administration and the American people might be content that no final answer had been given and that a dangerous breach in the American system had been filled. The three coordinate powers were not now at war; if there was no decisive victory, there was at least a truce.

CHAPTER XI

GIVEN the background of the new Administration, and the current public temper which saw in certain great public utilities the most manifest enemies of the public weal, it was certain that "something would be done about power." It was highly probable that part of that something would involve dealing with the long controversy over the Wilson Dam at Muscle Shoals on the Tennessee River. Since the Presidency of John Quincy Adams, state and Federal authorities had attempted to lessen the obstacles to navigation presented by Muscle Shoals. In the First World War, it suddenly acquired a new importance. Faced with what men feared might be a crippling shortage of nitrates, the Government hastily erected two plants at Muscle Shoals to fix nitrogen by the Haber process. To provide power for the plants, the Wilson Dam was begun.

But the war ended before either plant contributed nitrogen. Not until 1925 was the Wilson

Dam finished. As the dam neared completion, interest revived and Muscle Shoals became a center of bitter controversy. On the one hand those Americans who wanted to "get government out of business" were anxious to liquidate the project and dispose of the Federal assets on the best possible terms. On the other hand, the friends of "public power" wished to make sure that the Wilson Dam and nitrate plants were kept in the hands of the Government and used to help the farmer.

The controversy took the form of a duel between two distinguished Americans. The most attractive offer for the Federal properties at Muscle Shoals came from Henry Ford, and the chief opposition to the acceptance of the Ford offer or any like it came from Senator George Norris of Nebraska. Already important power developments existed on some tributaries of the Tennessee, and one important private dam had been built on the main river at Hale's Bar. The controversy ended in stalemate. Norris and his friends were strong enough to prevent the sale or leasing of the Wilson Dam to private interests but not strong enough to win their battle for Federal operation. Bills for this were passed by both houses, but vetoed first by President Coolidge and then by President Hoover.

The defeat of the Hoover Administration changed the situation. The President-elect was taken in January, 1933, to Muscle Shoals by Senator Norris, and on May 18, 1933, Congress passed the act setting up the Tennessee Valley Authority.

The Federal corporation thus set up was certainly enough of an innovation to deserve scrutiny. Its official purposes, as described in the preamble, were not very revolutionary. The TVA was set up to

improve the navigability and to provide for the flood control of the Tennessee River; to provide for reforestation and the proper use of marginal lands in the Tennessee Valley; to provide for the agricultural and industrial development of said valley; to provide for the national defense by the creation of a corporation for the operation of Government properties at and near Muscle Shoals in the State of Alabama, and for other purposes.

But the preamble did not mention (though the body of the Act did) that one function of the new Federal corporation would be to produce and market power. At once the agency set to work building new dams. It constructed no fewer than sixteen, and in time came to control twenty-one dams in all.

From the beginning the friends and enemies of the TVA concentrated on the power aspects of the authority activities. The TVA, according to its friends, was the Perseus who would free the Andromeda menaced by the predatory power interests. It would save from private exploitation the great power resources of the Tennessee Valley and, producing power at the lowest possible rate, with no watered stock, no pyramiding of holding companies, no opportunities for manipulation by speculators, would provide the American people with a "yardstick" which would measure the true price of electricity against those charged by the privately owned utilities. The enemies of the TVA saw in this enterprise a blow struck, with all the resources of the Federal Government, at corporations doing a legitimate business, already controlled by the public authorities. Competition was to be subsidized out of taxes, and the great mass of investment in the utilities was threatened with destruction. This fear was reinforced by the threatened use of the great Western hydroelectric systems at Boulder and Bonneville as yardsticks.

But although it was the power policy of the TVA that attracted most attention, the preamble was not a mere Constitutional fig leaf. Congress, the President, and the rulers of the new corporation *did* intend to improve navigation, flood control, and the conditions of life of the people of the valley.

The primary aim was that of rehabilitating the natural resources of the valley and of its greatest asset, its population. The northern end of the valley was mountainous, beautiful, and desperately poor. Its rural population represented a pioneer stock left behind in the great Western migrations and suffering increasing impoverishment. At the southern end of the valley lay the flat and once fertile lands of Alabama and Georgia, now afflicted with all the ills of the cotton kingdom. In the mountainous north an archaic system of agriculture reduced the level of life. In the cotton lands, bumper crops, low world prices, soil exhaustion, tenancy, share-cropping, malnutrition, all called for a remedy. Inevitably, some of the propaganda for this side of the TVA's activities provoked resentment; loose talk of "social salvage" angered people who wanted to be helped but did not want to be regarded as wreckage. But there was a great problem in human engineering, and the TVA was an agency for rehabilitating a very depressed region. There was a problem—and a possibility—for it was noted that most inhabitants of this region were of "old Anglo-Saxon stock," a type whose low estate could not be explained by any racial stereotypes.

Nor was the problem of navigation fictitious. The project of creating a permanent channel from Knoxville to the Ohio and so to the Mississippi had been recently studied by the Army Engineers, whose report, published in 1930, suggested two ways of doing it. One was a system of cheap low dams producing no power, one a system of costlier high dams which would produce power. Flood control was by no means a fictitious objective. The whole Mississippi Valley paid dearly for the uncontrollable rivers that fed the Father of Waters. The immensely expensive system of levees along the Mississippi, and the other partially effective engineering devices designed to control the great river, did not begin to solve the problem. The waters had to be impounded and controlled before they reached the Mississippi at all. The way to control the Tennessee was in the Tennessee Valley. If at Paducah its crest could be kept down by three feet at flood time, that would be reflected at Cairo in a diminution of the potentially disastrous contribution made by the Ohio to the flood waters moving down to New Orleans.

Closely connected was the problem of reforestation and the control of marginal lands. The destruction of the timber cover of the upper valley let the flood waters pour off the hillsides (some areas in the Great Smokies had an annual rainfall of eighty inches). The water that poured into the rivers carried away a great part of the topsoil. Erosion was universal in the valley, ranging from mere loss of good topsoil to the practical destruction of all fertility. The Clinch, the Holston, and the Tennessee itself showed that this was so in their turbid, coffee-colored waters. (It was to be one of the chief boasts of the TVA in later years that the water now ran blue between the dams.)

Breadth of function was not only the novel characteristic of the TVA. It was given extensive legal powers. It could sue and be sued. It was exempt from all civil service laws in the recruiting of personnel. It could exercise the right of eminent domain. It could make power and make fertilizer. Of course, a major duty was "to regulate the stream flow primarily for the purposes of promoting navigation and controlling floods." But it could also "provide and operate facilities for the generation of electric energy in order to avoid the waste of water power, to transmit and market such power." The rulers of the new organization were a triumvirate of directors who had (a revealing novelty) to "be persons who profess a belief in the feasibility and wisdom of this Act."

In this novel provision, some of the spirit behind the new Authority is made plain. This was no mere Federal agency; it was a great crusading enterprise whose success or failure would, it was thought, demonstrate the possibility of free, democratic planning in a world in which "planning" had become a panacea, but a panacea whose effective use seemed confined to authoritarian states. The three original directors, all in different ways, manifested this faith. The first chairman, President Arthur Morgan of Antioch College, was not merely an expert in flood control, but an apostle of the possibilities of amicable cooperation in a great social task. His second colleague, Dr. Harcourt Morgan, President of the University of Tennessee, was not merely a noted agricultural expert, but one of the leading public figures of the region, never forgetting that it was with the actual people of the valley that the TVA had to succeed or fail. The third and youngest member, David Lilienthal, was a product of the Harvard Law School, trained in controlling public utilities in Wisconsin.

The enthusiastic and sometimes uncritical spirit of the early days of the TVA extended far down the line. The long depression had been a sobering experience for thousands of young technicians, who had lost their faith in the ability of private industry to find a use for them. In working for the TVA they were toiling (so they thought) for a purpose larger and more attractive than any offered by a private profit-making concern. On the other hand, they were not working for a "mere" Federal agency. Business frustration, bureaucratic frustration, both would be avoided in this novel, exciting attempt to remake one of the sore spots of the American economy.

That crusading zeal had its drawbacks. The TVA was set up in one of the most conservative parts of the United States. The bright band of eager young men and women who crowded into

Knoxville (headquarters of the authority) were in some cases too candid and loud in their astonishment at the "folkways" of the valley.

Another cause of resentment was the employment policy of the Authority. Freed from all civil service rules, the TVA had to make its own. It rigorously excluded all political pressure; there was not any shadow of the spoils system. That was a novelty in Tennessee, and not a welcome one to all the local politicians.

From the beginning, the TVA decided to do all its own construction by what was called "force account." It did not delegate the task of dam building to contractors as had been done at Bonneville and Boulder. It recruited all types of labor, from highly qualified engineers, chemists, and agronomists to the simplest type of manual labor. Its employment roll rose to 40,000 when construction was at its height, and a series of tests enabled it to recruit and maintain its labor force with few labor disputes. The young men who joined the TVA in its early days found that their faith was justified, since promotions were mainly from the ranks and men rose high and fast. Not all labor policies were equally successful. Two-thirds of the labor force were recruited from the valley and that meant importing into the TVA the exacerbated local version of the color problem. The TVA tried to hold the scales even. It employed Negroes in about their proportionate numbers in the total population of the valley, or around 10 per cent. But it could not attack local prejudices; the Negro workers were seldom to be found in any but the more menial jobs; their recreational facilities were segregated from those of the white workers and sometimes were omitted altogether. The TVA decided that setting up a brand new pattern of race relations in the valley was not one of the "other purposes" mentioned by the Act.

From the beginning, the TVA was subject to violent attack. It was accused of being a version of state socialism (as it was), and part of a vast Communist conspiracy to undermine the American way of life. The TVA was only a few months old when it announced that "the interest of the public in the widest possible use of power is superior to any private interest. Where the private interest and this public interest conflict, the public interest must prevail." This was taken by friends of the utilities as a declaration of war. The normal American weapon was seized on, an appeal to the courts, and for the first four years the TVA was harassed and its plans delayed by endless litigation.

Not till the Ashwander decision in 1936 could the Authority begin to breathe easily, and not till the victory in the case of the "18 companies" in 1939 was the final battle won. The litigation concerned not only the direct activities of the TVA, but also its encouragement of municipalities to set up independent power systems or threaten to do so if the local utilities did not agree to sell out at the price offered. This seemed to the utilities—and to many sympathizers—an outrageous abuse of public power to ruin legally constituted corporations. Loans were made by WPA and by the Rural Electrification Administration set up in 1935. Aided by the cheap money thus provided, the TVA was able to fight the power companies and force them to deal with municipalities and rural cooperatives, which finally borrowed more than $100,-000,000 to finance projects of public ownership. These projects, it was maintained, were a polite method of robbing the investors in the utilities of the region. The utilities, meanwhile, had found a spokesman with telling powers of persuasion—Wendell Willkie, head of the Commonwealth and Southern. The battle was fought to a draw; Willkie finally consented to a sale of the Tennessee utility properties, but he obtained a price, $78,600,000, which was much higher than TVA originally proposed. Other privately owned utilities in Mississippi and Alabama were bought up.

Some of the controversies were not stilled by the victory. There was, for example, the very obscure series of problems represented by the "yardstick" theory. The utilities argued (and many agreed) that the TVA could not serve as a yardstick since there could be no valid basis of comparison between so highly privileged a producer of power and privately owned utilities without such exceptional privileges. For example, TVA calculated the interest rate that it should pay on the sums advanced by Congress at 3 per cent. The utilities contended that this was only half what they had to pay for money borrowed in the open market. Whether a yardstick existed or not, the TVA expanded its business until 1943 found it selling power to more than eighty municipalities, including Chattanooga, Knoxville, Memphis, and Nashville.

The multiple purpose of the Authority's activities made computation of capital costs, and so of reasonable rates, extremely difficult. The TVA was forced to take into consideration many problems not part of the business of a private utility. In strict law, it was created to build dams whose power product was only incidental to flood control and navigation. It was unfair, said the TVA, to charge to power the extra cost of providing for the primary purposes of the enabling act. It was still more unfair, replied the critics, to charge exorbitant sums to these alleged primary purposes, and thus keep down, for bookkeeping display, the capital allotted to producing power. The controversy was long and bitter. No rate case before the Supreme Court ever produced more fine-spun theorizing than did the assessment of the value of the TVA as a yardstick. But Congress and vocal sections of public opinion insisted on an assessment. The TVA had to accept a cash valuation of more than $700,000,000 for assets built by the Government. Power, the TVA computed, accounted for 65 per cent of the total cost, and on that computation the rate base could be examined. The yardstick was not the infallible measuring rod that a few enthusiasts had thought it might be in 1933. For as at Boulder and Bonneville, it was always possible to argue that the allocation of cost to power was still inadequate. Moreover, on the TVA basis, the rates were hardly, if at all, lower than those of the privately operated utilities. But that was not the answer, for the final rates made by the municipal and cooperative distributors were often much lower than the existing rates. And it was not a matter only of low rates but of greatly increased consumption, of the introduction of modern technical aids to farming and home-making into one of the most backward regions of the United States. In much of this area the home consumption of electricity increased by nearly 200 per cent during the years 1934–42.

The municipal or cooperative power plants introduced a new and healthy element of real democratic management into a political system that was backward and sterile. The meetings of the farm cooperatives were more effective educators in

democratic ways than the noisy oratory of the
political barbecue. There was, of course, another
side to the picture. The success of the TVA in
keeping "politics" out of its operations was not
always achieved in the local distributing units,
where patronage, pressure, and disregard of good
administration for political reasons were far from
unknown. The TVA also seemed to threaten the
financial stability of many local government units.
As a Federal agency it was exempt from local
taxation, and until the decision of the Supreme
Court in the case of *Graves v. New York* in 1939,
its employees were exempt from local income tax.
The loss of revenue caused by TVA withdrawals of
land and other assets from local taxation was a
legitimate ground for grievance, and it was some
years before an acceptable basis of compensation
was found.

Other critics, looking at the TVA from a very
different angle, felt that it had not completely fulfilled its early promise because, when its power
system was in full operation, it sold just as much
power to private business as to the municipalities
and cooperatives. This, they suggested, was not in
keeping with the priorities of the original Act, and,
like the rates charged to small consumers, showed
a greater desire to make a good financial showing
than was compatible with the general commission
to seek first the elevation of the living standards

of the poor and handicapped, and only secondly the approval of rigorous accountants.

Yet it was politically prudent to keep an eye on the views and susceptibilities both of private business and of the Treasury and Congress. Congress, although it gave the TVA a remarkably free hand in spending its funds, nevertheless had views as to how they should be spent, and the directors of the TVA took account of them. Although exempted from the normal accountancy rules applying to Federal Departments, TVA was involved in a series of disputes with the Comptroller-General. A friendly critic objected to the system whereby, instead of paying all its revenue into the Treasury and getting an offsetting grant, the TVA saved some of its income and asked for less than otherwise it would have needed. The whole accounting system was finally overhauled by the Authority itself, a system comparable to that used in private business was adopted, and the high degree of fiscal autonomy originally granted the TVA was, despite Congressional grumblings, preserved.

It was inevitable that public attention and public controversy should center on the great dams, and their use and cost. Taken together, they were far greater works of man than the famous Russian dam at Dnieprostroy, or even than Bonneville and Boulder. But the trinity of power, navigation, and flood control was not the only function of the TVA.

It was to "provide for the agricultural and industrial development of said valley," and that commission was taken seriously and widely. Too seriously, too widely in the first enthusiastic years. The
cultural as well as the agricultural and industrial
life of the Tennessee Valley was to be remade.
General programs of education were launched with
little regard to the size of the effective demand.
New industries using new techniques were to cause
a burgeoning of economic life that would enable
the long-depressed region to rival the old established industrial regions of the East.

The rigors of the power battle, the need for con-
ciliating Congress, the discovery that more was
involved in remaking the valley than good maps
and plans plus enthusiasm, caused a decline in the
first, fine, careless rapture of the TVA. The Authority had to husband its resources and not invite
dangerous criticism. So the lavish educational programs were cut down and the industrial projects
were reduced to more modest and manageable
proportions. Encouragement was given to the
exploitation of local resources like kaolin, though
critics in and out of Congress were unable to see
why the existing ceramic industry of the United
States should have to face subsidized competition.
Fish culture and afforestation were dealt with. But
the provision of abundant cheap power plus the
improved navigation facilities of the Tennessee

River were the chief contributions to the industrial growth of the valley.

It was in the improvement of farming that the TVA showed most persistence and ingenuity. No rural cooperative could be solvent on the revenues raised by selling power merely for light and radio. The farmer had to be induced to use electricity for other purposes, to drive farm and household machinery. Here the Electric Home and Farm Authority came in as an ally of the TVA, financing the purchase of cheap electrical machinery which would both lighten the work of the farmer and his wife and increase the demand for power until it reached an economically profitable level.

But more was needed. The standard of life of the farmer had to be raised and his diet improved. Hence communal refrigerators were fostered, and experiments with new machinery for treating cottonseed were subsdized. Most important of all, one of the original projects of the Muscle Shoals plants was revived. The TVA began to manufacture not nitrate but phosphate fertilizers. These were issued to farmers who agreed to make their farms demonstration units, keep records, and show their neighbors that modern science could restore the exhausted soil. It was to the obvious advantage of the TVA to reduce erosion, and one of the best ways was to train farmers to plough on the contours, to use soil-holding grasses like lespideza, to plant trees bred in the great tree nurseries run by the TVA. Thus, all kinds of farm problems were handled. Not all were handled with equal success, and not all the activities of the TVA got an equally warm welcome from the people of the valley.

Yet the servants of the TVA had learned a lot since the brash confident days of 1933. The directors, like all its officers, lived in the valley, not in remote Washington. They knew how much could and could not be done with the conservative valley folk. They knew that steady progress, fully adjusted to the local ways of thought and action, was far more valuable than more dramatic successes without local roots. They knew, too, that attention must be paid to all kinds of related problems that were not the business of any one section of the TVA: thus a power policy that incidentally bred malaria was not a good policy for a body like the TVA. So when the necessities of power development drowned the graves of the valley, the bones of the fathers were reverently removed to new sites, and when a farmer had to be expropriated, it was not enough to pay him money compensation, he had to be found a new farm. Whatever the original suspicions of the valley, by the time power began to pour from the dynamos and the great engineering works began to repay some of the investment, the valley had fully accepted the Author-

ity. The efficient auxiliaries of TVA, the Electric
Farm and Home Authority which helped people
to buy electrical equipment, and the Rural Electrification Administration, which promoted the
extension of public or cooperative current into
neglected areas, played a part in making it popular.

CHAPTER XII

By the time of Roosevelt's second inauguration in 1937, many of the undertakings of his first four years seemed to have weathered the storms which had beat fiercely about them. A good example was provided by the Securities and Exchange Commission set up in 1934. Few enterprises were more complex and difficult than that of regulating in the public interest the tremendous volume of security transactions—stocks and bonds, new issues and old, listed and unlisted. All brokers were required to register with the SEC; all stock exchanges were placed under its authority; company officers and holders of more than one-tenth the stock in any company had to file monthly statements of their trading in their own securities. Since the great stock exchanges, led by that of New York, were powerful and jealous, the SEC was certain of a troubled career. Its first head, Joseph P. Kennedy, proved too amiable to carry through the necessary reforms. The second chairman, James M. Landis, was more vigorous, and compelled the exchanges to toe the line. Then in 1937 came William O. Douglas, who demanded that management of the New York Stock Exchange be taken from the hands of insiders and confided to those who, doing business with the general public, were more ready to look after its needs. The new chairman had a stroke of luck when a former head of the Exchange, Richard Whitney, was convicted of larceny and sent to prison. Broad reforms were effected, the exchange was completely reorganized, and the SEC gained a position of secure power.

In various areas of the New Deal, it was now possible to raise fresh structures on the foundations laid by pioneer agencies. The SEC itself furnished an illustration of this. In 1936 it was given wide new responsibilities by the Public Utility Holding Act. All utility companies were compelled to register with the SEC and to furnish full information as to their operations. Beginning January 1, 1938, the SEC was to take steps to put an end to the sprawling activities of many holding companies. As the scandals attending Samuel Insull's career showed, the holding company was capable of great abuses. The Commission was now to see that each one limited its activities to a single well-integrated system, unless control of two or more was necessary to economical management and was confined to contiguous geographical areas.

This "death-sentence law" for holding companies provoked bitter antagonism. Many utility corporations fought it with desperation. It was upheld by the Supreme Court in the Electric Bond and Share Case (1938) and was kept genuinely effective. The SEC administered the law with moderation, and, in general, let the large companies work out their own plans of reorganization subject to Government approval.

Another great agency of the second term had its first-term antecedent. On the basis of the work done by the Federal Housing Administration created in 1934, the United States Housing Administration of 1937 was reared. Its main objective was the destruction of the ghastly slums which disfigured cities large and small. Not in Naples or Glasgow were worse housing areas to be found than in parts of Chicago and Los Angeles. The USHA was given authority to offer long-term loans at low rates of interest to state or local agencies which would undertake to raze noisome slums and erect low-rent housing in their place. Before the Second World War began, nearly three hundred of these housing projects were under way. This constituted only a small beginning—but at any rate, it was a beginning in a field too long neglected. Once more, the pioneering work of the TVA made possible the creation in 1936 of the Rural Electrification Administration. At first it operated with a hundred million dollars in relief funds; then in 1937 Congress passed the Rural Electrification Act which gave it wide authority and adequate resources. The REA did not intend, in general, to build its own power-generating plants. Its aim was rather to encourage the formation of cooperative groups of farmers which would buy electricity from existing sources. It did not take long to prove that many farming communities were hungry for electricity. Before 1944, nearly a thousand farmers' cooperatives had been set up, and electric lines were winding into remote communities of Vermont, Alabama, and Oregon.

The AAA had done much for the farmer; but a new step was now possible in the creation of the Farm Security Administration, which in 1937 began to look after the needs of the underprivileged in rural districts. It was established to help lift the tenant farmers, share-croppers, and farm laborers out of their poverty and insecurity. FSA loans were made available at 3 per cent interest to tenants and share-croppers who never before had possessed money enough to buy decent machinery, seed, and livestock, or to put fertilizer on their land, or to repair house or barn. Like the REA, the FSA encouraged the formation of rural cooperatives. When once set up, these associations were given funds to buy good breeding bulls, tractors and combines for community use, water facilities for arid localities, and other aids. Among tenants in particular, the FSA was of incalculable benefit. The fact that it really accomplished much rehabilitation —that it enabled poverty-stricken folk to begin to pay their own way—was demonstrated by the prompt repayment of about 90 per cent of the loans as they fell due.

In many ways the Second New Deal—the New Deal which laid its main emphasis on social welfare—seemed an assured success as the year 1937 passed into 1938. The labor force of the country was making use of the Wagner Act. The farmers were reassured by the Conservation and Domestic Allotment Act, and accepted Secretary Wallace's idea of the ever-normal granary with interest if not enthusiasm. A notable law was passed in 1936 to give the country a maritime fleet worthy of its strength; and the next year found a new Maritime Commission setting to work on ships that before long would be more desperately needed than anyone dreamed. In the air, too, the Government was striking out novel and constructive programs. The creation of the Civil Aeronautical Authority in 1938 was followed by a rapid increase in subsidies paid for the air carriage of mails.

Yet the Roosevelt Administration, even after its tremendous victory of 1936, had still a sea of difficulties to breast. The Democrats who had followed Al Smith remained unreconciled. And when the

Supreme Court bill brought a split between those who trusted and those who distrusted the President, Democratic harmony was irretrievably ruined. By 1938, in the face of the mounting discontent and of the business recession, Roosevelt began talking to intimates of his intention to retire at the end of his second term. He intimated to Hull, to Hopkins, and perhaps to others, that the Democratic nomination in 1940 was open.

It was not only the Court bill that was beaten; other measures as well met opposition. The Chairman of the Rules Committee of the House, representing both the old suspicions of Tammany and the general rise in Congressional temper, was a formidable obstacle to the enactment of the Presidential program. The role of Representative O'Connor attracted popular attention because he was a symbol of a great deal of opinion in both houses of Congress and because his brother, Basil O'Connor, had been the President's law partner. Within a year of the greatest personal triumph in American history, President Roosevelt had to fight for almost every measure, and not always successfully. He was able, over O'Connor's opposition, to get the Wage and Hours bill out on to the floor of the House where the rank and file, men who knew that they had been elected to support the President, passed it. He was able, too, but at the cost of further Senatorial irritation, to make Senator Barkley of

Kentucky floor leader over Senator Harrison of Mississippi; but the days of open or concealed dictatorship were over.

The decline in the President's power was made most manifest in the storm raised by a bill to give him authority to reorganize the civil service. There was little in the Administration proposals that had not been advocated by every President in recent times. Yet enemies of the President, inside and outside his own party, were able to stir up almost hysterical hostility to the measure. Catholics were aroused (especially by Father Coughlin) to the alleged danger of Federal control of parochial schools. Financial purists were alarmed by the threat to the independence of the Comptroller-General, though few competent students of government accounting thought that this officer was doing what was needed to make the financial vigilance of Congress effective. Horsemen in appropriate costume rode from Boston as modern Paul Reveres to stimulate Congressional independence and fears of Executive encroachment. Congressional eloquence on the technical details of the bill was emotional and irrelevant, and a Democratic President, with an overwhelming majority in Congress, suffered humiliating defeat. He was denied powers that were necessary, because his own party did not trust him—or so the American public interpreted the vote.

Among the many forces making for a Democratic victory in 1936 was the most potent of all—the return of good times. That argument was still potent in the spring of 1937 when the President and other Administration spokesmen decided that the American economy was in danger of a premature boom. There was, the Administration thought, too much discounting of future profits and too much hedging against a future rise in prices. The Administration would not be a party to this rush back to the bad old days of boom and slump, and Government purchases of such basic goods as steel would be cut down as far as possible. So, too, would be the expenditures for relief, less and less necessary as private business took up the slack. The balancing of the budget promised in 1932 would be achieved in 1938. The American economy would be kept on an even keel.

Unfortunately for the country and the Administration, it proved much easier to stop the incipient boom than to stabilize prices or employment. Workers, turned off relief, found no new jobs with private industry. The unions, emerging from the ordeal of the great strikes, found themselves tried even harder by the return to idleness of so many tens of thousands of members. Dues and confidence declined in the ranks of organized labor, and employers found their hands strengthened. In a year, national income fell by ten billion dollars. Industrial production fell from 118 to 78 (it had been 71 in 1933) ; payrolls from 100.1 to 70.9; only retail sales seemed to be holding up. It was a blow to the nation. Above all, it was a blow to the Administration that had rashly boasted: "We planned it that way."

The Administration was confronted with a condition and several theories. Some men inside the Government supported the view so vehemently advocated by conservatives outside, that there should be no return to large-scale expenditure of Federal funds. That had been tried; it had failed. Made work was no answer to the American economic problem. Direct relief, so recently damned as "the dole," was now seen as a prudent recognition of the fact that the Federal Government must see that no one starved. But it was not the business of the Federal Government to provide jobs. That must be left to the natural forces of recovery. If these natural forces had worked faster, the experiment might have been tried. But by the spring of 1938, the President's mind was made up. Recovery was not coming along fast enough; misery was increasing; the new social security system was too weak to carry the burden. There must be a return to large direct expenditure on relief works. WPA must be furnished adequate funds to meet the new needs. The ideas of John Maynard Keynes prevailed, and Secretary Morgenthau bewailed the defeat of conservative elements in the Administration. The spending policy was a challenge to the opposition, who were not slow to point out that this was a year of Congressional elections. And it was a sign that the Administration was on the defensive.

Indeed, Roosevelt seemed to be dogged by bad luck. The dissensions within the party ranks in Congress had their parallel within the governing body of the TVA. That friction had arisen inside the triumvirate was no secret. There had been friction almost from the beginning. Some of it arose from the giving of general administrative powers, as well as the right of supervision and inspection, to three men, none of whom was directly responsible for the day-to-day running of the administrative machine. The governing body of the Authority was soon divided; it took more the appearance of a bi-partisan Congressional committee than of a normal board of directors. And there was no doubt that the minority member was the Chairman, Dr. Arthur Morgan. For a time he suffered in comparative silence, but an explosion had to come. Finally, in speech, magazine articles, and open controversy, the Chairman of the TVA opposed the policy of his colleagues.

This opposition was both painful and dangerous in the eyes of the friends and supporters of the TVA. First of all, it provided ammunition for enemies and critics. But it did more than that; it brought into the open a real conflict of policy. Chairman Morgan, in the eyes of the public, was not only the head of the TVA; he was the sponsor of its most generous and attractive side. Thanks to him, the TVA stood for more than cheap power and rural economic rehabilitation. It stood for free cooperative planning to remake most of the folk-ways of the region, and it stood, too, for an intelligent conservatism, to holding fast to that which was good. In this light much of the public saw the case, and so did Chairman Morgan.

His colleagues were less convinced that all the problems of the valley could be cured by friendli-ness and negotiation. Nor did they think that the TVA could wait until all forces in the region had been converted. Important elements in the Tennes-see Valley and the nation had no interest in the success of the TVA. They had to be fought until they surrendered on reasonable terms. And what were reasonable terms was a matter of bitter dis-pute. The utilities hoped that the courts would declare either the TVA unconstitutional or that its offers for the assets of the private utilities in the region were so inadequate as to be flagrant violations of due process of law. There were some hopes, too, that the Government of the United States might pass in 1940 into more friendly hands. So the utilities, above all the great holding com-pany, the Commonwealth and Southern, used every

legal device to hinder the acquisition by the TVA
of local utilities and to prevent the creation of publicly owned power plants in the valley. From the
autumn of 1936, it was open war. The TVA withdrew from a proposed power pool, and the energetic
Wendell Willkie used all his skill in winning favorable publicity to dramatize the issue as an attempt
by a lavishly subsidized Government corporation
to force a private corporation to sell, at a price far
below the real value of the assets, the property of
the bondholders and stockholders.

In a sense, the issue was insoluble. For the "real"
value of the properties of the Commonwealth and
Southern involved all the most metaphysical questions of true value that had bedeviled the courts.
True, Commonwealth and Southern had wiped out
the most flagrant examples of the "write-up" in
the bookkeeping of its subsidiaries. Whether this
was wisdom and virtue (as some said), or merely
due to the holding company's having been formed
just as the great bull market collapsed, was a
matter of controversy. But there was a real danger
that genuinely innocent investors would suffer.

So thought Willkie; so thought Arthur Morgan.
His colleagues seemed bent on playing a game of
poker which they might win, but only at the cost
of kindliness and justice. They were not only playing poker, they were apparently playing politics.
They were discussing an impartial investigation of

a claim that the chairman was convinced was baseless; and they were discussing it, so Arthur Morgan
said, because the claimant, Major George Berry,
was both a United States Senator from Tennessee
and a leading New Deal supporter in the ranks of
the AFL.

President Roosevelt tried in vain to make peace
between the triumvirs. He listened to the complaints of the chairman and did what he could
to calm his fears. But the President was at heart
on the side of Dr. Harcourt Morgan and David
Lilienthal. He thought it hard to be unjust to a
utility, and he could see very well that a claim by
a United States Senator, however flimsy, had to be
handled with discretion. The cracks were papered
over for a time, but the chairman was too sincere
and passionate to keep silent. In an article that
made an open breach inevitable, he accused his
colleagues of dishonesty. So, at any rate, the public
read his statement. Roosevelt was notoriously reluctant to admit that personal deficiencies and dis-
agreements had reached a point where decisive
action must be taken. But that point had come.
The chairman and his colleagues were summoned
to Washington and Dr. Arthur Morgan was ordered to justify his charges. This he refused to do.
Only by testimony before a Congressional committee could he do justice to his case. It was obviously impossible to leave in office men so totally

opposed to each other, and there was no doubt which of the directors would have to go. The chairman was removed by Presidential order, over his protest. The President was fortified by the opinion of the Attorney-General as well as by many precedents, and the removal was upheld by the courts.

But the removal did not end the controversy. Enemies of the TVA were anxious to exploit their chance to discredit it, and a Congressional committee was set up under Senator Donahey of Ohio. It was the last effective victory of the enemies of the Authority. Errors of judgment and practice were exposed; obscurities of bookkeeping were criticized; the staff of the TVA were forced to remember that their autonomy had its limits. But no scandals, no serious errors were revealed. The courts, too, deceived whatever hopes had been placed in their intervention. The Administration emerged from the crisis less damaged than its enemies had hoped, but by the time the final decisions were handed down and the final financial settlement made, the politics of 1938 were nearly forgotten.

The TVA crisis, nevertheless, was one sign that the Administration was on the defensive. It was not the only one. One of the fields in which the President had delighted to show his mastery of the political arts had been in his press conferences. If most owners of the press were against him, most

working journalists were with him—as were the
voters. The triumph of 1936 over the massed battalions of the press had given the President more
confidence than ever in his ability to disregard or
circumvent the machinations of the publishers. But
under the stress of defeats in Congress and the
unexpected defeat on the economic front, press conferences now took on an occasionally acrimonious
note. He was no longer indifferent to what the
press said; even what the editorial pages said mattered now.

Another sign of the times was the President's
reaction to bad party discipline. Convinced that
he had been chosen by an overwhelming majority
to carry out a coherent program, he found the
repeated defiance by prominent Democrats in both
houses a breach of faith with the electors. As the
election drew nearer, it became obvious that the
President was not going to observe a dignified
neutrality. He was going to take the risk Wilson
had taken in 1918. This time, however, it was the
risk of intervention in the Democratic primaries,
not the Congressional elections. Some advisers
thought that the satisfaction of punishing muti-
neers would be outweighed (even supposing the
attempt to succeed) by the loss in Democratic
harmony and efficiency. The fact that the party was
an inconsistent alliance had better be accepted,
and discipline be restored by more cordial con-

sultations between the White House and Capitol
Hill, by the use of patronage, and by all the traditional weapons of the Presidential armory.

Such was the counsel of the party managers, and,
above all, Mr. Farley. The advice was not taken.
In Georgia, Maryland, and New York, the President openly supported candidates who were trying
to unseat the incumbents. In Kentucky, he threw
his influence on the side of Senator Barkley, who
was fighting desperately against the energetic Governor Chandler. It was a sight to please the Republicans, who had other grounds for pleasure.

The election results justified most Republican
hopes. True, by old standards there were still overwhelming Democratic majorities in both houses.
But there were great Republican gains—and it was
ten years since there had been Republican gains.
The party was no longer a dwindling remnant,
almost too weak to do its share in manning the
Congressional committees. Some of its gains were
significant and, for the Democrats, ominous. In
New York, Governor Lehman, the miraculous vote-
getter, had barely defeated the youthful Republican candidate, Thomas E. Dewey. That almost
infallible political barometer, Ohio, was equally
worth study. There an unpopular Democratic governor had been defeated by a Republican candidate, John W. Bricker. More significant was the
defeat of a capable New Deal Senator by Robert

Taft, victor in joint debate before he was victor at the polls. The American farmer, all over the Middle West, had forgotten the desperate days of 1932. What he remembered was the new limitation of his freedom of action, the comparatively meager rewards of adherence to the new agricultural policy. He was jealous of the town worker, angered by strikes, afraid that organized labor would invade his preserves. Even in states where the unions were or should have been strong, where the great industrial battles had been fought, the reaction was striking.

In the labor field, too, the Administration was encountering difficulties. The role of the National Labor Relations Board under the Wagner Act was difficult and certain to be misunderstood. It had no power to promote labor peace as such; it was not a mediation board or the agent of a system of arbitration. Its function was to implement, by quasi-judicial methods, the intent of the Wagner Act that workers should be free to organize in trade unions without suffering pressure from employers or from rival unions. It was difficult to secure this right effectually without undertaking an elaborate investigation of the practices of the employers and without imputing motives and assessing intentions.

Unfortunately, it was plain that many American employers were as hostile to the concept of independent unionism as slave owners a century before had been to the concept of freedom for Negroes. Union organization did severely limit, and not always for good reasons or with good results, the right of a man to do as he liked with his own plant, his "own" workers. Strike action often took the form of violence, and it was easy for a businessman, after quieting his conscience with the excuse that he could not rely on legal protection, to hire spies, gunmen, and thugs from agencies which sold these services to employers, along with such equipment as poison gas and tommy guns.

Not all the methods of these defenders of the free enterprise system involved the use of arms or even gas. Espionage was even better, and to plant a wrecker in the union ranks or offices was a device in which the experts in this field had much experience. A subcommittee of the Senate presided over by Senator La Follette uncovered many of these ingenious ways of keeping the American workers loyal to the good old ways and revealed chains of command ranging from eminent business leaders through a series of intermediaries down to mere thugs and gangsters.

It was not, of course, a world of innocent lambs into which these wolves were insinuated. Some unions had their thugs, some had their crooks, some had established a useful partnership in anti-social conspiracy with their employers. A well-known journalist, Westbrook Pegler, constituted himself a one-man committee to expose labor racketeers, and his vigorous articles forced action on the police and put the American Federation of Labor on the defensive. The public could not readily understand the passion for union autonomy that kept the AFL from effectively cleaning house.

The feud between the AFL and the CIO continued despite peacemaking efforts by the President and the Administration and despite offers of compromise on the part of the AFL, offers which were rejected for several reasons, one being the refusal of John L. Lewis to consider return to the federation. A jurisdictional war between the two groups led Oregon to express its irritation by a constitutional amendment, ratified by popular vote, which severely limited union rights. The AFL won the local battle against the CIO but both sides lost the campaign. Both sides, too, not content with attacking each other, attacked the NLRB. The Board's most delicate job was to determine which was the proper bargaining unit; often it also decided whether the AFL or the CIO had won the elections called by the Board, and each decision made one enemy and often one ingrate.

Politics also embittered the quarrel; John L. Lewis was already critical of what he thought the excessive and unshakable loyalty of most union leaders to the President. The few remaining Republican union leaders, like William Hutcheson of the Carpenters, shared this view. And, especially in the CIO, Communist infiltration had secured many levers of command for members, or for friends of the party like Harry Bridges of San Francisco.

The numerous enemies of the Wagner Act, in and out of Congress, insisted on action. There was an abortive investigation of the NLRB by Senator Burke of Nebraska and a more thorough inquiry by Representative Howard Smith of Virginia. The Smith committee did not return from its quest quite empty-handed. But the Wagner Act withstood the attack. After all, the NLRB had no executive powers; its "cease and desist" orders had to be enforced by courts and the bad record of many American employers kept public if not Congressional temperatures down. More harm was done by the continuous failure of the leaders of the two great federations to make peace. David Dubinsky withdrew his International Ladies' Garment Workers when it became plain that the rulers of the CIO were determined on a fight to a finish, a fight which might be fatal to a labor movement still under suspicion as "un-American," and whose compulsory relationship with the employers, imposed by the Wagner Act, had all the emotional instability of a shot-gun marriage.

In 1938 politicians learned that labor support had its drawbacks. Democrats lost control of that recent and precious prize, the state government of Pennsylvania. In Michigan, Governor Murphy was punished for his alleged tolerance of the sit-down strikes, and in Connecticut Governor Cross was punished for his intolerance towards them. Either way, the Republicans gained. And it was not only the Democratic party which lost. For its great leader failed in his attempt to punish and reward inside his own party. The candidates he had supported were defeated; the candidates he had denounced were triumphantly nominated. There were two exceptions. In Kentucky, Senator Barkley was renominated; in New York, Representative O'Connor was defeated. But experts noted that, after all, Senator Barkley was a veteran Senator in office; his victory was to be expected anyway. And in New York, the President was interfering in the politics of his own state and, it was believed, had vigorous support from Farley.

The rank and file of the Democratic party required more encouragement than mere sporting spirit could give them. And at the Jackson Day dinner in January, 1939, the President tried to give it. "Some of you Democrats today get scared and let the other fellows tell you you've lost an election just because you don't have majorities so big that you can go to sleep without sentries."

That the party needed sentries was evident, but more and more it was felt that what it needed was a new campaign under its old leader.

CHAPTER XIII

RECESSION IN A DARKENING WORLD

THE increasing stagnation in business, and the consequent decline in employment hit the Administration hard. They forced a more pesismistic assessment of the problem of relief and an abandonment of the austere financial program that had been planned. They forced, too, a reconsideration of the whole recovery program and made natural an attempt to discover what had again stalled the machine.

Conservative critics of the Administration and the New Deal were not at a loss for an answer. It was the Administration that was at fault. By its permanent hostility to business, its suspicion of the motives, competence, and good citizenship of the businessman, the Administration was thwarting the natural forces making for recovery. The labor policy of the Administration, throwing the whole weight of Federal authority on the side of the unions, was one source of economic unease and consequent stagnation. Another was unwillingness to balance the budget, the disregard for time-tested rules of sound finance. Another was the increasingly severe code imposed on the stock market by the SEC. It was idle to expect genuine recovery if fresh investment was made unattractive to the public and if the mechanisms by which money was pumped into the industrial system were made impossible to work by overrigorous regulation.

Naturally the Administration did not accept these charges. It refused to admit that reforms were the cause of the setback, or that the remedy was to give business its head. It was not by a return to the methods of 1929 that the malaise so disagreeably evident could be conjured out of existence.

The ills of the economic system were surely more complex, and in the disillusionment of 1937–38 an audience was provided for theorists who insisted that the "recession" was not surprising. If there was an inadequate flow of new capital into investment, that had been true of the "boom" economy of the 1920's. If the United States was still full of idle men, that was not a new and temporary weakness. If there was a shocking contrast between the possibilities of production offered by modern technology and the actual output, that, too, was no new story. Some of the critics who took this line were Marxians who affected to know that these

defects were inevitable in an age of finance capitalism. But the mass of American opinion was convinced that the evils (whatever they might be)
were not incurable.

The climate of opinion was deeply influenced by
modern economic theories that attributed the stalling of the economic machine, the cycle of "boom
and bust," to defects in the supply of capital and
in the distribution of purchasing power. Under the
impact of the theories of John Maynard Keynes
and above all of his distinction between saving
and investment, the assumption that the "free
enterprise system" produced its own remedies for
its own ills was not longer taken as axiomatic even
by normally conservative economists. Almost alone
among economists of the first rank, Keynes had
approved of the refusal of the Roosevelt Administration to underwrite general currency stabilization in 1933. And the use of "deficit spending" to
prevent the normal working of the trade cycle in
driving prices and production down was a Key-
nesian remedy that made his theories anathema
to orthodox economists and bankers.

The great speculative boom, it was said, had concealed the fact that long before the stock market
crashed, the flow of investment was falling off.
And this excess of mere saving was made possible
by a distribution of income that left the power of
investment in too few hands and reduced the pur-

chasing power of the great mass of the people to a point that crippled demand.

These explanations of the continuing crisis were not the only ones advanced. It was pointed out that in the great slump, the self-corrected mechanism of the price system that should have taken the United States out of the depression had, in fact, worked very irregularly. Prices for the farmer collapsed; so did wages in certain industries. But over considerable areas of the American economy, prices fell slowly if at all. The system of free enterprise failed to function because the basic price decisions were no longer made by the open bargaining of the market but by pools and rings, cartels and combines.

The chief exponent of this viewpoint was the Assistant Attorney-General in charge of the administration of the Sherman Act. Thurman Arnold had a remarkable talent for dramatizing a situation and great verbal facility in expounding his theories. The way to make the American system work was to restore its elasticity by breaking up the price-fixing agreements that ruled so much of American industry and that tied it, in some instances, to international cartels, doubly damned as being mainly German and therefore economic allies of Hitler in his undeclared war on the West. Despite hankerings after the price-fixing aspects of NRA, there was enough life in the old anti-monopoly principles to make Arnold's widely publicized assault on restrictive practices popular. It was especially popular in the West, which felt itself the victim of the price-fixing methods of the great Eastern corporations. West and South both thought of themselves as "colonies" of big business. Two Western Senators, Borah and O'Mahoney, had tried to give practical expression to this sentiment by proposing a system of licensing for corporations engaging in interstate commerce, one condition of keeping these licenses being obedience to the anti-trust laws.

The political necessity of doing something about business stagnation was obvious. The mid-term Congressional elections were approaching and the recession had given new hope to the defeated and discouraged Republicans. It was clear that the deeply disappointed American people would be tempted to seek out some villain and there were great political advantages in diverting the wrath of the voter to Big Business.

On April 29, 1938, the President's message on the concentration of economic power was sent to Congress. Concentration and the decline of competition, these were the linked phenomena to be studied. The Temporary National Economic Committee, which was the result of this message, was an unusual body. It was not (as some had hoped) a purely Congressional committee. It was not (as others had hoped) a committee of Administration experts. TNEC was recruited from the Senate, from the House, and from relevant executive departments such as Commerce and Labor. It included such public figures as Thurman Arnold, enemy of the trusts, and William O. Douglas, Chairman of the SEC and enemy of a type of corporation management that deprived stockholders of all real power. The Administration nominees were all good New Dealers. The Congressional nominees did not redress the balance, for the conservatives were outnumbered by members who had a congenital suspicion of the ways of big business. The same attitude marked many research workers employed by the Committee to study concrete problems; they brought to their task some of the attitude of a zealous district attorney.

From the beginning, conservative elements saw in TNEC more of a witch-hunting expedition than a scientific inquiry into the strength and weakness of American capitalism. It was not surprising that many industrial leaders were vague and sometimes inconsistent in their explanations of their own business policies. Business was not an academic and totally rational activity. The special talents of a business executive did not necessarily make him the match in wits and readiness of speech of a bright young economist who had nothing else to do but pry and probe. Merely providing the necessary documentation imposed a severe burden on the corporations involved. One executive asserted that it would be simpler to move the head office to Washington than to send down the mass of evidence asked for.

The Chairman of TNEC was Senator Joseph O'Mahoney of Wyoming, and his role was especially important, for the turn-over of committee members was abnormally rapid. Some died; some were defeated; some were promoted to new offices. The main direction of the Committee fell to the Chairman and the Executive Secretary, Leon Henderson, whose accurate prophecy of the approaching recession had earned him a reputation as critic of the existing order.

What was, in fact, given to the American public was not a program but a picture of American economic life that illustrated, in striking colors, the decline of economic competition and showed wide areas of the American economy controlled by a few great corporations. TNEC cast doubt, too, on the universal validity of the picture of the small businessman starting out to become the big businessman if he had the necessary qualities. It even cast doubt on the genuine freedom of the small businessman; the filling station proprietor was often as securely tied to the great oil companies as if he had been a salaried employee. It made the picture of the inventor profiting by his Yankee ingenuity seem out of date in a world where basic patents were often held by corporations willing to fight, with all the resources of the law, any newcomers rash enough to intrude. But TNEC did not provide an answer to the problem of poverty in the midst of plenty or give the American people any guarantee that the dilemma of modern capitalism was on the way to being solved. Even if a few witches were metaphorically burned, the problem of economic evil remained obscure.

The New Deal explanation of the stagnant state of the American economy was not allowed to go without challenge. But it was not the press or the politicians who most effectively stated the case for putting blame on the Administration. It was Wendell Willkie, the belligerent head of the Commonwealth and Southern, who fought with combative competence such spokesmen for the Administration as Robert Jackson. The corporation lawyer developed unexpected talents for debate, and millions came to associate him with the doctrine that it was in the "defeatism" of the Administration that the cause of the American economic sickness was to be found.

To the practicing politicians of the Democratic party, the outlook for 1940 was not bright. The margins for holding seats in Congress and the control of state governments were ominously narrow in the critical Eastern and Midwestern states. The elections of 1938 had dissipated many illusions, and to more and more party workers, there was only one chance of making sure of victory in 1940.

The prodigious character of the Roosevelt triumph in 1936 had at once suggested to many politicians that one miracle could be followed by another, and even in 1937 there was some discussion of the possibility of a third term. To politicians, rightly or wrongly confident in their own strength, the breach of the unwritten law against such a term was odious or deplorable. It was the conscious beneficiaries of the Roosevelt magic who began toying with the idea of another term for the President—and for themselves. But it was the election of 1938 that made the third term more than a remote possibility. It showed that the Democratic party was not securely entrenched in office, and revealed to many politicians that their own intrinsic strength was less than they had fondly hoped in 1936. They would find 1940 a hard fight—and it might be possible to win only by fighting under the President.

Moreover, it was getting harder and harder to answer the question, "If not Roosevelt, who?" No single heir apparent, no Van Buren, no Taft was in sight. There were veteran Congressional politicians like Vice-President Garner and Senator Wheeler. There was the great organizer of victory, Farley. There were rulers of important state machines like

McNutt of Indiana and there were leading New Deal executives like Henry Wallace, Harry Hopkins, Robert Jackson, and W. O. Douglas. But under the great shadow cast by the President, none of these saplings had grown to a height that made it easy for the public to measure them. It was obvious, too, that no one could be nominated in 1940 without the active support of the President. For a time the choice was thought to have fallen on Jackson and it was believed that he would be run for Governor of New York, so that he might meet the test laid down by the practical politicians of getting elected to something. But the New York politicians refused to accept him as a candidate, partly, it was assumed, because of the opposition of Farley.

Other possibilities were disqualified for other reasons. Wallace and Douglas suffered under the handicap that had counted against Jackson; neither had been elected to high office. Congressional leaders like Garner and Wheeler suffered from their known lukewarmness to the New Deal in its later stages, and they were opposed by the men around the White House. Farley had not only the handicap of being a Catholic, but of representing machine politics without policy. McNutt was vulnerable on the side of labor, and his hold on Indiana was not secure. Hopkins was desperately ill. Candidates canceled themselves out and the kinds of veto which proved effective also proved how much the Democratic party was a house divided.

So for zealous New Dealers and working politicians alike, the third term began to change from a possibility to a necessity. Loyal New Deal Senators like Joseph F. Guffey of Pennsylvania, practical politicians high in the ranks of what was now the greatest Democratic machine, the Kelly organization in Chicago, the voice of the Communists as heard in the *New Masses,* all began to talk lightly of the shibboleth that debarred the American people from calling for a third time on Roosevelt.

Speculation as to the President's intentions was, by the end of 1938, the chief staple of political conversation. At press conferences, any opportunity was taken to trick him into revealing his intentions. The President refused to say. So did his closest associates, who professed that they knew no more of his intentions than the Congressmen who were increasingly irritated by the monumental silence of the President. As long as the President's intentions were unknown, the potential candidates in his own and in the Republican party were at a disadvantage. Republicans for a time hoped that the Senate would go on record as opposing the innovation. A resolution condemning a third term would not only be ammunition for them, but embarrass such Democratic leaders as Barkley, who had voted for the La Follette resolution condemning a third term for President Coolidge. But the sponsor of the new version of the La Follette resolution was a Senator who knew that he had no chance of reelection, and his more hopeful colleagues were more circumspect. They were forced to hold their hands, for if the President did not run, his choice of a successor might be influenced by their conduct now. Public opinion polls showed a rise in the minority of Democrats who wanted a third term, while equally significant was the obvious calculation of the great city bosses that their fortunes and those of the President were inextricably intertwined. And to the calculations of Messrs. Kelly, Hague, and zealous Democratic voters was added the impact of the decision of Adolf Hitler to make war. By October, 1939, a majority of all voters and a large majority of Democratic voters would support the third term—and significant of a change in internal party conflicts, it was the traditionally conservative South that was now strongest for innovation.

When campaign plans were being laid in 1939 and in the early winter months of 1940, nobody was thinking of Willkie as a candidate, although his name had been mentioned more than once. The Republican revival of 1938 had brought into the limelight several contenders for the nomination who had good claims on attention. Governor Bricker of Ohio was a marked man in the eyes of those thousands of party workers who knew what Ohio had been in the history of the party. The "regulars" wanted a "regular," and there was every evidence that Bricker, in regularity, was a worthy successor of William McKinley.

Bricker was not Ohio's only candidate or its favorite son. That honor fell to Senator Robert Taft. He had only entered the Senate after the elections of 1938, but the dreadful havoc wrought in preceding elections in the ranks of Republican elder statesmen made his political youth of little moment. The Senate provided another possible candidate in Vandenberg of Michigan, who had fought the good fight in the darkest days of Democratic predominance. But the candidate in whom the public took most interest was Thomas E. Dewey, District Attorney of New York and defeated candidate for the governorship of the Empire State.

To come within less than a hundred thousand votes of defeating one of the strongest Democratic candidates, to force the Democrats of New York to rely for victory on an alliance with the unclassifiable American Labor party, these were very serious claims on the attention of the delegates to the Convention. Mr. Dewey's youth (he was only thirty-eight) was not against him; and he had a dramatic and adventurous record. It might seem that the conviction of criminals like Waxey Gor-

don, or even errant political bosses like Jimmie
Hines, was not proof of Presidential capacities, but
such achievements caught the popular taste. The
drab merits of Governor Bricker paled beside the
veracious story of the war against crime in New
York. Even the achievements of Taft and Vandenberg, even such triumphs as the coalition with conservative Democrats that had reversed much of the
Roosevelt fiscal policy and forced the President to
let a revenue bill become law without his signature,
were not the stuff of which heartwarming campaign
material could be made.

Mr. Dewey, however, suffered from two related
handicaps. He had become a candidate very early
and so was a target for a coalition of rivals. And by
taking the field early he, like the other Republican
aspirants, had committed himself to a view of
American foreign policy that was defensible, and
tactically shrewd in 1939, but became less defensible and less popular with every week that
passed after the outbreak of the European war.
The popular apprehension that was the driving
force behind the third term grew with each piece
of bad news from Europe. More and more Republican voters were becoming alarmed, both for the
fate of their party and the fate of their country;
they were looking for a new leader.

If it was largely Hitler who was making the third
term likely, it was undoubtedly he who was making

the nomination of Wendell Willkie possible. The rise in Willkie's chances was reflected in the Gallup polls; he was still running behind Dewey, but a month or two before, he had not, in any real sense, been running at all. The advantage of not having been running in 1939 now became evident. The invasion of Denmark and Norway in April put an end to any illusions that the conflict in Europe was a "phony war." It strengthened the popular opinion that the President knew what he was talking about and that his opponents did not. It was the leading Republican policy-maker on foreign affairs, Senator Borah, who had assured the President in the summer of 1939 that he was wrong, that there was going to be no war. Borah was now dead, but the memory of his ill-timed confidence in his private sources of information was not. Although it required some Democratic votes to prevent the amendment of the Neutrality Act in the summer of 1939, the bulk of the opposition came from the Republicans, and they fiercely opposed the amendments which the Administration had forced through when war broke out.

The President's repeated requests for more and more money for defense deepened the national sense of urgency, and when the German victories over the helpless Norwegians were followed by the *Blitzkrieg* that swept over Holland and Belgium and into the heart of France, the damage done to the

hopes of the leading Republicans was very great.
The authority of the President rose with each piece
of bad news.

To some extent, Republican policy could be
represented as the natural following of the old
maxim that "the duty of the Opposition is to oppose." But the American people were increasingly
critical of the old doctrine. They had had a lesson
in the extremes to which party spirit could go. The
American Communist party which, till the end of
August, 1939, had been active in every move to
give American support to the threatened democracies of Europe, had with perfect discipline followed the Russian lead and reversed itself. It went
into open and violent opposition to the Administration and into effective alliance with the friends of
Hitler.

Many voters began to love or at least tolerate
the President for the enemies he had now made.
And those enemies, ranging from Communists and
friends of Communists to defenders of the Third
Reich, included some vocal organs of Republican
opinion like the Chicago *Tribune*, as well as many
prominent members of Congress. It was difficult for
candidates who had taken what was now the increasingly unpopular isolationist line to disengage
themselves in time. And when the Republican Convention met in Philadelphia, the epic story of
Dunkirk and the catastrophe of French defeat were

themes competing with the news of delegates, primaries, and deals.

Wendell Willkie came to Philadelphia in person, to exercise on delegates and newspapermen and spectators those talents for making friends and influencing people that had got him so far, so fast. His big, bearlike figure became at once the chief sight of the convention. He was free, frank, talkative. Because of his temperament and because his only chance lay in the collapse of the old political order, he was not tempted to make the deals that the lesser candidates pinned their hopes on. Almost at once, the professionals saw that this newcomer to the game was one of the most formidable competitors. They did what they could to stop him. The foreign affairs plank was strengthened in a more isolationist sense; Senator McNary announced that the nomination of Willkie would alienate the West. But the Taft forces thought their job was to stop Dewey and they stuck to that plan of campaign just too long. On the sixth ballot, to the delirious delight of the spectators and to the wonder and apprehension of many of the delegates, the darkest of dark horses was nominated.

CHAPTER XIV

THE THIRD-TERM BATTLE

THE Republican convention, committed to so unorthodox a candidate, rapidly retreated to normality in nominating Senator McNary, representative of Western moderate progressive policy, for Vice-President. That he had strongly opposed the nomination of Willkie and that the candidates for President and Vice-President had never met mattered little. It was an abnormal year. This fact had been made manifest on the eve of the convention, when President Roosevelt, getting rid of his isolationist Secretary of War, while ill health removed his Secretary of the Navy, replaced them by two very eminent Republicans. Henry L. Stimson, Secretary of State under Hoover and of War under Taft, went to the War Department; Colonel Frank Knox, publisher of the Chicago *Daily News* and Republican candidate for the Vice-Presidency in 1936, went to the Navy Department. This was an admirable stroke, both men were very able, while their selection was a prelude to the President's non-

partisan conduct of the war effort. But to orthodox
Republicans, the appointments were doubly intolerable. Not only had two leading members betrayed the party by entering the Roosevelt
Cabinet, but this dramatic move fostered the growing belief that the United States *was* in danger. In
such a crisis it was almost pointless to harp on the
iniquitous novelty of the third term, a waste of
time to disinter the record of the New Deal.

The platform bound the Republican party to
firm opposition to "involving this nation in a foreign war"—although sympathy was offered to the
invaded countries; and it favored "the extension to
all peoples fighting for liberty, or whose liberty is
threatened, of such aid as shall not be in violation
of international law or inconsistent with the requirements of our own national defense." It denounced, too, the continuance of unemployment
and the inequitable administration of the labor
laws. It promised a "square deal" for Negroes and
interpreted the President's refusal to keep Congress in session as a plan that "we might be eased
into the war by word or deed during the absence
of our representatives from Washington."

Despite the widespread assumption that he
would stand for a third term, the President long
refused to speak. During 1938 he plainly indicated
to Morgenthau that he would not run; he encouraged Secretary Hull's hopes of the succession.

Democratic candidate after candidate made it plain that only if, by some totally unexpected miracle, the President did not run, was his own candidacy to be taken seriously. But from the White House came no public sign. The President had every day to face new developments of the European crisis, to ask Congress for more money for defense, to call into Government service such different types of Americans as Edward Stettinius of United States Steel and Sidney Hillman of the Amalgamated Clothing Workers.

Yet there were no real doubts by the time the convention met, and all was over when Senator Barkley read a brief message containing the decisive phrase. "The President," it ran, "wishes in all earnestness and sincerity to make it clear that all the delegates to this convention are free to vote for any candidate." That released such delegates as had been instructed in primaries to vote for the President, but it also made it possible to nominate the President. The convention acted; by an overwhelming majority the President was nominated on the first ballot. Only Postmaster-General Farley received more than a handful of votes. The Democratic party had broken the most venerable rule of American politics. It was after midnight, in the first hour of July 19, that the President spoke to the Convention from Washington, denying all ambition for a third term and accepting it now only as a

duty, as a sacrifice comparable to those he had
asked of other citizens. In the crisis, the President
would not "have the time or the inclination to
engage in purely political debate."

But the President had just been deeply involved
in a party battle, for it had taken all his power and
prestige to force the convention to accept as Vice-
Presidential candidate the Secretary of Agriculture,
Henry A. Wallace. Wallace was one of the amateurs the professional politicians disliked. That the
convention manager who put over the Wallace
nomination should himself be another of the
amateurs—the President's closest adviser, Harry
Hopkins—was another source of irritation. And
that the victorious chief of staff of 1932 and 1936,
Farley, should resign from the national chairman-
ship as well as from the office of Postmaster-
General bred some further fears. Yet Farley's successor as Chairman, Edward Flynn of the Bronx,
was as much a master politician as Farley had
been, and the great city bosses, Hague, Kelly, and
the rest, were not men to let mere resentment blind
them to the interest they had in another Roosevelt
triumph.

In the summer of 1940, all political news had to
compete with the intelligence of the French armis-
tice and the German preparations for the destruction of Britain. Some Republicans—and others—
thought that the British would see reason and

make the best terms they could and, if peace came before the election, Republican chances would be very much brighter. Conservatives might insist that it was principles not men that were indispensable, but if the war continued, it was probable that millions of doubting Americans would vote for a man.

But that man might not be the President. Despite the novelty of his situation, Wendell Willkie did not propose to do away with the old, formal ceremony of the notification to the candidate of his nomination. And that notification was to take place in his old home town of Elwood. An Indiana background, it was thought, was more helpful than one provided by the offices of Commonwealth and Southern.

The eyes of the country were on the new and still largely unknown candidate. He was a corporation lawyer but had been a Democrat and described himself as a La Follette Progressive. Of pure German descent, he was bitterly hostile to all that the Third Reich stood for. Vigorous enemy of the New Deal, he was a devoted believer in civil liberties whether they were threatened in the person of Florida Negroes or the Communist leader Earl Browder, or the leader of the Nazi Bund, Fritz Kuhn. But so little was known of him that politicians and public alike were intensely curious over the character, talents, plans, and possibilities of

this "dark horse in a loose box," to borrow a phrase
from English political vocabulary. He was a farmer
as well as a lawyer. He was a man of books and
thought, as well as of action. By August 17, Elwood
was the center of the nation's attention. That attention and expectation were disappointed, for
Willkie at Elwood was less effective than Willkie
at Philadelphia. For all his great ability he had
little to say that a standard candidate might not
have said, and his newness to the political game,
and to the art of public speaking to great audiences,
was manifest. His devoted supporters were distressed; the Democrats jubilant. Nor did the first
speeches which the Republican candidate made in
his tour of the nation do much to cheer his supporters, or shake the gloomy conviction of the regular Republican politicians that a dreadful mistake
had been made and that what they were sending on
tour round the country was a "dead whale." How
could the President, with all the terrible responsibility of the safety and peace of the United States
on his shoulders, take time off from observing the
Battle of Britain to answer the wild charges of the
Republican candidate? Such was the question put
by Ickes and other confident Democratic spokesmen.

It began to appear, however, that the Willkie
campaign, like the Willkie nomination, was not
normal. There was, for instance, the peculiar char-

acter of the direction of the campaign. It was very amateur; the candidate paid scant attention to the advice of the Republican regulars and relied far more on the help of the volunteers who had secured him the nomination. And it was they who largely secured him the cash.

Congress, in the two Acts that bore the name of Senator Hatch of Arizona, had recently tried to keep Federal officials from being active in politics and even tried to debar from open partisan activities state employees whose compensation was, in part, derived from Federal funds. The old days of conventions packed with office-holders were at an end. Less success attended the attempt of the law to keep the campaign expenditures down to a minimum. The national committees were not permitted to spend more than $3,000,000 each. But it was possible to aid the good cause by gifts to local state committees and by gifts to special bodies set up to forward the interests of parties and candidates. So money began to pour in to "Retailers for Willkie," to the "Willkie-for-President Club of Akron," to "Willkie War Veterans," as well as to the "Jeffersonian Democrats of California," the "Committee to Defend Life Insurance and Savings," and bodies with slightly varying titles expressing their opposition to a third term. The Willkie campaign was not, it was soon apparent, likely to suffer from financial anemia. Nor was the Democratic campaign; there, organized labor, despite the hostile silence of John L. Lewis, was the greatest single "angel." The admirably organized Democratic machine managed to collect and spend nearly six million dollars, and the Republicans nearly fifteen million dollars. It proved harder to reduce politics to a bread-and-water standard by statute than had been hoped.

It became evident, too, that the Willkie money was not being totally wasted. The candidate was still the despair of the regular party technicians. It was a plan of campaign for the regulars to stress the dangers of Rooseveltian war-mongering. True, the Democratic platform was as positive as the Republican. "We will not participate in foreign wars and we will not send our Army, Naval or Air forces to fight in foreign lands outside of the Americas, except in case of attack." But the Roosevelt Administration was sending arms abroad to aid Britain; it was exchanging destroyers for bases; it was setting up conscription for the Army in peace time. It was highly vulnerable, open to attack from unreconstructed isolationists as well as from the great German and Italian racial groups.

It was obviously good Republican tactics of the old type to say nothing, to let support flow in from all quarters that opposed the Administration. But Willkie was not an old-fashioned politician and he openly supported some of the politically dangerous measures of the Administration. He showed himself, in short, both independent and patriotic. It began to appear that these unorthodox tactics were not suicidal, that the public, in the fall of 1940 as in the summer of 1940, was attending very loosely indeed to the old rules of the political game. That the impulsive Willkie was making headway was soon indisputable, for the President threw overboard his role of complete absorption in his duties and announced that he would make five campaign speeches.

That the President felt bound to abandon his plan to stay out of the campaign was due in part to the nervousness of politicians who, in the last weeks of a Presidential campaign, inevitably become victims of morbid fears. And politicians had a right to be considered, for the President was not merely a candidate, but the head of a long list of candidates.

Willkie's policy was not necessarily tactically mistaken. For whatever he might do, he could not alienate the support of the elements in the voting public who were opposed to the foreign policy and defense policy of the Administration. The isolationists, the groups using the slogan "America First," the pacifists, the Socialists, the Communists, and the Nazi sympathizers were working for the Republican candidate. It was not by voting the Communist ticket that effect would be given to the new party line of "no aid to the imperialist war makers in London, Berlin, Paris, Tokyo and Rome." It was, in fact, only the "warmongers" of London who were aimed at by the American Communists—and the best way to hinder them was to do as much damage to the Administration as possible.

Less doctrinaire critics were also disturbed by the domestic results of the concentration of the President's attention on problems of war and defense. Each new appropriation for defense was made an excuse in Congress for demanding further reductions in relief. Left-wing friends of the Administration were quick to point out that the defense appropriations created a demand for a different type of labor from that normally employed on the relief rolls. The alienation of the farmers from the New Deal was growing more marked and the influence of John L. Lewis was being used to weaken the President's appeal to the organized workers.

Other critics saw in the defense program an unnecessary extension of the reckless debt policy of the New Deal. Yet, in many conservative areas and groups the President was more popular, or less unpopular, in 1940 than he had been since the summer of 1933. But many members of the more prosperous classes, especially in the East, who approved the President's foreign policy still thought it unlikely that the New Deal could organize America effectually.

The ostensible cause of the President's decision to come down from the heights and test the efficacy of his skill was the misrepresentation of his record by his opponent. But far more important than any refutation of campaign charges was the demand from the rank and file as well as the party leaders of the harassed Democracy. When the President did at last enter the campaign, friends and foes alike were stirred as the armies had been at Dresden in 1813 when the bearskins of the Old Guard revealed to both sides that the Emperor had taken the field in person.

The President did not confine his campaign to defenses of his actions or even to repeated denials that he designed to lead America into the war. The Democratic line in 1940 was a variation of that of 1916: "He *will* keep us out of war—with safety." The President was explicit. "Your boys are not going to be sent into any foreign wars. They are going into training to form a force so strong that, by its very existence, it will keep the threat of war far away from our shores. The purpose of our defense is defense." Such statements were of course subject to future contingencies. But the past record of the Republicans was reviewed too, and the upturn in business that had begun in 1939 and was now being nourished by defense spending, made it safer to recall 1932 than it would have been had the stagnation of 1938 continued to mock the hopes of

the New Deal. Nevertheless, the Administration
had not managed to organize the American economy to produce the desired national income of
$80,000,000,000, and there was a drift back to the
Republican party of the more prosperous urban
voters and farmers. Poll-takers and political workers alike found that rent and wages provided a good
basis for estimating the probable political action of
voters. Even though the Administration had not
prevented cuts in relief and although the expected
war boom had had comparatively little effect on
the great pools of unemployment, the poor were
still for the President.

So were events. The opposition candidate was
reduced to criticism, to promises; the President
could act and had the information, the responsibility. Hence the news of the invasion of Greece,
like the news of the nightly bombardment of London, told in his favor.

When John L. Lewis finally abandoned his neutrality and openly appealed for labor support for
Willkie, it was too late—even though he made his
continued leadership of the CIO depend on labor's
taking his advice. The leader's lieutenants did not
follow his directive, and his own miners affirmed
their acceptance of his leadership in industrial relations and their firm refusal to be marched over
to the other side in the political battle. Democratic hopes rose daily, and on the eve of the elec-

tion, the President was confident that he would be returned.

The American people spoke decisively. Willkie carried only ten states, although he got seven million votes more than Governor Landon and was left a figure of national stature. But over the greater part of the Union, the popular verdict was unmistakable. It was so interpreted by the defeated candidate. His loose organization of amateurs was dissolved, the Willkie clubs disbanded, and more startling still, money that had come in too late to be used was returned to the donors and the Republican party given back to its old owners and managers.

In Europe the campaign had been watched with fear and hope. For Roosevelt was, by November, 1940, a world symbol. His victory was a defeat for the Rome-Berlin-Tokyo Axis; a victory for Greece and Britain, the two European countries resisting Germany and Italy in arms; and a source of silent encouragement to fearful neutrals, to Belgrade, to Stockholm, to Moscow. That was the basic meaning of the victory outside the United States. And it was its meaning inside it too.

The New Deal was over. The tides of war that had washed away so many barriers all over the world were rising high round the ramparts of the United States, and the commission given the President by the electors was rightly interpreted by him as a modern version of the charge given of old to the Roman consuls, that they should take care that no ill befell the commonwealth.

CHAPTER XV

THE QUESTION OF NATIONAL UNITY

In the bewilderment bred by the depression, it was natural that both timid and optimistic men should see signs of a revolutionary movement among the workers and farmers hardest hit by the catastrophe. In the small groups of radicals, these easily alarmed conservatives saw a real threat to the good order of the United States and perhaps to the survival of its traditional institutions. And the timid were reinforced by the astute, to whom the red herring of a red menace was the most promising way of diverting the attention of the people from concentration on present discontents, as well as a time-tested mode of attracting the favorable attention of patriotic but frightened voters.

Even before the Roosevelt Administration took office, there had been a Congressional investigation under Hamilton Fish of subversive movements and dangerously radical individuals. But this was only one investigation among others, and the radical leaders were small fry compared with the business

magnates investigated and, in some cases, exposed
by the Pecora Committee. The American Communist party was probably more helped than hurt,
and it was free to carry out its plans for a recasting
of American society on the Russian model.

Those plans were more ambitious than practical.
Despite the energy and undoubted zeal of the party
faithful, the American "workers and peasants" remained hostile. If the workers could not be won to
revolution in the darkest days of 1932, they were
unlikely to be won to it in the comparatively hopeful days of 1935.

And in that year, the American Communist
party abandoned, with startling rapidity and admirable decision, its revolutionary program. It
ceased to assail rival radical bodies as the worst
betrayers of the workers and, willing to forget the
past, offered cooperation on its own terms to Socialist leaders like Norman Thomas. The change might
have been explained in terms of a failure of the
previous party line to get anywhere in America; but
observers noted that the change was world-wide,
that the same overtures were made to French as to
American Socialists, and were driven to conclude
that it was the increasing threat to the safety of
the Soviet Union that had forced so dramatic a
reversal of policy on the party everywhere.

The reversal was thorough enough. There was
still a danger of an imperialist war, but it was not

a war between rival and equally odious imperialisms, or a war of all the imperialists against the Soviet Union. What was threatened was a war of "Fascist Germany, Japan and Italy" against the Soviet Union and "the capitalist democracies of France, England, Czechoslovakia, Spain, the United States." The refusal of the Socialists to recognize the danger, to abandon their old opposition to armaments, was a proof of their inadequacy to the new situation.

By November, 1936, a powerful new emotional issue had given the Communist party a more secure position in American life. The outbreak of civil war in Spain and the open intervention of Nazi Germany and Fascist Italy alarmed millions of Americans. The counter-revolution was in arms in Spain, undoing the work of the Spanish Revolution of 1931. It was a young American Jew who later testified that he went to fight for the Spanish Republic against the forces that were threatening his people everywhere. But there were hundreds of thousands of Gentiles who felt that their way of life was threatened, too, and who saw, in the volunteers of the Abraham Lincoln Brigade, the front-line defenders of democracy. And the Abraham Lincoln Brigade was mainly a Communist creation.

The organizations that sprang up to aid the Spanish Republic and to develop resistance to the advance of Fascism, were from the beginning largely under Communist inspiration. The young men who died for the Spanish Republic were martyrs with much of the prestige of the Philhellenes of a century before. And it was as ungrateful a task to scrutinize the credentials of the American Communist party as it would have been to inquire, too closely, into the mixture of motives that sent Byron to die at Missolonghi.

But the rise in the prestige of the American Communist party was not due solely to the impact of the Spanish War. The depression had driven many members of the "intellectuals" out of the ivory towers they had inhabited in the twenties. It had sent many expatriates hurrying back from Paris to America; it had forced others to consider more critically the role of the writer, artist, teacher in the modern world. The absence of any visible coherent economic philosophy in the New Deal, the shock to faith given by the long crisis of American capitalism, and the alleged immunity of the Soviet Union from the apparently fatal ailments of a declining capitalism, all made Communism seem more understandable and to some more attractive. Not many of those thus attracted joined the party; not all who joined remained members; and not all who wanted to remain members were permitted to do so. But by the time of the second Roosevelt election, the prestige of the Communist party, its numbers, its resources, and its hold on certain important sections of the labor movements made it a decidedly more important body than when the depression had first gripped the nation.

Its power was much greater than its open membership (never more than about one hundred thousand) would suggest. It had far more helpers, far more sympathizers, than it had members. And the zeal, energy, and lack of respect for conventional bourgeois ethical restrictions made the Communists much more formidable, much more to be feared, than their numbers apparently justified. No more than a great boss of the old days had needed to be a mayor or governor to rule his city or state did Communists need to be in positions of formal power to control a society or a labor union. Zealous liberals and union leaders, aware how much of the immediate effectiveness of their organizations was attributable to Communist industry, courage, and single-mindedness, were not disposed to look the gift horse in the mouth. This was especially true in the fast-growing and understaffed Congress of Industrial Organizations, which was in desperate need of competent agents to organize the undisciplined masses pouring into the new giant unions.

Yet the external connection and exotic origin of the American party could not long be hid. Its regional party meetings had the strange title of "plenums"; and even a veteran American radical like William Z. Foster, once he was converted, employed all the technical terms of his new leaders. This progress "from Bryan to Stalin," of which Mr. Foster boasted, was not, in the opinion of some old radicals, necessarily all to the good, since the American worker and still more the American farmer was much more likely to respond to appeals couched in the words of Bryan than to documents and speeches that seemed like bad translations from Russian.

This was not the only criticism from the Left. The Communists had, from the beginning of their activity in America, tried to win the support of the most obviously underprivileged group, the Negroes. They organized the defense of such victims of race prejudice as the Scottsboro boys. Citizens of Chicago were startled to see Communists of black and white complexion working together on terms of apparently complete equality. Negroes were gratified to see one of their race nominated for Vice-President on the Communist ticket and others prominent among the open ruling members of the party. The claim of the Soviet Union to have abolished all forms of race prejudice was constantly repeated to win Negro hearts.

There were signs, some thought, that the zeal of the Communists for the rights of the American Negro were merely tactical. The early Communist solution for the problem, the creation in those parts of the South that had a Negro majority of a "Negro

Republic," seemed to realistic well-wishers of the colored people a plan for a race war in which the Negroes might well be exterminated. When the policy of collaborating with all enemies of Fascism was adopted and the program of the Negro Republic disappeared into the limbo of outmoded policies, the lesson that consistency was a weakness from which Communist leaders were exempt was learned by some disillusioned allies.

It was not the only lesson learned. Like all other Communist parties, the American party had had its heretics, including some leaders of the party. Not only were the open Trotskyites expelled and declared anathema, but one important group of militants, led by Jay Lovestone, were put down from their seats by an edict from Moscow. Many minor party members were forced out until, as leading party intellectuals put it, the party "expelled the last of the dissidents in 1929. Narrow sectarianism was sloughed off."

If the United States was still going through crises, it was soon evident that the Soviet Union was not, in fact, exempt from them. The great purges, the trials and confessions put a serious strain on the fidelity and credulity of party members. In the American scene, the crucial question for the new intellectual converts was the guilt or innocence of Trotsky. His case was made a test of orthodoxy of the most rigorous kind. The dean of American liberals, Professor John Dewey, became head of a committee that not merely refused to accept the word of Moscow as decisive proof of guilt, but conducted its own investigation of the alleged counter-revolutionary conspiracy and absolved the exiled heresiarch. But although there were signs of doubt and threats of breaks in the ranks as early as 1937, unity was to some extent enforced from the outside by the violent attacks of the "red baiters," above all by the assaults of the Chairman of the House Committee on un-American Activities, Representative Martin Dies of Texas.

The creation of the immediate ancestor of this committee was one of the first signs that the Nazi Revolution in Germany was going to affect the internal as well as external politics of the United States. The accession of Hitler to power, the burning of the Reichstag, the first unmistakable signs of the character of the new regime in Germany all had had to fight for attention from the American people, deeply involved in its own great crisis of the winter of 1932–33.

But American Jews could not take so philosophical an attitude in face of the threat to the well-being of their kin in Germany, and their first reaction was to organize a boycott of German goods. It was imperfectly effective, and it helped to provoke the organization of German-American opinion in defense of the New Order in Germany. A society of "Friends of the New Germany" was founded to counter the propaganda that, it was asserted, blackened the name of Germany. Some politicians, either from genuine sympathy with the German people or a lively appreciation of the importance of the German vote in their districts, were ready to defend the Third Reich, and by 1934 there were charges and counter-charges in the House between Congressmen from districts with a large Jewish population and Congressmen with considerable numbers of German-American voters.

The organization of German-Americans for the defense of the New Order in Germany did, in fact, create a problem. But above all, it was the character of the new government in Berlin which made the problem serious. The claim that all healthy states were founded on a community of race was, if the theory were extended to the United States, fatal to American unity. There was, therefore, a good deal of support in Congress and the country for a proposal to investigate subversive activities and, although the prime mover in the House, Representative Dickstein of New York, had evidently in mind the exposure of Nazi activities, there were other Congressmen, notably Representative Dies, who were at least as anxious to renew the work of the Hamilton Fish Committee and investigate the Communists.

The Committee was presided over by Representative McCormack of Massachusetts. It took a sober view of its duties, and its report, when finally published in 1935, told little that had not been known or guessed. There was a good deal of Nazi activity among the German-Americans. There were youth camps that recalled those where the boys and girls of Germany were indoctrinated with the new gospel. Anti-Semitic and quasi-Fascist organizations had received encouragement from Nazi sympathizers in America. On the other hand, the promise made by the Soviet Government that, in return for recognition, it would halt all encouragement of subversive propaganda had not been kept. There were no grounds for panic, although there was reason for vigilance. Its report published, the committee died.

This was not the ending of the question or of the political profits and risks of agitating it. By 1935, a considerable section of the American public was genuinely alarmed at the spread of "un-American ideas," although many might have been at a loss to define their own conception of Americanism. The readiness of politicians to cater to this anxiety was reflected in the passing of various state "teachers' oaths" laws. These statutes forced teachers to swear allegiance to the Federal, and occasionally to the state, Constitution. Teachers were indignant that they, as a class, had been singled out for such exceptional treatment, while the cynical were amused at the assumption that revolutionaries of the Left and Right would be seriously handicapped by being forced to disclose themselves or to commit perjury.

Alarmed patriotism, professional patriotism, political strategy, all combined to secure the easy passing by the House of the resolution creating the Dies Committee. More than most special committees, this one deserved to be known by its chairman's name. For Representative Martin Dies was not merely a veteran hammer of the Reds; he took a view of his duties as chairman quite as autocratic as any attributed to the President by the bitterest enemies of Roosevelt. He directed the work of the committee's investigators and issued their reports without going through the formality of checking their reliability or consulting his colleagues. He carried out some important investigations single-handed. Indeed, it was perhaps a misnomer to call his methods "investigations," since he often thought it sufficient to let a witness testify with more or less plausibility, and to release this testimony to the press as if it were the most perfectly authenticated matter of undisputed record.

These usurpations of authority often raised protests both among other members of the Committee and the victims of the reckless denunciations. But Chairman Dies was only occasionally apologetic, and he had some reason for ignoring his critics; for public opinion in and out of Congress approved of the activities of the committee, and as the European sky became darker, this approval grew. No matter how loudly the intellectuals raged, Congress renewed its mandate and its funds.

If the Nazis were limited to recent German-American immigrants and a few fairly open agents of the Third Reich, most of their allies among Americans of non-German stock were obviously members of the lunatic fringe. It was difficult to take seriously the panacea of General Moseley, which was a (military) strong hand, and even more difficult to take seriously the outpourings of Representative Thorkelson, with his preoccupation with the dangers threatening from the activities of the "Hebrews." In a wider sense, many of the materials for Fascism were lying around in the United States, but they were not being effectively assembled or used by the self-appointed Fascist leaders. In so far as the various, fantastic, crackpot, fanatical anti-Semitic, antiradical, pro-Nazi organizations were exposed to the public eye, it was done far less effectively by the Dies Committee than by such private enterprises as the investigation of this curious underworld by individuals like "John Roy Carlson" whose best-seller *Under Cover* was to complete this unfinished business of the Committee.

It was very different with the Communists. Here

was the real game of the majority of the committee. Here, it was maintained, was a highly disciplined party under orders from a foreign government many of whose members were planted in important strategic positions in the American Government. Because the Communist party encouraged its members to take "party names" and often permitted them to keep their membership secret, it was no easy job to determine who were, in fact, Communists. And in his zeal for the expulsion from Government service of persons whose real allegiance was to the Soviet Union, Representative Dies was not hampered by any regard for the principle of giving the accused the benefit of the doubt. A test of constructive guilt was adopted that defied all the principles of Anglo-Saxon jurisprudence. Because Communists undoubtedly created and controlled societies apparently independent of the party machine, it was convenient to make mere membership in such societies a proof of guilt. Because Communists had undoubted influence in some societies that they had not founded, membership in such societies was proof of being at least a fellow traveller.

The Dies Committee achieved some of the objects of some of its members, for it did help to associate in the public mind the New Deal, or at any rate New Dealers, with the propagandists of novel, seditious, "un-American ideas." As far as the Dies Committee helped to create a climate of opinion alarmed at the dangers to American institutions from organizations or individuals devoted to a foreign government or governments, it was in part responsible for that formidable statute, the Alien Registration Act of 1940, which imposed severe penalties on both citizens and aliens for attempts to seduce members of the armed forces from their duty.

Not all of the committee's fears were unreasonable. It was a novelty in American history to find so many citizens, native-born as well as naturalized, who had so deep a devotion to another government. Even the member of the Dies Committee whom the assailed radicals most trusted, Representative Voorhis, did not deny that there was an evil, however skeptical he was of the simple remedies of suppression proposed. For the remedies suggested were too simple to be effective. It was foolish to impose test oaths on people who were, at the same time, accused of perfect readiness to perjure themselves. It was of less than no avail to bar the Communist party from the ballot, as was done in some states. A Communist was willing to run on the Republican ticket if it suited the party line, and he could escape with ease through the wide meshes of the nets set for him by the Congressional fowlers.

As the Dies Committee itself admitted, the overwhelming majority of the American people, black or white, had proved immune to the seductions of Nazis and Communists. Indeed, in mere voting strength, radical third parties had never made so poor a showing as they had done in the Presidential elections since the depression. The internal threat to the American way of life came not from agitators or conspirators, but from its failure to give assurance to many of the American people that the pursuit of happiness was a race in which they were not hopelessly handicapped. And the most effective barrier to the growth of such skepticism was the widespread conviction among the underprivileged that the Administration contained many men who had a deep concern for the poor and unfortunate.

CHAPTER XVI

THE war naturally determined the character of the third term from the moment of the President's re-election was assured. What the preservation of the Union had been to Lincoln, the defeat of the Axis now was to Roosevelt. It was the preservation of the possibility of democratic government that was the primary task of the Administration.

If this were so, the test of any policy was its relevance to the rapid mobilization of American resources for aid to the countries resisting the Axis in arms, and the preparation of the American people for the time that might soon come when the United States would have to accept belligerency or withdraw in face of a triumphant and deeply alienated group of powers. By 1941 not many supporters of the Administration would have denied this. New Deal supporters who held to the disdain for the outside world that had marked so much of the policy of the first Administration had been alienated long before. Support for the President's foreign policy was now the mark of the orthodox Democrat, and it was easy to be an orthodox Democrat without being a New Dealer.

It was the memory of 1917—and after—that alarmed many who yet approved of the President's policy, for they remembered the abandonment of the "New Freedom" in the second Wilson term, the return of Big Business to control, the harassing of radical thought, the witch hunts run by the Department of Justice. If there had to be a war, they wanted one that did not involve abandonment of the New Deal. Mere technical efficiency was not enough. Any left-wing leaders who were inclined to overlook political backsliding had to face the constant criticism of the Communists and their allies. The invasion of Russia on June 21, 1941, was overnight to diminish this pressure, but it did not totally disappear. Even if the intellectuals were converted, there was the massive exception, John L. Lewis. He had carried out his promise to resign the leadership of the CIO, to the alarm of his colleagues, who thought he might well be more formidable out of office than in. In any case, he was very much in office in the Mine Workers, and that union was not likely to be betrayed in any negotiation by leaders too susceptible to Governmental appeals to national discipline.

The Republican party had been reduced to formal unity during the Presidential campaign, but Willkie's defeat freed its permanent leaders. They were not united, but no more was the Democratic party. By the fall of 1941, the Republicans were in general opposition to the foreign and military policy of the Administration, minimizing the seriousness of the world situation and skeptical of the necessity of the measures taken by the Administration to cope with it. They were skeptical of the need for unpopular measures like the extension of the service of men drafted into the army under the law of 1940, and hostile to the modifications of the Neutrality Act that the President got in the fall of 1941. They were skeptical, too, of the value of the "Atlantic Charter," and reluctant spectators of the extension to Russia of aid under Lend-Lease.

The war crisis provided an excuse for a slowing-up of the New Deal, but that slowing-up was bound to happen in any event. The conservatives of both parties in Congress had acquired the habit of working together. They did not share, for example, the President's desire for a more thorough reform of the tax laws; for a campaign against the "high bracketeers" who by legal tricks escaped the Treasury net.

Nor was it clear what the New Deal policy would have been, even if it had been supported by convinced majorities in both houses. It was

possible to develop such administratively successful policies as those applied by the Department of
Agriculture to the varied ailments of the American
farm economy. It was possible to extend further
Federal aid to rehousing, schools, and child welfare,
and a different kind of Congress would doubtless
have voted far more money than was now made
available by the thriftier elements in both parties.
Experiments of more doubtful value, like the model
communities which were to set an example of
higher rural living or the "green-belt" ventures in
town planning, would have had their achievements
scrutinized with a less skeptical eye and might have
been encouraged to expand on a large scale. But
there was little chance of that in face of permanent
deficits and with the increasing pressure of defense
spending on the Federal budget.

Even the Administrative simplifications of the
overlapping New Deal agencies that had been
loudly called for had been mainly completed by
1941. Thus in 1939, two important consolidations
produced the Federal Security Agency and the Federal Works Agency. The first took over the National Youth Administration, the Office of Education and the Civilian Conservation Corps with
other minor offices; the new FWA took over the
PWA, the WPA, and the Public Roads Administration. The most famous or notorious of the agencies
thus swallowed up kept its initials as the Work

Projects Administration, but its activities steadily diminished in volume and interest. And the CCC at last in 1941 began to acquire something of a military character. Its main field of activity moved from forestry and conservation to preparing sites for the rapidly expanding army, and, although still unarmed, it acquired more discipline.

Of course, all problems of economic organization for defense involved political considerations. The President was conscious that it was his duty to carry the people along with him, especially after a series of naval "incidents" made it plain that a "shooting war" was likely to occur and was not very far away. But the appeal now was to the workers. "Our nation cannot be hampered by the selfish obstruction of a small but dangerous minority of labor leaders who are a menace . . . to the true cause of labor itself, as well as to the nation as a whole." In speeches like this, the public took more note of the novel spectacle of the President chiding labor than of the familiar spectacle of his chiding management.

Pearl Harbor for a moment silenced all but the most bitter opponents. Indeed, some of the most vehement critics of the Administration professed to rejoice that the nation had at its head so bold and talented a commander-in-chief. But after the first few weeks, the political opposition to the President gained ground. The early disasters of the war were a shock to a very confident people that had not really thought itself vulnerable, and there was a human temptation to find a scapegoat. There was the effect, too, of the first intrusive regulations of the military economy forced on the United States. Gasoline rationing was a barely explicable nuisance in communities like Los Angeles where the oil had to be forcibly kept underground. Other forms of rationing were met by a skepticism bred by years of criticism of New Deal experimentation. In a politically harmful sense, this seemed to many millions "a New Deal war," run by amateur brain-trusters, bureaucrats, even by dangerous radicals. The farmer, especially, was irritated by regulations that seemed to have been made for and by towns-men, which deprived him of his sons, his hired men, of spare parts for his farm machinery, of the gaso-line that for him at least was a necessity, not a luxury to be dispensed with. Equally important, he was becoming more solvent. Prices for farm prod-ucts were rising and he saw himself deprived of his right to profit by the rise.

With the drafting of millions of young men into the Army, with the switching of millions of workers from their permanent abodes to the new war plants and war towns, political organizations were upset. That hurt the Democrats more than it did the Republicans, for it was largely the lowest paid workers who were now sucked into the new plants away from home—and, equally important, taken off the relief rolls. One politically important group of the underprivileged which made an important part of the New Deal strength in some critical Northern cities was not merely indifferent, but angry. The Negroes found it very difficult to get jobs in the new war plants; they were still on relief; they remembered the race maxim that described their situation, "Last to be hired, first to be fired"—and they had not even been hired yet.

The Republicans saw a chance to win the Negroes back to the party of Lincoln, and they were helped by some notorious figures of the party of Roosevelt. Listening to the diatribes of Southern politicians like Senator Bilbo and Representative Rankin of Mississippi, Negroes might be pardoned for skepticism concerning American denunciations of the racial policy of Hitler. "What punishment should be meted out to Hitler?" a high school class was asked and the winning answer came from a colored girl. "He should be let loose in America as a Negro." So thought tens of thousands of strategically placed Negro voters.

A good many normal and one or two exceptional circumstances aided the Republicans in their Congressional campaign. There was not only the "swing of the pendulum," but the obvious disunity of the Democrats. The rapid shift of John L. Lewis away from the CIO, as well as his open opposition to the

President, was an omen that alarmed the party managers. For if most of the leaders of the AFL were still loyal to the Administration, some were hostile, some were good Republicans, and the AFL was politically less effective than the CIO. Any weakening of the CIO was a blow to the Administration.

The activities of some Democratic leaders chilled labor, for there were many politicians from the South whose hostility to labor unions exceeded that of all but the most backward-looking Northern Republicans. But it was in the President's own state that the cleavage was made most manifest. Governor Lehman was determined to retire in 1942 and the President's candidate was Senator Mead. Farley had other views, however. His candidate, John S. Bennett, was nominated and was denied the support of the American Labor party, whose 400,000 votes had been decisive in 1938 and 1940. The left-wing supporters of the Administration were not willing to ratify Farley's choice, and the regular Democratic machine preferred to run the risks of defeat with its own candidate rather than try for victory with the President's choice. The Democrats barely kept control of the House and were lucky to escape serious losses in the Upper House. One loss to the New Deal, if not to the Democratic party, was particularly distressing, for George Norris was defeated in Nebraska. He was the most generally admired Senator, the most famous for probity and independence; but Nebraska was in no mood to overlook the sins of the Administration even if it meant rejecting its most distinguished citizen. This was ominous for 1944. Even more ominous was the defeat of the Democratic candidate for the Governorship of New York by Thomas E. Dewey. Not for twenty-two years had the Republicans elected a Governor of the Empire State.

The bare Democratic victory of 1942 was followed almost at once by the landing in North Africa which marked the turn of the tide of war. Maybe, the optimists calculated, the good news would have made all the difference. Those who thought that stressed the magnanimity of the President, who had refused to adjust the time table of war to the necessities of the American electoral system. The more sober commentators, however, were not so sure. For them the lesson was the lesson of 1938; the millions of voters who had stayed away from the polls in 1942 would only be brought out by the magic of the great name. Roosevelt must run again.

The result was even more of a blow to the political ambitions of the labor movement than the losses of 1938. Congress was fuller than ever of representatives of both parties who wanted to "put labor in its place"—and a state of war might well seem to them an appropriate time to attempt it.

Practicing politicians who had defied labor hostility had felt no reason to regret it; practical politicians who had voted as labor wanted had not had their fidelity rewarded. One such politician put the point of view of the average candidate clearly: "If you vote as labor wants you to, lots of people will take the trouble to vote against you, but nobody takes the trouble to vote for you."

The first job of the founders of the Committee for Political Action was to prove the falsity of this analysis. They knew that politicians had no use for sectional blocks that could not deliver the vote, and they determined to deliver the vote. The Political Action Committee (or PAC) was a descendant of Labor's Non-Partisan League, the political weapon of John L. Lewis when he was head of the CIO. This Non-Partisan League had not only suffered from its association with Lewis and from bitter internal disputes bred mainly by conflicts between Communist and non-Communist elements, but had become an independent political party in New York (the American Labor party) and had proved ineffective outside New York after the election of 1940.

The situation confronting the founders of the PAC in July, 1943, was not one to be dealt with in long-term plans. Congress had just passed the Smith-Connally Act greatly limiting the freedom of the unions, imposing a thirty-day period during which no strike could be called, and making compulsory a strike vote conducted by the National Labor Relations Board. It also gave powers to the President to seize plants and forbade direct union contributions to campaign funds. The bill was, in fact, the first serious move in the long-heralded Congressional offensive against the "privileges" conferred on labor by the Wagner Act. It was so obviously this that the President vetoed it, but it was noted that the veto was delivered on a Friday when most of the Representatives from New York and from the other Eastern industrial cities went home to mend their fences. There was hence an adequate majority of members present to override the veto; a result not totally displeasing to the White House—or so suspicious left-wing Congressmen thought.

The labor movement must impress on Congress and the President the importance of its hostility or friendship. The degree to which the President was unaware of or indifferent to the opinions of organized labor was made very plain when in his address to Congress on January 11, 1944, he asked for a national service law, for Governmental control of labor—or for labor conscription—the destruction of the basic rights that unions existed to preserve, as labor leaders saw it. But Congress, more politically minded than the President, refused to enact a law that would have given the executive control over far more than organized labor. Yet labor was not grateful to Congress or permanently alienated from the President. Even the miners did not bear the President malice, although they paid no attention to his protest when John L. Lewis brought them out on strike. It was by adroitly planned strikes that their leader had extended the bargaining rights of the United Mine Workers over all the soft coal fields, the unionization of the "captive mines" being decided on the morning that the Japanese attacked Pearl Harbor. And nothing had happened to make it wrong to strike after Pearl Harbor.

Lewis, however, was not content with this divided allegiance and with his wrath mounting against his old colleagues of the CIO he undertook to reunite the CIO with the AFL. A year or two before, such a reunion was the panacea preached by all Administration "friends of labor." They were not so sure now. In a reunited labor movement, Lewis might well be dominant and, in that event, labor could not be relied on to support the fourth term effectually. The projected union broke down and the PAC went into battle with little open support from unions outside the CIO.

It was from the CIO that the first contribution of $700,000 came—a contribution not barred by the Smith-Connally Act, so lawyers advised the PAC leaders, since it was for educational purposes. The

Chairman of the PAC was Sidney Hillman of the Clothing Workers, close associate of John L. Lewis in the founding of the CIO and now chief labor adviser of the President. The PAC had its own program, with victory in the war leading all the rest. Its objectives were not very different from those the President had outlined in his "Economic Bill of Rights," but there was a more marked insistence on the necessity of planning and on the dangers of letting the turn-over from peace to war be made without general control by the Government. Above all, post-war planning must provide "jobs for all." "Freedom from want" was the first freedom.

The lesson of 1942 was learned, the lesson of the millions who had neither registered nor voted. As the PAC song put it:

Let's go out and ring doorbells and get the neighbors
to vote.
Is your Congressman stalling, is he getting your goat?
Let's go out and ring doorbells and get the neighbors
to vote.

The song was put into action. Zealous workers rang the doorbells, spoke at meetings outside the great war plants, gave few excuses to avoid registration—and registration was half or more than half the battle. In the Democratic primaries the PAC got credit (some of it deserved) for the defeat of some bitterly anti-labor Congressmen and for the decision of Representative Dies not to run. These victories were the more striking when they occurred in the deep South. Into the rotten boroughs of the Gulf states there had poured thousands of workers for the new industries that the war had created, and many of these newcomers, though white, had no loyalty to the old Southern folkways. Long before the election, the PAC was recognized as a power.

It was a power working one way. Theoretically it could endorse Republicans and very occasionally did. Theoretically it could work with AFL leaders and sometimes it did. But it was basically an organization working to give practical expression to the CIO support for the fourth term. That there would be a fourth-term campaign was certain. The simple-minded wondered why there was less opposition to a fourth than to a third term. "Well, there is a law against bigamy but no law against trigamy," said a Democratic leader. There was, of course, plenty of resentment in Democratic ranks. In the South, the alleged favoritism of the Administration to the claims of the Negroes was bitterly resented and there came into existence a whole myth attached to the name of Mrs. Roosevelt. "Eleanor Clubs" were supposed to have been founded by Negro women who had determined to fight for social equality and to make refusal to work in white women's houses the first stage in the campaign. Had there been any effective organization of revolt in the South, it might have been serious. But only in Texas did the irritated conservatives get temporary control of the party machine and attempt to choose Presidential electors who would cast the vote of Texas for Senator Byrd. But in Texas as well as elsewhere the Roosevelt forces were too strong, the demand for the fourth term too genuine.

In 1944 as in 1940, the interest of the Democratic Convention was not centered on the Presidential nomination, but on the fight over the Vice-Presidency. Vice-President Wallace had certain claims to a renomination. He had been one of the prominent if vague "liberal" interpreters of American war aims and some of his slogans had caught the public ear. He was trusted by most union leaders and by the intellectual left-wingers working with the PAC. A bitter public quarrel with Jesse Jones, the Secretary of Commerce, had pleased many who disliked the enemies Wallace had made. But despite four years as presiding officer of the Senate, Wallace gave professional politicians an impression of being as much an incurable amateur as ever. He had nowhere managed to create anything like an organization that could work effectively for him; his judgment was widely and deeply distrusted—even by Roosevelt. It was only too evident that his own state of Iowa and the other farm states were safely back in the Republican fold. Indeed, it was a paradox that a candidate whose background and achievements linked him closely to rural America should, by 1944, have been strong only with the industrial workers and their intellectual mentors. Many politicians warned Roosevelt that he could not win with Wallace—and they believed it.

CHAPTER XVII

THE FOURTH CAMPAIGN; ROOSEVELT'S DEATH

THE Democratic convention of 1944 repeated the struggle of the convention of 1940; then the battle had been to get Wallace the second place on the ticket, now it was a struggle to keep him off it. The issue could only be determined, in 1944 as in 1940, by one man, by the President. Wallace could go to Chicago and fight his battle there, but the experts had no real hope (or fear) that he could win it without some equivalent of the vigorous support given in 1940, and they had good reason to believe that such support would not be given.

There was no new heir-apparent, for the President's support of James L. Byrnes, on which so much hope had been placed, was no more determined and decisive than his formal support of Wallace. Byrnes was an impossible candidate in the eyes of the CIO. He was a Southern liberal of the older school, not to be confused by either side with the new Southern radical leaders of the type of Senator Pepper of Florida. He had been an effective New Deal party manager in the Senate; he was a close friend of the President's; he had stepped down from the bench of the Supreme Court to undertake the politically thankless task of directing the war economy on the home front. And it was in that role that he had finally burnt his boats by opposing wage increases. The leaders of the PAC, on whose zeal and money so much depended, were most determinedly opposed to a Byrnes nomination. He suffered, too, under another handicap in that, born of a Catholic family, he had become a member of the Episcopal church. This, it was asserted, would be a serious handicap in the great industrial cities of the North. The convention was conscious, too, that a Vice-Presidential nomination might be far more important this year than normally. It was well understood that Roosevelt might not serve out his fourth term, and the succession was of the greatest interest to all sections of the heterogeneous alliance which made up the Democratic party.

It was a chance for manipulation, and the chance was taken. The new party Chairman, Robert Hannegan of St. Louis, was active on behalf of his candidate, Senator Harry S. Truman, although Truman was a strong supporter of Byrnes. The other compromise candidate favored by the President, Justice Douglas, was widely believed to be determined not to accept a Vice-Presidential nomination. The main claim of any candidate in this confused situation was "availability," and Truman was eminently available. He was now serving a second term in the Senate, having been rather narrowly reelected in 1940. His record as a voter on New Deal issues was nearly perfect; and if he had entered the Senate as the nominee of one of the most notorious political machines in America, the Pendergast organization in Kansas City (Missouri), a tacit alliance between great city machines and the New Deal had been one of the oddities of American politics for a decade past. It was the war, however, that had projected Senator Truman into the limelight, for as Chairman of a Senate committee on war expenditure, he had performed a most useful public service, quietly, modestly, effectively. The "Truman Committee" became well known and its Chairman had as many claims on the Vice-Presidential nomination as candidates for that office normally have.

The supporters of Wallace were bitterly disappointed by the defeat of their hero. He had shown more strength among the delegates than had been expected, and the more naive may have thought that the convention was to be swept off its feet. But the real managers knew better; and when the opposition to Byrnes had canceled out the opposition to Wallace, the adjustment was made. Truman was nominated for the Vice-Presidency—and, so many felt, for the probable reversion of the Presidency. The public was puzzled but not overexcited by the result. It was, however, interested and excited by the role attributed by commentators to Sidney Hillman, head of the CIO. The consent of this labor union leader was essential to the combination that had ended in the shelving of Wallace and the nomination of Truman. And some commentators thought it would be the success of this leader and his organization that would determine whether the fourth term would become a reality or a desperate maneuver that failed.

There could be little doubt as to the identity of the Republican candidate in 1944. It would be Governor Dewey of New York. He had almost been nominated in 1940, when his claims were far slighter. Then he was merely a candidate who had nearly been elected Governor of New York. Now he had been given the chance to demonstrate his executive ability as head of the greatest state in the Union. And, equally important, he had secured control over the political machine in the Empire State. The public paid more attention to the fact that Governor Dewey now had views on international problems while in 1940 he seemed to have had none, or none that were relevant. Then he had seemed a "young man in a hurry"; now his ambition seemed more legitimate.

By the time the convention met, the lead was

so great that all but the most determined partisans were ready to rally to the side of the victor. Two of the most conspicuous candidates had already thrown away their chances. In the years since his defeat, Wendell Willkie had become more of a national and still more of a world figure than in 1940. Acting on his doctrine of "loyal opposition," he had supported the Roosevelt policies; he had seen the warring outside world at first hand; he knew London, Moscow, and Chungking. His book *One World* was a best-seller, and by 1944 liberals and radicals had forgiven him most of the harsh things they had felt bound to say of him in 1940. Indeed, he probably ranked next to Wallace in the esteem of the left. No Republican leader was so popular among Democrats, a popularity that hurt him with his own party. He was especially the spokesman of the younger politicians in both parties, who thought that the time had come for a bolder, more constructive, and more internationally minded foreign policy. In 1940, the support he had won from Governor Stassen of Minnesota had angered many old-time Republicans, and Stassen's friends had come to be regarded as representative specimens of a special type, the Willkieites.

But devoted friends, passionate partisans, press support, world fame, were not enough. The miracle of 1940 could not be repeated without an organization, and there was no effective organization. It could not be repeated without proving to the regular politicians that the Willkie magic had not lost its vote-getting power. So, against the advice of friends, Willkie decided to fight the decisive battle on difficult ground by entering the primary in Wisconsin, reputedly the most isolationist of states, where both progressive and conservative Republicans combined in opposition to the internationalism of Willkie, Wallace, and Stassen. It was magnificent but it was not politics. He was disastrously defeated, and with the same dramatic decisiveness that he had entered the Presidential campaign, he withdrew.

The withdrawal of another leading aspirant was less voluntary. In the dark winter and spring of 1941–42, General Douglas MacArthur had been the chief hero of the American people. To the elements in the American press, in politics, and among the people that thought the Pacific war the only purely American war, he remained the chief hero. Praise of MacArthur could be combined with suggestions that the global strategy of the war was being used as an excuse for keeping from him the means of speedy victory. There was nothing new in this. All American wars have produced the problem of the political general or of the general whom politicians propose to use. General MacArthur was not totally unreceptive. He had on his staff, in Colonel Philip La Follette, ex-Governor of Wis-

consin, a zealous partisan who was also an energetic
politician, and he had, all over the country, supporters who disliked all the available political personnel. But in the great struggle now approaching
its climax, the old rules of American politics
seemed, to millions of Americans, decidedly out of
place and out of date. The allocation of resources,
the choice of objectives, the choice of commanders,
were no fit themes for the stump—and they would
inevitably be themes if General MacArthur were
nominated. There were grave doubts, too, if a soldier's approach were needed for the direction of
the United States in war and the transition to
peace. A letter to a friendly Congressman seemed
to show that the General's political judgment was
far inferior to his military ability, and the Mac-
Arthur candidacy died.

Long before the Republican convention met, it
was as certain as such things can be that Governor
Dewey would be nominated. As with the Democrats, the Republican uncertainty was over the
second place on the ticket, and that was pressed
on Governor Warren of California. But the smooth-
running Dewey machine suffered its first upset
when Warren firmly declined the honor. It was,
some thought, ominous. It meant, presumably, that
Governor Warren had a poor opinion of Republican
chances and a reason given for the refusal, that
Governor Warren had promised the people of Cali-

fornia to serve out the full four years of his term, was thought to be a reflection on Governor Dewey of New York, who was proposing to leave Albany for Washington despite a similar promise. Governor Bricker of Ohio, as a good party man, stepped into the breach and the ticket was complete.

It did not seem in the early summer of 1944 to matter much, for the invasion of France was under way at last, and the attention of the world was on the great battles in the West and in the Pacific. As in 1940, the President declared his unwillingness to campaign. But as the campaign got under way, it became even harder than in 1940 to remain above the battle. Alarmed reports began to pour into party headquarters, and apprehension increased in quarters close to the White House. It was impossible, for one thing, to estimate the effects of a sudden ending to the European war. The argument of necessity might cease to work for the President. Dewey was not nearly so glamorous a candidate as Wendell Willkie had been, but he was proving more effective. His campaign was admirably organized; he now had as secure a hold on the national machine as he had had for two years past on the machine in New York. The Republican candidate stood up well to hostile anecdotes, to disparaging references to his height and manner, to indifferent or hostile crowds in Democratic cities like San Francisco, to the self-regarding caution of politicians who

thought that too warm support of the national
ticket would harm, not help them. It was time for
the President to revise his decision. The election
was not going to be won by statesmanlike reports
from the Pacific front, like the radio address delivered from Bremerton Navy Yard.

There was worry, too, about an issue injected
into the campaign that had great explosive possibilities. The Republicans had no intention of letting it be forgotten that one of the main roles, in
the Democratic convention, had been played by
Sidney Hillman. "Clear everything with Sidney,"
so it was said, was the battle order given at Chicago by the President. Sidney Hillman had had
the last word because his control of the PAC meant
control of the Democratic party. The Republican
attack on the "Hillman-Browder axis" (Earl Browder was the Communist leader) was not ineffective, if only measured by the degree of panic it
bred in the Democratic high command. The zeal
of the Communists fed the suspicions of their foes.
Gone were the days of revolutionary slogans and
bitter war on class enemies. Since the President
had met the ruler of the Soviet Union at Teheran,
the one desire of the American Communists and
their allies had been to get on with the war. As a
party they were now more than loyal—and they
ceased to be even a party. After the dissolution
of the Communist International, came the ostensi-

ble transformation of the American Communist party into a mere educational association!

It was not enough to denounce the authors of "Clear everything with Sidney" as liars; it was not enough to denounce the open exploitation of anti-Semitism that lay behind the repeated insistence on Hillman's "Lithuanian" birth. There must be attack as well as defense. The Negroes in the great Northern cities must be kept from straying back to their traditional Republicanism. The Irish Catholics of Boston must be reminded of the campaign of 1928, when Al Smith had been the victim of the same forces that were now harping incessantly on the nefarious influence of Sidney Hillman. Above all, the endless rumors that the President's health was such that he was unfit to serve a fourth term must be scotched. "Do you want to vote for Truman for President?" was a question frequently put if seldom printed.

When he returned to the political battle, the President showed that absorption in war and high politics, Casablanca and Teheran, had not lessened his delight and skill in the tactics of American political warfare. He had great advantages; though the European war was not ending in a sudden German collapse, it was ending victoriously. The war was being won, too, in the Pacific, and before the election came, the American flag was again flying in the Philippines and General MacArthur

was redeeming the humiliations and underscoring
the heroism of Bataan. Governor Dewey could not
ignore or rival such triumphs. If he said all he knew,
made all the controversial points he might have
made, that was unpatriotic; if he kept silent, he
seemed ignorant and obviously outside the small
circle within which world history was being
made.

The PAC was proving effective in getting out
the vote and that was ominous for Republican
chances. Nor did it seem likely that the failure of
Congress to enact a general soldier's voting law
would keep as many serving soldiers and sailors
from the ballot as had been feared or hoped. And
by asserting that Republicans and conservative
Democrats had conspired to make soldier's voting
as difficult as possible, the Administration succeeded in spreading the view that the only hope
of a Republican victory lay in the indifference of
the voters.

Two deaths reminded the country of great
careers—and of old and new divisions in party
ranks. For Al Smith, "the Happy Warrior," died
in the middle of the campaign, and within a week
the extraordinary career of Wendell Willkie was
ended. The death of Al Smith was no great surprise,
but that of Willkie in the full flower of his career
was both a shock and an event. The Republican
candidate of 1940 had not yet endorsed the Re-

publican candidate of 1944. Governor Dewey had
been careful to exclude his predecessor from the
national convention, but as the campaign approached its climax, a word of approval from Willkie became a boon greatly to be desired. Such
approval would reassure hundreds of thousands of
doubtful "liberals" suspicious of the depth of
Dewey's conversion to international cooperation,
and their votes might be decisive. Willkie's death
was a personal blow to devoted followers who had
given him a passionate devotion that no other
public figure commanded. All their resentment at
the treatment of their hero by the Republican high
command might now boil over. Some leading Willkieites did come out for the President; others went
further and declared that the dead leader had been
planning to endorse Roosevelt. Others, equally close
to Willkie, declared that he was merely biding his
time to announce his support of the Republican
ticket; others that he would have refused to support either candidate. It was a matter of debate
whether this last attitude would now be reflected
in the abstention of thousands of voters who would
normally have voted the Republican ticket, or in
silent support of the President.

By election eve it was plain that there would be
no indifference to the issues. The Negroes were
swinging back to the Administration, which now
seemed to mean business in its support of the

FEPC (the Fair Employment Practices Committee). Driving through New York in torrents of drizzly rain, the President for hours showed the great crowds that he "could take it" and, on the air, conveyed to millions that he could "dish it out" with all his old power, adroitness, and eloquence. He defended the war record of the Administration; more important, he recalled the past —1932 and the miracles of the early New Deal. And for the future, who were the men to trust? "I believe that we Americans will want the peace to be built by men who have shown foresight rather than hindsight."

For the last time the magic worked. Nearly fifty millions voted and the President got twenty-five and a half million to Governor Dewey's twenty-two millions. In electoral votes the difference was much greater, for Dewey added only seventeen votes to Willkie's eighty-two. It was the vote of the great cities, the great industrial areas, the less privileged classes that, for the fourth time, chose Franklin D. Roosevelt. It was a victory for a great national leader, but it was a class victory too.

A fourth inaugural, like a third, was a momentous novelty and the brief inaugural speech was devoted to the great problem of peace. It was an appeal for the banishing of suspicion also, and this was the theme of the Presidential report to Congress on the conference with the allied leaders at

Yalta. But post-war problems were not to be covered by the mere invocation of the spirit of peace. And, to some Americans, the most significant Presidential decision was the removal of the Secretary of Commerce, Jesse Jones, and his replacement by the former Vice-President, Henry Wallace. Each man was a symbol; Jones represented one of the last links of the Administration with big business, especially in the South. To replace Jones by Wallace was not only a public acknowledgment of the claims of the PAC and of Wallace on Presidential gratitude; it was a sign that the post-war economic policy of the Administration would be directed by a man sympathetic to the claims of small business and of labor, and suspicious of the great corporations. It was a sign that the days of "Dr. Win-the-War" were numbered, and that the immediate post-war problems would be handled in the general spirit of the New Deal, not in blind trust in the recuperative powers of business. The fourth term was to have a meaning; it was not to be a mere liquidation of the war.

Rumors about the President's health were not stilled by his appearance before Congress, or by the newsreels that showed him at the Yalta conference, aged and weary. But the President, relaxing at Hot Springs, having his portrait painted, preparing his speech for Jefferson Day, jesting about his job of making laws, had no apprehensions, nor had his immediate entourage. As suddenly as if an assassin had struck him down, Franklin Delano Roosevelt died on April 12, 1945.

The news went round the world; people wept in the streets of Moscow, stood stunned in the streets of London, and in a score of American cities could not believe the first, incredible dispatch. Three thousand miles away in beleaguered Berlin, the desperate Führer rejoiced hysterically. His stars had not deserted him; his great enemy was dead; the Third Reich could still survive. But all over the world, to millions of simple men and women, inside America and outside, a great symbolic figure had been removed and with him a ground of confidence and hope. To these, "untimelier death than his was never any."

When men suddenly realize that a profound change has occurred in the circumstances of their lives, it is their natural human weakness to set the exact moment in time at which the change took place. Before that date and after that date are easily treated as two decisively different historical situations. And such sudden dramatic changes are all the more easily believed in if they can be associated with one man. So it was with the New Deal and with Franklin Roosevelt. There was a catastrophe; there was a dramatic change; there was an easily definable beginning to a legally determined epoch. And the first view of the new Administration was soon confirmed by two types of partisan commentary, the commentary of friendly partisans who attributed to it not only all the virtues but gave it the credit for all the innovations that the situation evoked. And, on the other hand, once the brief honeymoon was over, the rapidly growing flock of enemies of the new Administration imputed to it, as its own dangerous inventions and as proofs of its own inherent incompetence and malice, whatever devices, expedients, reforms, and principles were evoked to meet the crisis. For all of these, the Administration obviously had no exclusive claim to praise or blame.

The experience of other great changes in human societies suggests that the friends and enemies of the New Deal attributed too much to it and to its leader. We know that no revolution is complete or new.

So it was with the New Deal. Had the Republicans won in 1932, faced with the crisis of 1933 they must have resorted to expedients that would only have differed in detail from some of those adopted by the Democratic Administration. Party theories and even deeply rooted principles would have given way under the pressure of events. For we may be sure that a Republican President and Congress would have considered themselves no more bound by party precedent or platform than were the Democrats of 1933 by the platform of 1932, by the practice of Grover Cleveland, or by the enunciated principles of Thomas Jefferson.

It is easy enough to show that some of the instruments of the New Deal, like the RFC, had been manufactured by the Hoover Administration and that even some of the wielders of those instruments, most associated in the public mind with the New Deal, actually began their official service under Hoover. Even that most characteristic instrument of Roosevelt policy, the "Brain Trust," the collegiate executive of experts, had its precedents in the Hoover Administration.

If, as has been often argued, the depression was well on the way to being cured in 1932 and if that cure was only delayed by the election, by events outside the United States, and by the mistakes of the New Deal, it is possible to conceive a second Hoover Administration that would have reaped the reward of the fortitude of the first, in its clinging to sound if unpopular principles. But even had this occurred, the depression had opened too many wounds, had forced the asking of too many questions for even the return of "normalcy" to heal the wounds or silence the questioners. The American banking system, even without the last crisis of 1933, the American system of ownership and control of public utilities, even without such extravagant scandals as the collapse of the Insull empire, the American system of poor relief, of local taxa-

tion, of school financing, of rural credit—to name
only a few of the cracks in the social structure—
would have called for drastic and dramatic remedies. Some kind of new deal was inevitable.

Indeed, seen from a longer historical perspective,
it was the Harding-Coolidge epoch that was the
interruption of a long-term historical process. It
had not been a universally accepted American doctrine that "the business of the United States is
business." All of the early twentieth century was
filled with protest and action against this view. But
for a brief, ecstatic period, the American people, all
criticisms stilled by the euphoria of the boom, forgot truths and passions and prejudices that, all the
same, were merely sleeping.

Even the political history of the boom years
showed that the superficially unchallenged Republican supremacy was, in fact, seriously challenged.
The La Follette vote in 1924 was expressive of a
widespread rural discontent that worse times might
embitter still further. The remarkable strength developed by Governor Smith in the great cities in
1928 was ominous, too, ominous of a change in
temper that men of old political habit refused to
take into account. There was plenty of discontent,
skepticism, anger in the America of the twenties; it
was hard to hear it in the din of the bull market but
it was there. And inevitably the Republican party,
the party in power, was destined to be the victim

of any increase in pitch and intensity of the voice of protest.

Against such a background the New Deal assumes its due proportions. Whether it was true in fact, it was true in popular belief that the control of American life had been turned over to the businessman; and in 1932 the people demanded an accounting. They forced the old political order into bankruptcy and were ready to enforce drastic changes in the economic order. So the old barriers against trade unions, against social legislation, against state interference in, and competition with, business broke down, the more easily that the pressure against them was now at least a generation old.

Even had the United States been isolated in the world, unaffected by the rest of human society, great changes would have come about in some form or other. But it was greatly affected by a world that, in turn, it profoundly influenced. In a world like that which followed the first World War, when it was darkly suspected that the waters of the great deep had broken up, it was idle to expect to postpone, for more than a few years, the confrontation of American ways of life with those of the outer world. It was idle to expect that all questions would be posed and could be answered in terms set by American traditional forms. It was again the special mark of the New Deal that this confrontation was made suddenly and speedily, but it would in any case have had to be made.

On the other hand, the New Deal was basically, in intention and effect, conservative. In the winter of 1932 and 1933, the old political order in the United States might seem, and to many did seem, to be doomed. The Roosevelt Administration was thought of as a mere stopgap, as a mere expedient to be swept away, as in past crises in other lands comparable compromising evasions of a revolutionary situation had been swept away. But it was not to be so. Not only did the Administration survive, but the Republican party survived and after further disasters recovered, inside six years, most of its old prestige and a great deal of its old power. And this suggests both that the situation was not as revolutionary and the New Deal not as fundamentally novel as friends and enemies of the old and new orders had believed. Not only did the old party system survive, but so did such threatened institutions as the Supreme Court.

In personnel, in policy, in attitude the New Deal was not one doctrinaire experiment or even the expression of one party philosophy. That it was empirical, flexible, inconsistent, temporizing, as well as boldly, even recklessly experimental and disdainful of precedent, merely proved that it was a genuinely American way of meeting not one but a series of problems. To some of the problems it provided what are probably final answers. It is unlikely that the old restrictive ideas of the functions of the Union and of the states to which parties had paid lip service, will ever effectually revive. It is unlikely that the extensions of Federal authority secured by the coercion or bribing of states and cities will be undone except in detail. The basic problems of making democratic capitalism work and the still more basic problem of securing the survival of American institutions in a world in which democracy was more and more a dangerous trade, were left unsolved—as was perhaps inevitable. But they were not left insoluble; the time that had to be bought was bought. Whether the price was too high and the time inadequately used are questions that this generation cannot answer. All that can be said is that, in a great crisis, time is bound to be bought dear and that no free society can solve all its problems to the satisfaction of all the people.

That the New Deal had not saved America from every serious threat to its prosperity and security was evident by 1939. That it had not destroyed the power of American society to save itself in a still greater crisis than that of 1933 was evident by 1945. That it had, on the whole, helped, not hindered that society to make ready for the crisis of World War II is not provable though it is probable. One basic thing it had done, *the* basic thing it had done, was to keep alive in the breast of the average

American the faith that this was still the last best hope of earth and that the poorest and most disinherited were sharers in the common assets of the American people and their own salvation part of the general welfare.

BIBLIOGRAPHICAL NOTE

FROM its beginning the Roosevelt Administration attracted an exceptional amount of attention from writers and phampleteers. Attempts to write its history began almost at once, and some books of real merit were produced. Among these should be noted Ernest K. Lindley, *The Roosevelt Revolution: First Phase* (1934), Louis M. Hacker, *A Short History of the New Deal* (1934), Charles A. Beard and George H. E. Smith, *The Old Deal and the New* (1940), and Basil Rauch, *The History of the New Deal 1933–1938* (1944). An excellent survey of the whole period is provided by Dixon Wecter's *The Age of the Great Depression 1929–1941* (1948). The social history of the time is described by Frederick Lewis Allen in *Only Yesterday* (1931) and *Since Yesterday* (1940), and general economic history by Broadus Mitchell in *Depression Decade from New Era through New Deal 1929–1941* (Vol. IX of *The Economic History of the United States,* 1947). Two good narratives of twentieth-century American history deal with the Roosevelt Administration: Harvey Wish, *Contemporary America* (1945), and Foster Rhea Dulles, *Twentieth Century America* (1945).

The extraordinary interest evoked by the New Deal

and its chief led to the publication of more than the usual number of lives of the President. Of books of this type, Ernest K. Lindley, *Franklin D. Roosevelt* (1934), Don Wharton (editor), *The Roosevelt Omnibus* (1934), and Gerald W. Johnson, *Roosevelt: an American Study* (1942) are the most notable. An English view is presented by Compton Mackenzie in *Mr. Roosevelt* (1945).

President Roosevelt organized the publication during his tenure of office of *The Public Papers and Addresses of Franklin D. Roosevelt* (5 vols., 1938; 4 vols., 1941). These volumes run from 1928 through 1940. This great collection was compiled and arranged by Judge Samuel Rosenman, but its course was vigilantly watched by the President. It should be noticed that not only was editorial choice exercised in the selection of speeches and official papers to be printed, but the texts are not always complete or identical with those given in the contemporary press. The introductions to each volume by the President make a kind of brief autobiography of great value, but probably the reports of the press conferences (seven hundred and ten are reported in whole or part) are the most valuable part of the two series. For the speeches delivered after 1940, there is a good selection in *Nothing to Fear: the Selected Addresses of Franklin Delano Roosevelt 1932–1945,* edited by B. D. Zevin (1946).

Close associates of the President published both personal narratives and collections of speeches and other documents. Among these especially notable are Hugh S. Johnson, *The Blue Eagle from Egg to Earth* (1935); Raymond Moley, *After Seven Years* (1939); Frances Perkins, *The Roosevelt I Knew* (1947);

Charles Michelsen, *The Ghost Talks* (1941); and Harold I. Ickes, *The Autobiography of a Curmudgeon* (1943). See also Henry A. Wallace, *Democracy Reborn;* Selected from Public Papers and Edited with an Introduction and Notes by Russell Lord (1945), and Rexford G. Tugwell, *The Battle for Democracy* (1935). The comment of an intelligent journalist may be found in Marquis W. Childs, *I Wrote From Washington* (1942). A more full, candid and hostile account of the politics of the New Deal and the methods of President Roosevelt was given by James A. Farley in his book *Jim Farley's Story: the Roosevelt Years* (1948). A less disgruntled account of the politics of the era can be found in Edward J. Flynn's *You're the Boss* (1947). Probably the most important book yet published on the internal history of the Roosevelt Administration, its ways of working and its personalities is Robert E. Sherwood's *Roosevelt and Hopkins* (1948). Although the greater part of the book is devoted to the war period, it is of great value for the New Deal and for the political history of the Administration.

Departmental reports, especially those of the Treasury, the Department of Agriculture, the Department of Labor, are of great interest. The Brookings Institution of Washington published a series of valuable and critical studies of which the most notable are Leverett S. Lyon (and others), *The National Recovery Administration: an Analysis and Appraisal* (1935); Edwin G. Nourse (editor), *The Recovery Problem in the United States* (1936); Edwin G. Nourse (and others), *Three Years of the Agricultural Adjustment Administration* (1937); Harold W.

Metz, *Labor Policy of the Federal Government* (1945); and Lewis Meriam, *Relief and Social Security* (1946).

From the beginning, the Roosevelt administrations attracted a great deal of foreign interest. Among the more notable surveys from the outside are E. M. Hugh-Jones and E. A. Radice, *An American Experiment* (1936); Louis R. Franck, *L'Expérience Roosevelt* (1937); A. S. J. Baster, *The Twilight of American Capitalism* (1937); and Robert Waithman, *Report on America* (1940). The polemical literature is overwhelming in quantity. Among the more interesting critical commentaries are: Herbert Hoover, *The Challenge to Liberty* (1934); Ralph Robey, *Roosevelt versus Recovery* (1934); Norman Thomas, *After the New Deal What?* (1936); Benjamin Stolberg and Warren Jay Vinson, *The Economic Consequences of the New Deal* (1935); John L. Spivak, *America Faces the Barricades* (1935); and Frank R. Kent, *Without Grease* (1936).

The early measures of recovery were described and appraised in a very bulky literature. Notable studies are Charles Frederick Roos, *NRA Economic Planning* (1937); A. A. Berle (and others), *America's Recovery Programme* (1934); Michael F. Gallagher, *Government Rules Industry* (1934). For the agricultural measures, Joseph S. Davis offers a critical study in *Agricultural Policy 1926–1938* (1939), and E. G. Nourse a balanced view in *Government in Relation to Agriculture* (1940). Wesley McCune discusses the political background in *The Farm Bloc* (1943). A good discussion of the background of the problems of American agriculture can be found in

Wilson Gee, *The Social Economics of Agriculture* (1947).

The novel problems of Federal relief policy produced a large and, on the whole, valuable literature. Abraham Epstein's *Insecurity . . . a Study of Social Insurance in the United States and Abroad* (1933, 1936, 1938) in its successive revisions shows the development of institutions and of thought about the problem. Paul H. Douglas, *Social Security in the United States* (1936, 1939), also illustrates the development of Federal legislation. Josephine Chapin Brown has provided a good historical account in *Public Relief, 1929–1939* (1940); Donald S. Howard, in *The WPA and Federal Relief Policy* (1943), and Bryce M. Stewart (and others), in *Planning and Administration of Unemployment Compensation in the United States* (1938), deal with the application of legislation; while Grace Adams, *Workers on Relief* (1939), and Elizabeth W. Gilboy, *Applicants for Work Relief: a Study of Massachusetts Families under the FERA and WPA* (1940), treat of the human problems behind the statistics.

The rise of organized labor has also been elaborately studied with more or less objectivity. Robert R. R. Brooks, in *When Labor Organizes* (1937), *Unions of Their Own Choosing* (1939), and *As Steel Goes . . . Unionism in a Basic Industry* (1940), gives a good picture of the new unionism. More uncritical accounts are *Labor's New Millions* by Mary Heaton Vorse (1938), and J. Raymond Walsh, *C.I.O. Industrial Unionism in Action* (1938). The split in the movement is dealt with by Herbert Harris, *Labor's Civil War* (1940), and McAlister Coleman, *Men and*

Coal (1943). The political activities of the CIO are described by Joseph Gaer in *The First Round: the Story of the CIO Political Action Committee* (1944), while there is an admirable summing-up in Selig Perlman's reprinted lectures, *Labor in the New Deal Decade* (1945). The legal position created by the Wagner Act and its administration is described in Joseph Rosenfarb, *The National Labor Policy and How It Works* (1940), and in Charles O. Gregory, *Labor and the Law* (1946). For the darker side of the labor picture see Harold Seidman, *Labor Czars: a History of Labor Racketeering* (1938).

Financial policy is dealt with in James Daniel Paris, *Monetary Politics of the United States* (1938), and Paul W. Stewart and Rufus S. Tucker, *The National Debt and Government Credit* (1937). Other aspects of fiscal policy are treated in Sidney Ratner, *American Taxation* (1942), and Harley Leist Lutz, *Public Finance* (1947). The spirit of Federal control of the stock markets is expounded in *Democracy and Finance; the Addresses and Public Statements of William O. Douglas as Member and Chairman of the Securities and Exchange Commission,* edited by James Allen (1940), and Rudolph L. Weissman, *The New Wall Street* (1939).

The Supreme Court controversy produced an abundant literature. The best collection of opinions is to be found in the *Hearings before the Committee on the Judiciary, United States Senate* (1937). A narrative of considerable merit is Joseph Alsop and Turner Catledge, *The 168 Days* (1938). A very effective contemporary pamphlet is by Walter Lippmann, *The Supreme Court, Independent or Con-*

trolled? (1937). More partisan is Drew Pearson and Robert Allen, *The Nine Old Men* (1936). Two able statements of the case against the Court are to be found in Edward S. Corwin, *Court over Constitution* (1938), and Robert H. Jackson, *The Struggle for Judicial Supremacy* (1941). E. S. Corwin has described the outcome of the controversy in *Constitutional Revolution, Ltd.* (1941).

The reports of the Tennessee Valley Authority are of great interest as are the *Hearings* before the Joint Congressional Committee. Two good academic studies are C. Herman Pritchett, *The Tennessee Valley Authority: a Study in Public Administration* (1943), and Herman Finer, *The T.V.A.: Lessons for International Application* (1944). An able statement for the defense is in David Lilienthal, *T.V.A.—Democracy on the March* (1944), and a hostile account is to be found in Frederick L. Collins, *Uncle Sam's Billion-Dollar Baby: a Taxpayer Looks at the T.V.A.* (1945).

The question of soil erosion and the rehabilitation of rural labor is dealt with in Russell Lord, *Behold Our Land* (1938), in Stuart Chase, *Rich Land, Poor Land* (1936), and in Carey McWilliams, *Ill Fares the Land: Migrants and Migratory Labor in the United States* (1942). For the impact of the New Deal on the Negro rural population of the South see Gunnar Myrdal, *An American Dilemma* (1944).

The relation of foreign affairs to the domestic scene is illustrated in Charles A. Beard, *American Foreign Policy in the Making* (1946); S. F. Bemis, *The Latin American Policy of the United States* (1943); T. A. Bisson, *America's Far Eastern Policy* (1945); Carl Kreider, *The Anglo-American Trade Agreement*

(1943); Phillips Bradley, *Can We Stay Out of War?* (1936); Allen W. Dulles and Hamilton Fish Armstrong, *Can We Be Neutral?* (1936); also Frank P. Davison and George S. Viereck, Jr., *Before America Decides* (1938). Excellent chapters on pre-war and wartime economy are to be found in Allan Nevins and Louis M. Hacker, *The United States and Its Place in World Affairs* (1944). *The Memoirs of Cordell Hull* (2 vols., 1948) offer an exceptionally full and careful, if sometimes partisan, study of the foreign relations of the United States, 1933–1945.

The housing problem is dealt with in Langdon Post, *The Challenge of Housing* (1938), and in Robert Lasch, *Breaking the Building Blockade* (1947).

INDEX

Abraham Lincoln Brigade, 314
Acheson, Dean, 50
Agricultural Adjustment Administration, 52, 74, 149, 160 ff.; amendment *re* currency, 62, 66 f.; crop controls, 150 ff.; cash payments, 153; policy and program, 161 ff.; Supreme Court vs., 219
Agriculture, farm debt, 50 f.; improved methods, 143 ff.; curbs on production, 150 ff., 162 f.; soil erosion, 154 f., 245, 256; "mining methods," 161; surpluses, 163 f., 165; subsidies, 164
Agriculture, Department of, 123
Air-mail carriers, 140
Akron, Ohio, 11, 18, 191
Alabama, 244
Amalgamated Association of Iron, Steel, and Tin Workers, 180
American Communist party, 295, 312 ff.; rise in prestige, 314; vs. Trotskyites, 317; *see also* Communists
American Federation of Labor, 168, 173 ff., 178 ff., 277, 333
American Labor party, 213, 335
"American plan," The, 111 f.
Anti-trust laws, 73, 76 ff., 283
Army, Dept. of the, 123
Arnold, Thurman, 285
Arthurdale, 156

Art projects, 101 f.
Ashurst, Henry F., 230
Authorities, local, for PWA projects, 126
Automobile industry, 180; strike, 185 ff.

Baker, Newton D., 31
Bank failures, 13 f., 39 f., 44 f., 148
Bankhead-Jones Act, 157
Banking legislation, 45 ff., 53 ff., 64
Bank of United States, 13, 69
Barkley, Alben W., 30, 100, 264, 274
Baruch, Bernard, 72
Beer, 56
Bennett, John S., 333
Berle, Adolf A., 50
Berry, George, 271
Black, Hugo, 192, 231, 237
Black-Connery bill, 72
"Blue Eagle," 71, 80, 219
Bond codes, for PWA, 125
Boom, 266, 281, 359
Borah, William E., 230, 284
Boulder Dam, 124
Brains Trust, 34, 50, 129, 358
Brandeis, Louis D., 40, 232
Bricker, John W., 274, 291 f.
Bridges, Harry, 170
Brophy, John, 179
Bryan, William Jennings, 47
Budget, Federal, 52; deficit, 15